DAY

SYDNEY

First Edition

John Chapman
Monica Chapman

Bullimah Beach, Walk 28

CONTENTS

Published by
John Chapman
PO Box 5042, Laburnum, Victoria 3130

First Edition 2011

National Library of Australia card number and ISBN
978 1 920995 08 9

While the authors have endeavoured to ensure that the information presented is as up-to-date as possible, they cannot accept any responsibility for any loss, injury or inconvenience sustained by any person using this book. Like many other outdoor activities, walking has its hazards and it is the responsibility of each walker to use common sense to reduce risks. There are potential dangers on some of these walks from both weather and the terrain. The walks in this book may also alter as both natural and man-made changes will occur with time. Personal judgement should be exercised about capabilities and safety in undertaking any walk. The maps in this book are intended to be used only as a guide of where to walk. All walkers should also carry and use the recommended maps as these show more information and cover a larger area.

For updates to this book either send a stamped, self-addressed envelope to the publisher or visit the website www.john.chapman.name

Front cover – Garie Beach, Walk 5
Front cover background – Sandstone, Walk 3
Back cover – Terrace Falls, Walk 13

INTRODUCTION

Sydney is world renowned for its stunning harbour, the bridge and opera house. It is perhaps not so well known for the myriad of walking possibilities on its doorstep. There are walks with spectacular coastal views, including beautiful beaches, and others through attractive forests and heathlands.

There are 40 day walk areas in this guide ranging from easy walks to longer, more strenuous trips that venture through temperate rainforests to visit waterfalls or for a delightful view. Fit walkers with limited experience can undertake most of the walks as they follow marked tracks or well-used routes. For the experienced bushwalker, a few more difficult walks have been included.

The Walk Index provides a quick reference to the walk grading, distance and public transport availability. All walks include variations that provide extensions to the specific walk or alternatives to shorten the walk. Access to each walk is described in full and notes on safety aspects for walks are provided as necessary.

The colour topographic maps contained in the book are designed with bushwalkers in mind, being either 1:12,500, 1:25,000 or 1:50,000. Nevertheless, it is recommended that they be used in conjunction with the suggested maps for each walk. Where possible, circuit walks have been described to avoid the problems of arranging car shuffles. Some walks use train or bus transport to complete the loop.

Every attempt has been made to ensure the accuracy of the information in this book. However, change is inevitable and care still needs to be taken when venturing into the bush.

More information on Sydney and other areas of Australia can be found on the website at www.john.chapman.name. The website also contains information on:

- Bushwalking History
- Climate
- Bushwalking clubs
- Extensive links to other sites of interest

There are so many good day walks within close proximity of Sydney. Those that follow are a selection that represent a range of destinations. Enjoy the experience of discovering some of the beautiful scenery, flora and fauna in Sydney's environs.

WALK INDEX

	Walk Name	Length km	Style	Hours	Grade
	SOUTHERN SUBURBS				
1	**Cape Banks**	**7.4**	**Circuit**	**3**	**E-M**
	Henry Head	4.4	Return	1½	E
2	**Kurnell to Cronulla**	**14.3**	**One-way**	**4½**	**M**
	Kurnell to Cape Solander	5.6	Circuit	2	E
	Cape Solander to Cape Bailey lightstation	5.0	Return	2	E-M
	Cape Solander to Potter Point	7.0	Return	2½	M
	Kurnell to Potter Point	12.6	Return	4	M
	ROYAL & HEATHCOTE NATIONAL PARKS				
3	**Port Hacking Point**	**6.3**	**Circuit**	**2½**	**E-M**
	Jibbon & Shelley Beaches	4.8	Circuit	1½	E
	Port Hacking Point & Marley Beach	15.1	Circuit	5	M
4	**Marley Beach Circuit**	**11.8**	**Circuit**	**3½**	**M**
	The Waterrun	6.6	Return	2	E
5	**Curra Moors Circuit**	**11.2**	**Circuit**	**3½**	**M**
6	**Otford to Burning Palms**	**12.3**	**Circuit**	**3½**	**M-H**
7	**Heathcote Audley Circuit**	**15.4**	**Circuit**	**5½**	**M-H**
	Heathcote to Karloo Pool	5.4	Return	2	E-M
	Heathcote to Uloola Falls	10.0	Return	4	M
8	**Kangaroo Creek**	**14.8**	**Circuit**	**6**	**M-H**
	Waterfall to Kangaroo Creek Falls	4.4	Return	2½	E-M
	Waterfall to Karloo Pool & Heathcote	9.2	One-way	4½	M-H
	Waterfall to Audley & Heathcote	19.2	One-way	8	H
9	**Bullawarring Track**	**10.8**	**One-way**	**3½**	**M**
	Kingfisher Pool	5.0	Return	2	E
	Mooray Track	6.3	Circuit	2½	M
	BLUE MOUNTAINS				
10	**Glenbrook to Red Hands Cave**	**12.8**	**Circuit**	**5**	**M**
	Glenbrook Pools	4.7	Circuit	2	M
	Red Hands Cave	8.1	Circuit	3	E-M
11	**Warrimoo to Glenbrook**	**9.3**	**One-way**	**5**	**H**
	Warrimoo to Blaxland	6.0	One-way	3	E-M
	Blaxland to Glenbrook	6.7	One-way	4	M-H
12	**Sassafras Gully & Magdala Creek**	**10.2**	**Circuit**	**3½**	**M**
	Sassafras Gully & Wiggins Track	5.9	Circuit	2	E-M

Grade: E Easy, E-M Easy-Medium, M Medium, M-H Medium-Hard, H Hard

WALK INDEX

Public Transport	From Sydney	Closest Town or Suburb to start	Features	Page Number
Bus	**14**	**La Perouse 0km**	**Coastal views, shipwreck**	**20**
Bus	14	La Perouse 0km	Lookout, gun emplacements	20
Train+bus	**36**	**Cronulla 10km**	**Forest, coastal cliffs, beach**	**24**
Train+bus	36	Cronulla 10km	Monuments, coastal forest	24
None	39	Cronulla 13km	Lightstation, coastal cliffs	24
None	39	Cronulla 13km	Lightstation, rock platforms	24
Train+bus	36	Cronulla 10km	Forest, coastal cliffs	24
Train+ferry	**54**	**Bundeena 0km**	**Coast, views, heathland**	**29**
Train+ferry	54	Bundeena 0km	Aboringal engravings	29
Train+ferry	54	Bundeena 0km	Heathland, views, beach	29
Train+ferry	**54**	**Bundeena 0km**	**Cliffs, heathland, beach**	**32**
Train+ferry	54	Bundeena 0km	Waterfall, heathland	32
None	**47**	**Sutherland 19km**	**Wildflowers, coastal cliffs**	**36**
Train	**56**	**Otford 1km**	**Rainforest, coastal views**	**40**
Train	**36**	**Heathcote 0km**	**Woodland, heathland, views**	**45**
Train	36	Heathcote 0km	Woodland, rock pool	45
Train	36	Heathcote 0km	Waterfall, woodland	45
Train	**42**	**Waterfall 0km**	**Woodland, cascades**	**50**
Train	42	Waterfall 0km	Waterfall, woodland	50
Train	42	Waterfall 0km	Woodland, cascades, pools	50
Train	42	Waterfall 0km	Woodland, heathland	50
Train	**42**	**Waterfall 0km**	**Forest, pools, gullies**	**55**
Train	42	Waterfall 0km	Pools, forest	55
Train	42	Waterfall 0km	Pools, forest	55
Train	**63**	**Glenbrook 0km**	**Gorge, aboriginal paintings**	**60**
Train	63	Glenbrook 0km	Sandstone gorge, rocky pools	60
None	65	Glenbrook 0km	Aboriginal paintings	60
Train	**69**	**Warrimoo 0km**	**Untracked gorge, forest**	**65**
Train	69	Warrimoo 0km	Sandstone gullies, cliffs	65
Train	66	Blaxland 0km	Untracked gorge, pools	65
Train	**75**	**Springwood 0km**	**Sandstone gorge, forest**	**71**
Train	75	Springwood 0km	Sandstone cliffs, forest	71

WALK INDEX

Walk Name	Length km	Style	Hours	Grade
BLUE MOUNTAINS (continued)				
13 **Lawson & Hazelbrook Waterfalls**	**9.9**	**Circuit**	**4**	**M**
Lawson Waterfalls	2.5	Circuit	1	E-M
14 **National Pass & Nature Walk**	**6.7**	**Circuit**	**4½**	**M**
Nature Walk	1.9	Circuit	1	E
National Pass	4.6	Circuit	3½	M
15 **Vera Falls**	**6.2**	**Circuit**	**5**	**H**
KATOOMBA & BLACKHEATH				
16 **Katoomba Cliff Walk**	**11.3**	**Circuit**	**5**	**M-H**
Prince Henry Cliff Walk	4.0	One-way	2	E
Echo Point & Giants Staircaset	6.8	Circuit	3	M-H
Echo Point & Leura Forest	7.1	Circuit	3	M
Katoomba Cliffs & Scenic Railway	9.6	Circuit	4	M
17 **Ruined Castle**	**15.0**	**Return**	**5**	**M-H**
Scenic Railway to Ruined Castle	12.8	Return	4	M
Golden Stairs	7.8	Return	3	M
18 **Devils Hole**	**8.7**	**Circuit**	**3½**	**M-H**
19 **Centennial Glen**	**6.7**	**Circuit**	**3½**	**E-M**
Porters Pass Circuit	5.1	Circuit	3	E-M
20 **Grand Canyon**	**5.4**	**Circuit**	**3**	**M**
21 **Blue Gum Forest**	**18.1**	**Circuit**	**8½**	**H**
Rodriguez Pass Track	10.7	Circuit	6	M-H
Blue Gum Forest & Grand Canyon	20.1	Circuit	10	H
NORTHERN SUBURBS				
22 **Pennant Hills Circuit**	**8.2**	**Circuit**	**3½**	**M**
Pennant Hills to Cheltenham	8.9	One-way	4	M
23 **Thornleigh to Hornsby**	**9.2**	**Circuit**	**4**	**M-H**
24 **Mt Kuring-gai - Berowra Circuit**	**17.5**	**Circuit**	**8**	**M-H**
Mt Kuring-gai to Berowra via Cowan Creek	9.1	One-way	4	M
Mt Kuring-gai to Berowra via Berowra Creek	8.4	One-way	4	M
HAWKESBURY RIVER				
25 **Smugglers Ridge**	**12.6**	**Circuit**	**5**	**M**
26 **Cowan to Brooklyn**	**10.9**	**One-way**	**5**	**M**
Jerusalem Bay	4.6	Return	2½	M
Campbells Crater	11.5	One-way	5½	M

Grade: E Easy, E-M Easy-Medium, M Medium, M-H Medium-Hard, H Hard

WALK INDEX

WALK INDEX

Walk Name	Length km	Style	Hours	Grade
HAWKESBURY RIVER (continued)				
27 **Piles Creek**	**8.1**	**Circuit**	**4**	**E-M**
Girrakool Loop	1.3	Circuit	½	E
Piles Creek Circuit	4.5	Circuit	2½	E-M
28 **Putty Beach to Bouddi Spur**	**12.0**	**Circuit**	**4½**	**M**
Putty Beach to Maitland Bay	7.9	Circuit	2½	E-M
Maitland Bay & Bouddi Spur	5.7	Circuit	2	E-M
KU-RING-GAI CHASE NATIONAL PARK				
29 **Elvina Bay**	**5.1**	**Circuit**	**2**	**E-M**
30 **Sphinx to Bobbin Head**	**10.2**	**Circuit**	**4**	**E-M**
31 **Centre & Duck Hole Tracks**	**11.2**	**Circuit**	**3½**	**E-M**
GARIGAL NATIONAL PARK				
32 **Belrose Circuit**	**8.5**	**Circuit**	**3½**	**M**
33 **Two Creeks Track**	**10.9**	**Circuit**	**4**	**M**
Gordon & Moores Creeks	6.9	Circuit	2½	E-M
34 **Forestville Circuit**	**13.4**	**Circuit**	**5**	**M**
NORTH-EAST SUBURBS				
35 **Mona Vale to Manly**	**18.8**	**One-way**	**5**	**M**
Mona Vale to Collaroy	8.4	One-way	2½	E-M
Collaroy to Manly	10.8	One-way	3	M
36 **Manly Dam Circuit**	**7.9**	**Circuit**	**3**	**E-M**
37 **Spit Bridge to Manly**	**9.7**	**One-way**	**4**	**E-M**
Manly Scenic Walkway	8.9	One-way	3½	E-M
CENTRAL SYDNEY				
38 **Lane Cove Three Bridges**	**15.5**	**Circuit**	**5**	**M**
Fullers & De Burgh Bridges	10.4	Circuit	3½	E-M
Fullers & Epping Bridges	5.7	Circuit	2	E-M
39 **Iron Cove**	**7.1**	**Circuit**	**2**	**E**
40 **Bondi to Maroubra**	**11.5**	**One-way**	**4**	**E-M**
Bondi to Coogee	6.6	One-way	2	E
Coogee to Maroubra	5.9	One-way	2	E

Grade: E Easy, E-M Easy-Medium, M Medium, M-H Medium-Hard, H Hard

WALK INDEX

Public Transport	From Sydney	Closest Town or Suburb to start	Features	Page Number
None	**73**	**Gosford 11km**	**Sandstone gully, mangroves**	**145**
None	73	Gosford 11km	Aboriginal engravings	145
None	73	Gosford 11km	Deep sandstone gully	145
None	**96**	**Woy Woy 12km**	**Lookouts, rocky coast, beaches**	**149**
None	96	Woy Woy 12km	Sandy beaches, lookouts	149
None	96	Woy Woy 12km	Lookout, coastal forest	149
Bus+ferry	**33**	**Terrey Hills 8km**	**Heathland, waterfall, views**	**154**
Train+bus	**25**	**North Turramurra 1km**	**Carved rock, tidal creek**	**157**
None	**28**	**Terrey Hills 2km**	**Views, engravings**	**160**
Bus	**19**	**Belrose 0km**	**Forest, cascades**	**164**
Train or bus	**14**	**Lindfield 1km**	**Tidal creek, rock overhang**	**168**
Train or bus	14	Lindfield 1km	Waterfalls, mangroves	168
Train+bus	**15**	**Forestville 0km**	**Tidal creek, picnic grounds**	**172**
Ferry+bus	**31**	**Mona Vale 0km**	**Rocky coast, views**	**177**
Ferry+bus	31	Mona Vale 0km	Beaches, views	177
Ferry+bus	22	Collaroy 0km	Swimming baths, views	177
Train+bus	**15**	**Brookvale 3km**	**Dam reserve, waterbirds**	**184**
Ferry+bus	**10**	**Seaforth 1km**	**Harbour views, bushland**	**187**
Ferry+bus	10	Seaforth 1km	Views, aboriginal engravings	187
Train+bus	**13**	**Chatswood 2km**	**Creek valley, bridges**	**192**
Train+bus	13	Chatswood 2km	Narrow valley, rock shelters	192
Train+bus	13	Chatswood 2km	Historic site, golf course	192
Bus	**4**	**Rozelle 1km**	**Shoreline track, views**	**197**
Bus	**8**	**Bondi 0km**	**Scenic coastline, pools**	**200**
Bus	8	Bondi 0km	Historic cemetery, coast views	200
Bus	12	Coogee 0km	Coast views, swimming baths	200

Day Walks Sydney Walk Locations

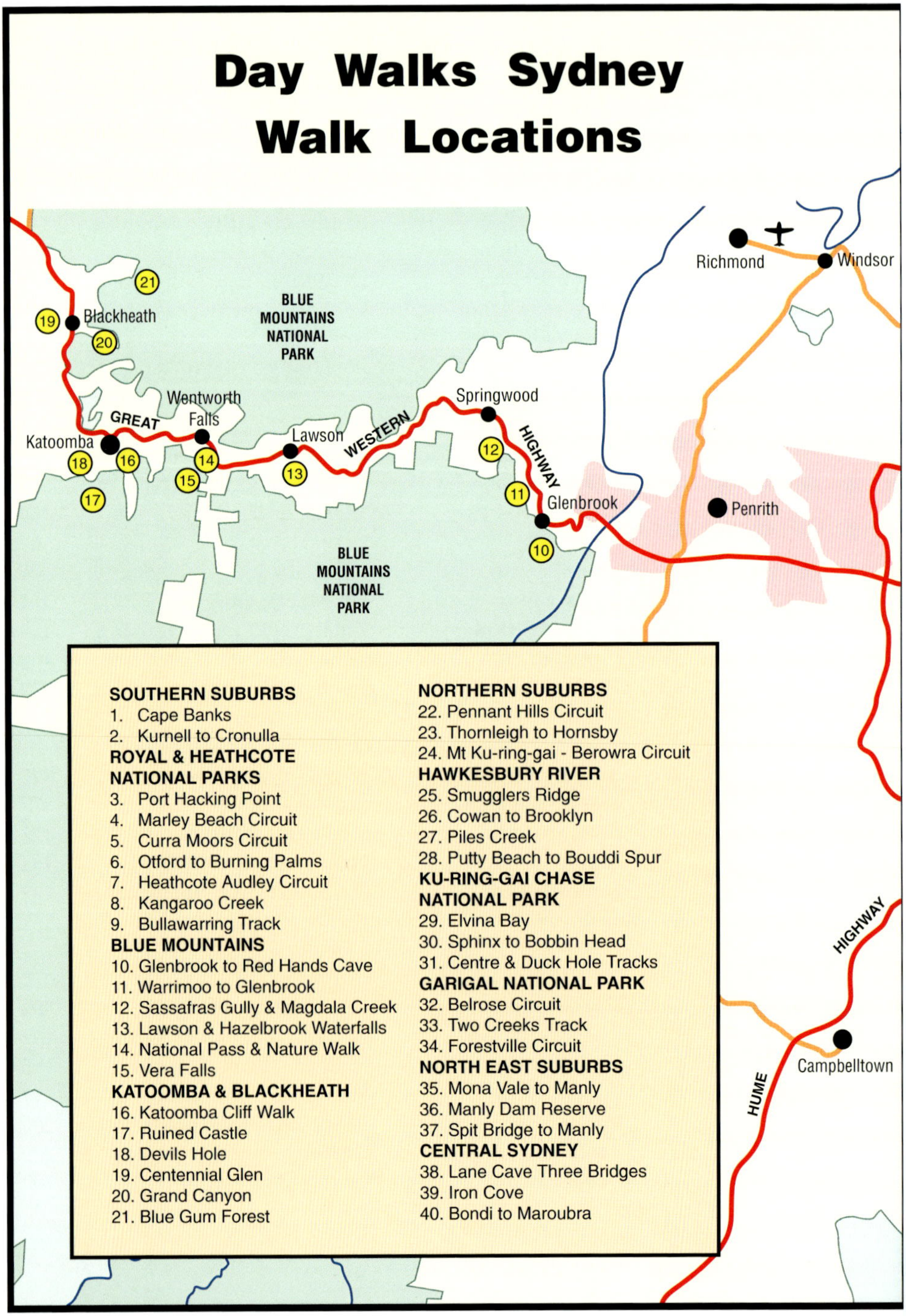

SOUTHERN SUBURBS
1. Cape Banks
2. Kurnell to Cronulla

ROYAL & HEATHCOTE NATIONAL PARKS
3. Port Hacking Point
4. Marley Beach Circuit
5. Curra Moors Circuit
6. Otford to Burning Palms
7. Heathcote Audley Circuit
8. Kangaroo Creek
9. Bullawarring Track

BLUE MOUNTAINS
10. Glenbrook to Red Hands Cave
11. Warrimoo to Glenbrook
12. Sassafras Gully & Magdala Creek
13. Lawson & Hazelbrook Waterfalls
14. National Pass & Nature Walk
15. Vera Falls

KATOOMBA & BLACKHEATH
16. Katoomba Cliff Walk
17. Ruined Castle
18. Devils Hole
19. Centennial Glen
20. Grand Canyon
21. Blue Gum Forest

NORTHERN SUBURBS
22. Pennant Hills Circuit
23. Thornleigh to Hornsby
24. Mt Ku-ring-gai - Berowra Circuit

HAWKESBURY RIVER
25. Smugglers Ridge
26. Cowan to Brooklyn
27. Piles Creek
28. Putty Beach to Bouddi Spur

KU-RING-GAI CHASE NATIONAL PARK
29. Elvina Bay
30. Sphinx to Bobbin Head
31. Centre & Duck Hole Tracks

GARIGAL NATIONAL PARK
32. Belrose Circuit
33. Two Creeks Track
34. Forestville Circuit

NORTH EAST SUBURBS
35. Mona Vale to Manly
36. Manly Dam Reserve
37. Spit Bridge to Manly

CENTRAL SYDNEY
38. Lane Cave Three Bridges
39. Iron Cove
40. Bondi to Maroubra

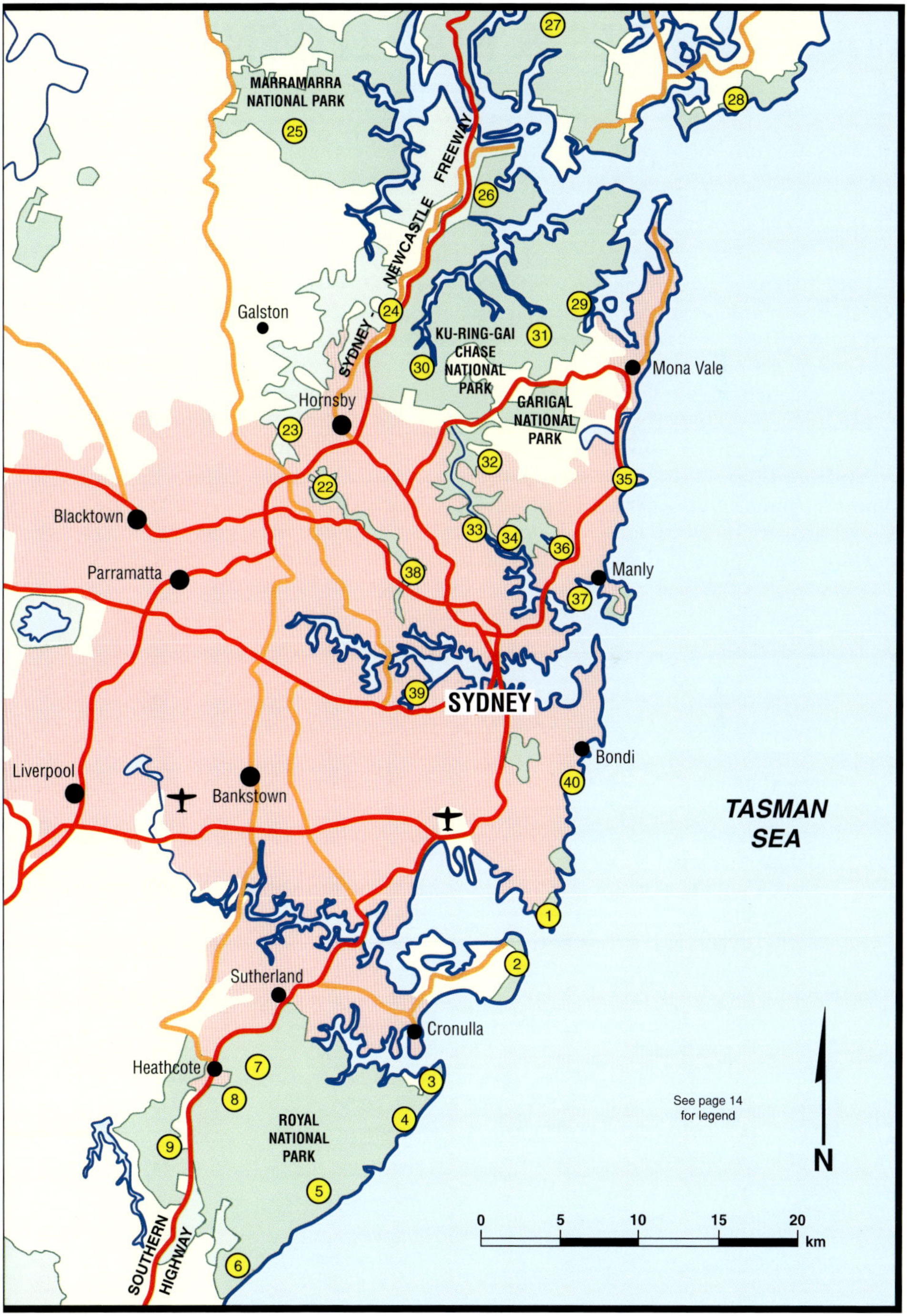
MARRAMARRA NATIONAL PARK
25
27
28
26
SYDNEY - NEWCASTLE FREEWAY
Galston
24
29
KU-RING-GAI CHASE NATIONAL PARK
31
30
Mona Vale
Hornsby
GARIGAL NATIONAL PARK
23
32
35
22
Blacktown
33
34
36
Parramatta
38
Manly
37
39
SYDNEY
Bondi
Liverpool
Bankstown
40
TASMAN SEA
1
2
Sutherland
Cronulla
Heathcote
7
3
8
ROYAL NATIONAL PARK
4
9
5
SOUTHERN HIGHWAY
6
See page 14 for legend
N
0
5
10
15
20
km

WALK GRADES & MAP LEGEND

Gradings are influenced primarily by distance and the amount of climbs and descents with other factors such as track condition and navigation requirements being taken into consideration. These grades are similar to those used by many bushwalking clubs.

Easy – follows constructed, well-defined, level or gently undulating tracks to 7km in length and are able to be completed by walkers of average fitness.

Easy-Medium – follows marked, constructed tracks to 12km. May have some short, steep climbs or descents or longer, gradual climbs. May also follow short sections of unconstructed track with simple navigational requirements.

Medium – requires a reasonable level of fitness with distances to 18km. May also follow long sections of unmarked tracks requiring navigational skill.

Medium-Hard – requires a good level of experience and fitness. May involve some long climbs or descents or be primarily level with distances up to 21km. May also follow very rocky, rough or unmarked tracks requiring navigational skill.

Hard – for experienced, fit walkers. Can be primarily level with distances greater than 18km or require either some competent navigation or include long climbs and descents. May also involve some rock scrambling or wading of streams.

Major or access road	Hut or building
Minor road or street	Ruin or historic site
4 wheel drive track	Camping area
Walking track	Parking area
Unmarked track	Bus Stop
Described walk	Caravan park
Sidetrip/variation	Toilet
Distance marker (11.8)	Mountain or summit
Railway line	Lookout
Railway station	Gate
Park boundary	Golf Course
Urban area	Mine
Power lines	Aboriginal site
Contour line & height (50)	Swamp
Cliff-line	Walk start (START)
Creek	Walk finish (FINISH)
River	Cave
Waterfall or cascade	Tower
Dam, waterhole	Lightstation
Pipeline	Shipwreck
Sand beach	Picnic shelter
Ocean & coastal rocks	

Govetts Leap Brook, Walk 21

PREPARATION & PLANNING

How to get there

Many of the walks described can be reached by public transport. All descriptions include public transport details from the city centre of Sydney. The start and finish of each walk in this book are accessible by two-wheel-drive vehicles. If walking with a group it is better to share transport. Valuables should not left in vehicles before heading off on a walk.

Entry Fees

A fee applies for entry and parking of cars in many national parks and the access notes advise when fees are payable. Fees do not apply to pedestrians. Many of these walks start in the suburbs and many of the popular parking areas have restrictions – some are time based while in others fixed parking fees apply. Read all signs carefully before leaving a vehicle. Where possible, free, day long, parking areas have been suggested.

When to go

Any time! There is a large variety of walks and most are excellent all year round.

What to take

The following list of basic items should be carried in a suitable daypack:

- Waterproof jacket with hood
- Warm jacket or jumper
- Shady hat
- Maps & guidebook
- Compass (GPS optional)
- Whistle
- Torch & matches
- Water bottle
- Lunch & high energy food
- First aid kit
- Trowel & toilet paper
- Sit mat (closed-cell foam mat)
- Sunscreen
- Camera (optional)

Maps

The maps for each walk in this guide are provided to make it easier to follow the notes. They should be used in conjunction with the recommended UBD or SYDWAY street directories or LPI topographic maps. The recommended maps usually provide more detail and cover a larger area. Specialist map shops are listed under Maps in the Yellow Pages telephone directory.

Footwear

The most important item of equipment to ensure an enjoyable day in the bush is comfortable, sturdy footwear. Runners are used by many for walks near Sydney. However, some prefer lightweight walking boots as they provide more foot support, better grip on rough surfaces and more underfoot protection from sharp rocks.

Water

At least one litre of drinking water should be carried by each walker in mild weather conditions, but around three to four litres is suggested in hot weather. It is always safer to carry all water as most water sources along the described walks are unsuitable for drinking.

Boat Harbour, Walk 2

First aid

All walkers should have a sound knowledge of basic first aid. Problems such as blisters, cuts and minor injuries can be managed with what is carried in a personal first aid kit. If walking with a larger group, consideration should also be given to carrying a group first aid kit. Remember to use sunscreen.

Heat injury (hyperthermia)

Heat stress and heat-stroke can occur easily in the summer when daytime temperatures rise above 30°C. A shady hat, an adequate supply of water, and long, regular rests during the heat of the day are essential to avoid heat-related injury.

Cold injury (hypothermia)

Walking in cold, wet conditions for several hours without adequate protection, rest and nourishment can lead to the onset of hypothermia. The best method for treating exposure (as it's more commonly known) is prevention. To reduce the risk of exposure, avoid walking for long periods in cold, windy and wet conditions. Use good windproof and waterproof clothing, and eat and rest regularly to help maintain the body's ability to generate warmth.

Tides

Some coastal walks should not be undertaken at high tide or in rough seas. Tide information is found in daily newspapers (usually near the weather report), in books of tide tables (from map, boating and fishing outlets) or from the internet. The web site **www.bom.gov.au** provides sea conditions and tide forecasts for Sydney.

Cliffs

Sydney has many kilometres of sandstone cliffs and these feature on most of the walks in this guide. While some popular lookouts are fenced, the majority of cliffs are not. Many of the walks visit clifftops as they provide wonderful views and caution should always be taken when approaching any cliff edge.

Glenbrook Creek, Walk 10

Let someone know before you go

The best and simplest safety precaution is to "let someone know before you go". Leave details of the vehicle and its location or public transport details, walk details and expected time of return with a responsible person. Do not rely on walker intention books to initiate a search. Such books are mainly used for statistical purposes and are not checked for overdue walkers until an alarm has been raised by a concerned relative or friend.

What to do if lost

Stop and don't panic. Orientate the map to the features that are visible and try to determine on the map the last known point before becoming lost. Then estimate how long it's been since leaving that spot and the direction taken. This should narrow down the choices of the current location. To confirm the estimated location, either climb to the nearest, clear high point to get a better view, or if a track or creek junction is thought to be close, try to find it. Walk only a couple of hundred metres to check and remember to look around to ensure a return to the current location is possible.

If the current location is still not obvious, it is best to stay put and wait for assistance rather than getting further off course. If lost with a group, keep together. Seek shelter nearby and make a small fire for warmth and as a signal – smoky by day, flaming at night. If there is a need to get water, return as soon as possible. Don't camp too close to running water as searchers' calls may be inaudible. Conserve energy and listen for voices or other signals.

Minimum Impact Bushwalking

Tracks

If there is a track or route, keep to it. Minimise damage by not cutting corners or trampling vegetation to form a new path. Leave gates as they were found – either open or closed.

Toilets

Use toilets at picnic grounds where provided. If nature calls between these locations, dig a hole and ensure waste is buried at least 15cm deep and 100m away from streams.

Rubbish

Carry out all rubbish and dispose of it appropriately.

Useful websites

Bus timetables:	**www.sydneybuses.com**
Train timetables:	**www.cityrail.info**
NSW National Parks:	**www.environment.gov.au/nationalparks**
Bureau of Meteorology:	**www.bom.gov.au**

1 CAPE BANKS

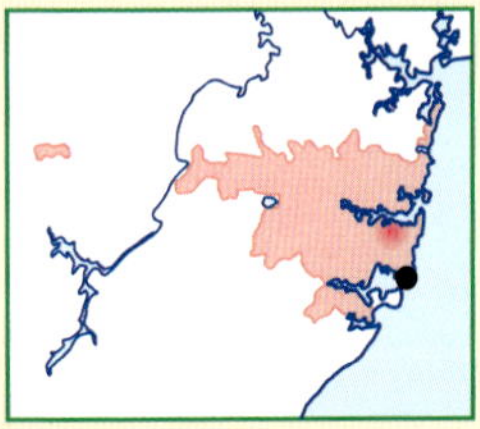

Length: 7.4 km, circuit
Time: 3 hours
Grade: Easy-Medium
Total Climbing: 100m
Maximum Height: 55m
From Sydney: 14km
Closest Suburb: La Perouse
Map: UBD 1:19,000 p296 or SYDWAY 1:20,000 p338

Botany Bay National Park includes the two rocky headlands at the entrance to Botany Bay. It is historically significant being the site where Europeans first met the local aborigines. The suburb of La Perouse is named after the famous French explorer Captain La Perouse who landed in 1788. A monument and museum located close to the start of the walk document his life and can easily be visited either at the start or end of the walk. The northern head of Botany Bay had a series of fortifications built on the clifftops to protect Sydney from attack from the sea. While the guns have been removed, the emplacements and associated lookouts and bunkers can be explored. This walk initially follows wide tracks to the fortifications on Henry Head. A rough, rocky track is then followed to Cape Banks then wider tracks and roads are used for the return. The cape is a popular site for viewing ships entering the bay and also for watching planes land at nearby Sydney airport.

Access:

From Sydney follow Liverpool then Oxford Streets then veer right onto Anzac Parade. Follow Anzac Parade south for 13km to the end of the road in La Perouse. Parking is available in several parking bays on the eastern side of Anzac Parade.

Public transport – from Sydney catch Bus 391 or 393 to the bus turn around at the end of Anzac Parade in La Perouse. Refer www.sydneybuses.com for timetables.

Variation:

1. **Henry Head**, 4.4km, return, 1½ hours, Easy. Follow the first 2.1km of the walk to Henry Head. After exploring the fortifications, return to the 0.7km point then turn right to cross the road and continue from the 6.5km point of the notes to the end.

0.0km At the southern end of Anzac Parade, follow the signposted walking track east onto Congwong Beach. Follow the sandy beach east for 100m then follow the signposted track to a track junction. To the right a short sidetrack leads to Little Congwong Beach. Continue on the left climbing gently through coastal scrub to another track junction. Turn right and follow the track through dense bushland to the next track junction close to a road.

0.7km Turn right and continue southwards towards Henry Head. Ignore unmarked, minor tracks as the path sidles through tall, coastal scrub above Little Congwong Beach. Continue until a sidetrack is met entering from the right and marked as leading to Browns Rocks – a popular fishing site above a small cliff. Follow the

Congwong Bay & Bare Island

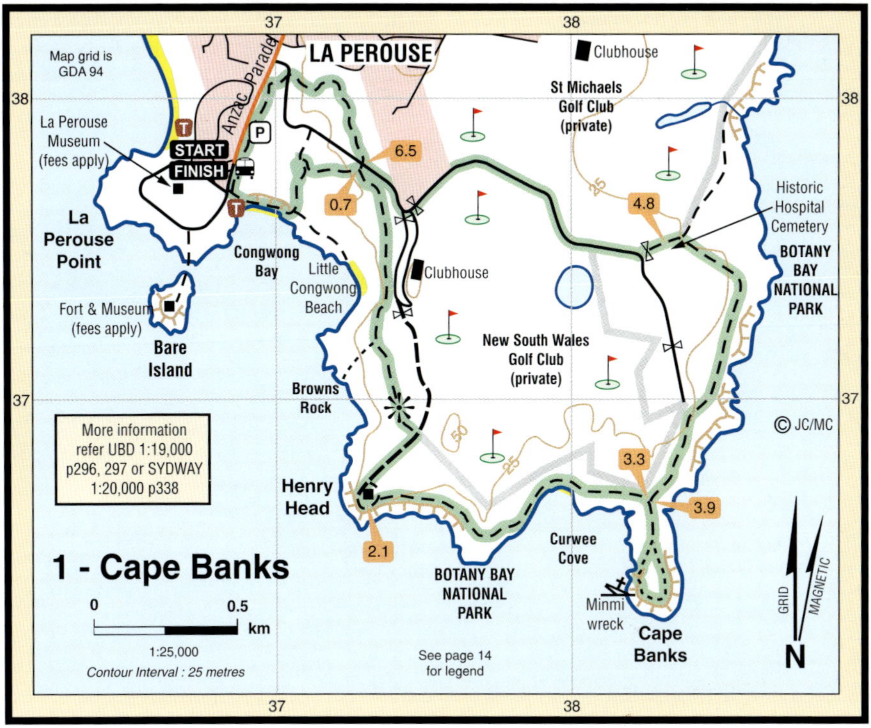

main track straight ahead into heathland where views open up to the west. Veer right at the next junction and follow a powerline to a second world war concrete lookout on a hill. After enjoying the view descend south-east to meet a sealed fire track, turn right and follow it south-west to Henry Head.

Coast Banksia

2.1km The head has a small lightstation for shipping and a series of concrete bunkers, gun emplacements and lookouts. These were constructed to defend Sydney from sea attacks. The fortifications began in the 1880s and were added to many times until finally abandoned after the second world war.

Continue from the eastern gun site on Henry Head and cross the open, rock slabs above the cliff. The rock slabs soon narrow and a well-defined walking track rises over a ridge then steps lead down to an open, sandstone pavement where the track divides. The left track remains above the coastal cliff, but is scrubby. Continue by veering right following the rock platform north-east just above the shoreline of Curwee Cove. Pass a cave then a tiny, sand beach and rise gently along the rocky shoreline to a bridge.

Henry Head bunker

Cape Banks shoreline

3.3km The bridge is the start of a return sidetrip to Cape Banks – the cape is a narrow peninsula that is close to becoming a small island. Cross the bridge and rise onto the narrow spine of Cape Banks. Descend west onto the rocky platform and follow it south under colourful, low cliffs to the rusting remains of the SS Minmi that was wrecked here in 1937. Past the wreck, avoid the rugged shoreline by scrambling east onto the low crest of Cape Banks where there are good views of Botany Bay. Head back along the top of the cape to return to the bridge.

3.9km From the bridge follow a sandy, vehicle track north-east ignoring the first two tracks to the left. The track passes more gun emplacements and lookout towers known as the Cape Banks Battery. The now grassy track continues north-east then north-west crossing low heathlands above coastal cliffs to the entrance to an historic hospital cemetery.

4.8km From the cemetery continue south-west for 100m to pass through a gate onto a road. Turn right and follow the road beside the golf course for 1.1km to a sharp bend to the right. Continue following the road a further 200m to the start of a walking track on the right.

6.5km Follow the walking track north-west through coastal heath. Ignore minor sidetracks as the main track rises to a lookout rock where there are views of Botany Bay. Descend westward to cross the road to the golf course, cross a small creek on a bridge then rise onto grassland beside Anzac Parade. Follow the parade south to the car parks or bus stop.

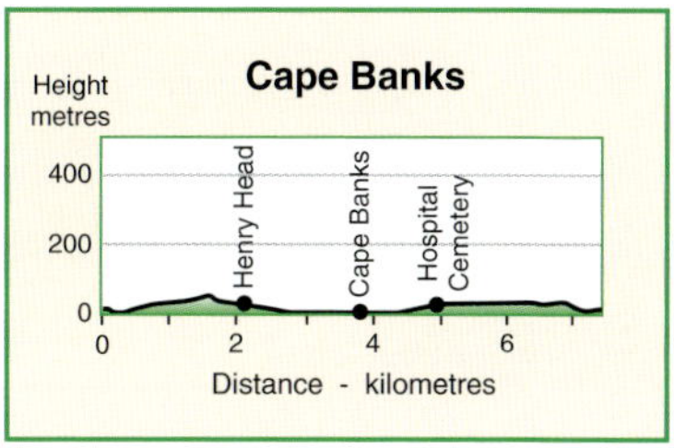

2 KURNELL TO CRONULLA

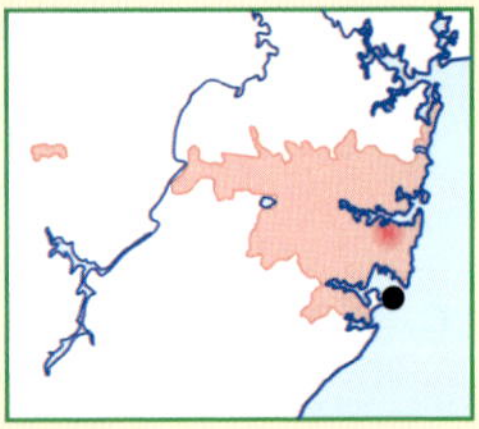

Length: 14.3 km, one-way
Time: 4½ hours
Grade: Medium
Total Climbing: 75m
Maximum Height: 35m
From Sydney: 36km
Closest Suburb: Cronulla 10km
Map: UBD 1:19,000 p316,334, 335, 336 or SYDWAY 1:20,000 p337, 338, 356, 357, 358

The southern half of Botany Bay National Park contains the site where Captain Cook's expedition first landed in Australia in 1770. The expedition stayed here for eight days collecting water and an enormous number of plant specimens. Monuments have been erected to Cook and the expeditions two botanists, Banks and Solander. South of the monuments, the park is undeveloped heathland edged by steep, sandstone cliffs that fall into the ocean. The coastal cliffs are dissected by some narrow gorges that are the remains of volcanic dykes that have been eroded by the sea.

This walk is very varied. Initially it follows a wheelchair standard track past the monuments then the rest of the walk follows rougher tracks. It passes through coastal forest, follows the top of a long cliffline, visits a lightstation, crosses wide, wave-cut platforms then leaves the national park to follow a sandy beach to the end of the walk at Cronulla. There are many excellent views of the rocky coastline.

Coast near Tabbigai Gap

Access

Old Man Banksia

From Sydney follow the Princes Highway south-west for 14km then turn left and follow Rocky Point Road then Taren Point Road south for 8km. Turn left onto Kingsway and follow it for 4km to Cronulla. Park near the railway station 500m to the south. To get to the start of the walk catch the Kurnell 987 bus from the railway station to the entrance to Botany Bay National Park – see www.veoliatransportnsw.com.au for timetables. Note that there are only three bus services on Sunday and public holidays. For the variations, drive from Cronulla along Elouera Road north for 1.5km then follow Captain Cook Drive north-east for 8km to the park entrance. Park left of the entrance for the start from Kurnell. For Cape Solander, enter the park and drive to the end of the road – an entry fee applies for vehicles.

Public transport – from Sydney Central, trains operate on the 'Eastern Suburbs and Illawarra Line' to Cronulla – this may require a train change at Sutherland – refer www.cityrail.info for timetables. From the railway station catch the 987 bus as above to Kurnell.

Safety

Avoid high tides as these make Cronulla Beach narrow and hard to walk along.

Variations:

1. **Kurnell to Cape Solander**, 5.6km, circuit, 2 hours, Easy. Follow the first 3.3km of the walk to Cape Solander then reverse the walk to Yena Track and turn left to follow it then the road to the park entrance.
2. **Cape Solander to Cape Baily lightstation**, 5.0km, return, 2 hours, Easy-Medium. Start at the 3.3km point of the notes and follow the notes to the lightstation at Cape Baily at the 5.8km point then reverse the walk to Cape Solander.
3. **Cape Solander to Potter Point**, 7.0km, return, 2½ hours, Medium. Start at the 3.3km point of the notes and follow the notes to the 6.8km point at Potter Point then reverse the walk to Cape Solander.
4. **Kurnell to Potter Point**, 12.6km, return, 4 hours, Medium. Follow the first 6.8km of the walk to Potter Point then reverse the walk to Yena Track and turn left to follow it then the road to the park entrance.

0.0km From the park entrance walk north-west along the park boundary for 200m then turn right to enter the park. Follow Monument Track north-east passing the historic sites of Cooks Well and monuments to Cook, Banks and Solander. This is the area in which Banks and Solander spent eight days collecting plant samples

Shore below Yena Picnic Area

in 1770. The path follows the foreshore then swings south to head inland to the visitor centre. From the visitor centre veer left across the car parking area to meet Cape Solander Drive. Cross the sealed road and follow Maru Track south-east to a track junction. Ignore the management only track to the right and continue on the left through kunzeas, hakeas and tea-tree forest to meet the sealed Cape Solander Drive.

2.0km Turn right to follow the road for 50m then turn left onto a minor road and descend gently to Yena Picnic Area. The rocky shoreline is easily accessed from the picnic area. Continue following the road as it loops back to the west to meet Cape Solander Drive again. On the opposite side of the road is Yena Track and that can be used as an alternative return track for some of the walk variations.

2.6km Turn left and follow Cape Solander Drive south-east to the end of the road. There is a public car park here – an entry fee to the park applies for vehicles.

3.3km On the left side of the toilet a walking track heads south along the coast. Initially it is not well-defined crossing open, rocky terraces above the coastal cliffs. Continue for 800m to Tabbigai Gap.

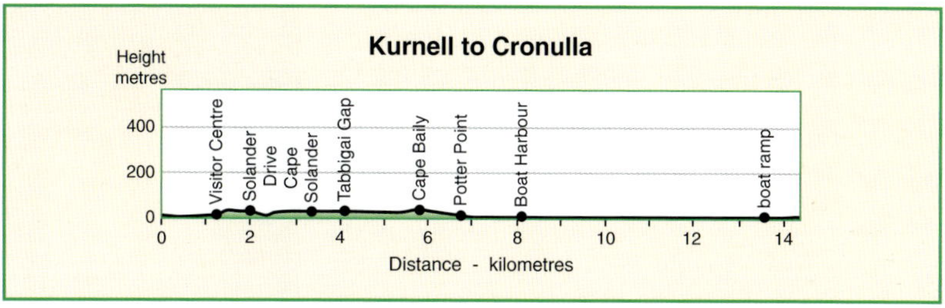

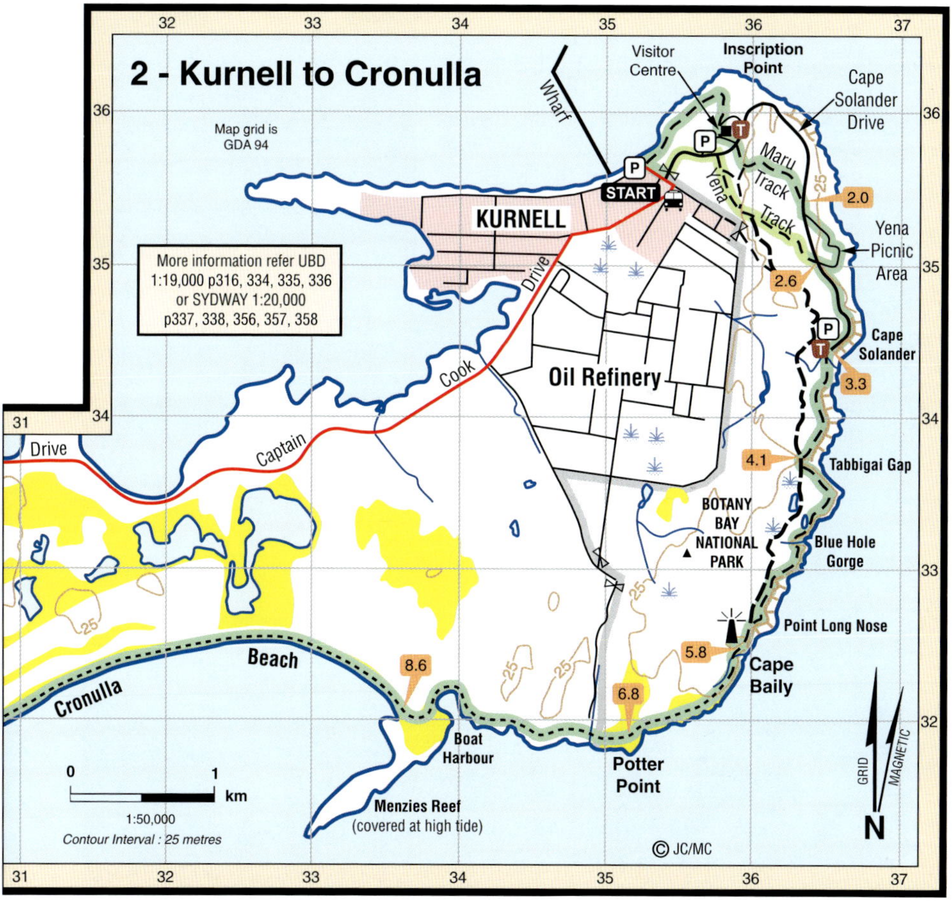

4.1km The gap is a narrow gorge in the cliffs and on the south side of the gorge on cliff ledges are remains of several shacks. At the gap the track divides – the right track is an old vehicle track. Turn left and follow the more minor walking track along the south side of the gap then follow open, rocky slabs southwards along the cliffs. Continue along the clifftops for 1.6km to merge with the old vehicle track, then continue a further 100m to a track junction.

Cape Baily lightstation

5.8km The track on the right is a 200m sidetrip to the automatic lightstation on Cape Baily. While the light is not very interesting, the site provides a good view of the coast. Return to the track junction and turn right and continue south-west following the open terraces between the scrub and the cliffs. The track soon starts descending gently to the extremely wide, rocky terrace behind Potter Point. Potter Point has some interesting rock formations and terraces that are popular with fisherman.

6.8km From Potter Point continue west along the trackless, rocky shoreline for 300m to a wide, shallow gully which contains a pipeline – this is marked by a set of tall riser pipes. Continue following the wave-cut platform west for 1.0km to the tiny cove of Boat Harbour. Follow the sandy shoreline round the small cove then across the back of Menzies Reef onto the sand of Cronulla Beach.

8.6km Follow the sandy beach north-west, west then south-west to its end. Continue west up a boat ramp onto a concrete path then turn south and follow the path underneath the multi-storey residences of Cronulla. Pass two tidal swimming pools then, at the South Cronulla Surf Life Saving Club (SLSC), turn right and head west to Cronulla Railway Station.

Boat Harbour

PORT HACKING POINT 3

Information panel, Jibbon Beach

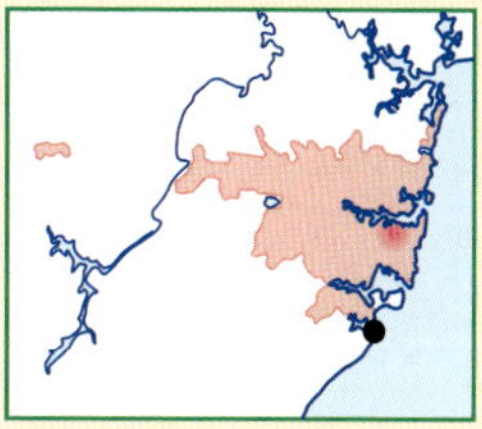

Length: 6.3 km, circuit
Time: 2½ hours
Grade: Easy-Medium
Total Climbing: 90m
Maximum Height: 50m
From Sydney: 54km
Closest Town: Bundeena 0km
Map: LPI 1:35,000 *Royal National Park*

The northern section of Royal National Park is a low headland covered with a mixture of sand hills, heathland and tea-tree forests. The headland separates the quiet waters of Port Hacking from the turbulent waters of the South Pacific Ocean. The contrast between the two bodies of water is best seen from Port Hacking Point. The point was also popular with aborigines and they left behind a series of rock engravings including a kangaroo, a tortoise, whales and a male figure. In warm weather another feature of the walk is the sheltered swimming at Jibbon Beach. Well-used walking tracks follow the coast around the point linking the area's major features.

Access

From Sydney follow the Princes Highway south for 28km to Sutherland. Continue on the highway another 3km then turn left into Farnell Avenue to enter Royal National Park – an entry fee applies. Continue for 3km to Audley then follow Bertram Stevens Drive southward for 10km before turning left and continuing north-east a further 10km to Bundeena. Park near the corner of Brighton and Loftus Streets near the ferry jetty. An alternative is to park near Cronulla Railway Station and catch the ferry to Bundeena.

Public transport – from Sydney Central, trains operate on the 'Eastern Suburbs and Illawarra Line' to Cronulla – this may require a train change at Sutherland – refer www.cityrail.info for timetables. From Cronulla Railway Station head east to the wharf and catch the ferry to Bundeena – this leaves on the half hour each hour and the return ferry leaves Bundeena on the hour – refer www.cronullaferries.com.au for current timetables.

Variations:

1. **Jibbon & Shelley Beaches**, 4.8km, circuit, 1½ hours, Easy. Follow the first 2.7km of the walk to Shelley Beach then follow the track to the west for 400m to Jibbon Beach. Walk west along Jibbon Beach and through the streets of Bundeena to the start.
2. **Port Hacking Point & Marley Beach**, 15.1km, circuit, 5 hours, Medium. Combines Walk 3 and 4 into a longer circuit. Follow the first 4.8km of the walk 3 then turn left and continue from the 1.5km point of Walk 4 to the end of Walk 4 at Bundeena.

0.0km Start at the corner of Brighton and Loftus Streets near the ferry jetty. Head north-east up steps into the park following a heritage walk. The track climbs onto a headland where there are some information panels. Continue to the end of the track then pass left of the RSL building into a narrow street. Follow the sealed street north-east – the street changes name three times. Continue for 700m to where Neil Street swings south-east to meet the end of Loftus Street.

1.0km Turn left and descend north-east following a walking track onto Jibbon Beach. Follow the rocky then sandy shoreline east then north-east to the end of the beach. Ignore the track to the east that crosses to Shelley Beach. Follow a well-used foot track north into heathland. The track stays close to the rocky coastline and initially crosses two, grassy openings then continues north-east to a tiny, sandy cove. Just past the cove there is an unmarked track junction.

1.9km About 25m south-east of the junction on flat rocks are some aboriginal rock engravings. The engravings depict a variety of animals, sea-life and one human figure – walkers are requested to not walk on the engravings. Return to the track junction and continue north-east above the coast through more heath to Port Hacking Point.

2.1km The point is a low, rocky headland backed by heathland and there are excellent views to the north of Cronulla and Kurnell Peninsulas. To the west are the sheltered waters of Port Hacking while to the east the restless waves of the South Pa-

Coast Track

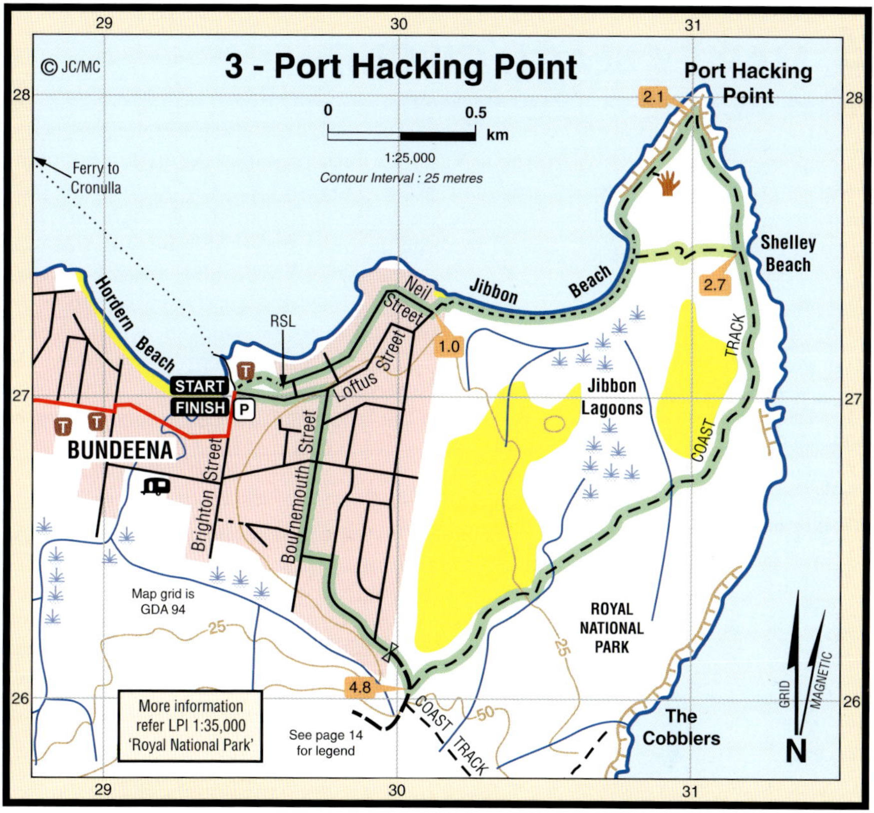

cific Ocean pound the coastline. From the point turn right and continue south-east along the top of the cliffs facing the ocean. Continue southwards for 500m through heathland and tea-tree forest to Shelley Beach.

2.7km At the back of Shelley Beach there is a track junction. Ignore the track heading west across the peninsula to Jibbon Beach. Head south and follow Coast Track which soon widens to become an old, sandy road. Follow this southwards for 700m then leave the coast to swing south-west. Follow the soft, sandy track as it rises gently onto old sand dunes. Continue for 1.4km passing through heathland to a track junction beside a closed, sealed road.

4.8km Turn right and after 100m pass through a gate marking the boundary of Royal National Park. The remainder of the walk is through the streets of Bundeena and there are several options. The suggested route is to keep left at the next two street junctions then turn right into Bournemouth Street and follow it north to Loftus Street. Turn left into Loftus Street to return to the junction of Loftus and Brighton Streets.

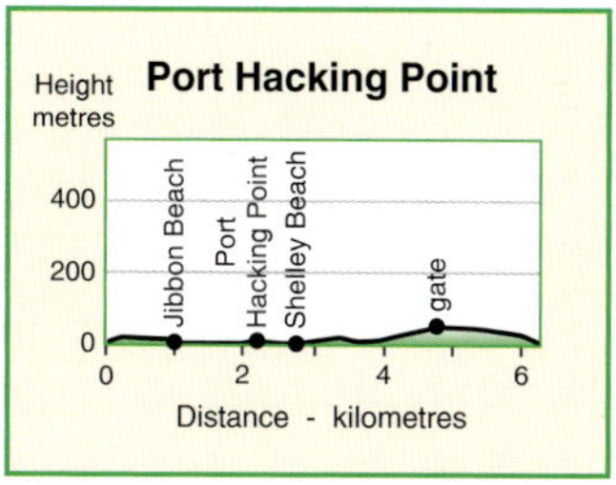

4 MARLEY BEACH CIRCUIT

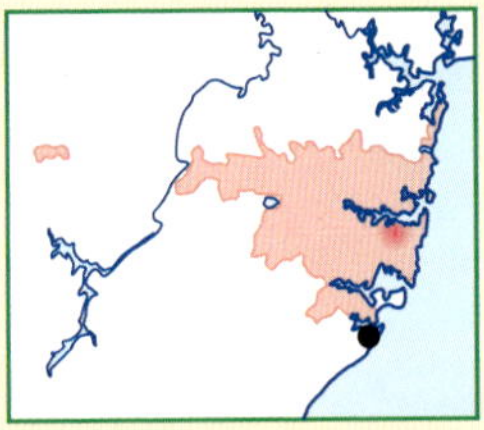

Length: 11.8 km, circuit
Time: 3½ hours
Grade: Medium
Total Climbing: 220m
Maximum Height: 70m
From Sydney: 54km
Closest Town: Bundeena 0km
Map: LPI 1:35,000 *Royal National Park*

Royal National Park provides the venue for many excellent walks. This circuit in the north of the park has some magnificent coastal scenery. It begins by a walk through the quiet streets of Bundeena, but soon enters the national park. Crossing a heath-covered ridge, the track meets the coastal cliffs which are then followed south to the sandy beach at Marley. There are plenty of magnificent views along the way. The surf beach at Marley is not suitable for swimming, but it is interesting as behind the beach are moving sand dunes that hold back a shallow lagoon. The walk returns by following a closed, sandy management track.

Much of the track passes through heathlands and there are always some wildflowers to be seen. The heath is also home to many birds and the observant walker should see fantails, pigeons, honeyeaters and waterbirds. Animals are harder to find, but reptiles such as dragons, skinks, geckos and snakes are often seen basking on the track.

Access

From Sydney follow the Princes Highway south for 28km to Sutherland. Continue on the highway another 3km then turn left into Farnell Avenue to enter Royal National Park – an entry fee applies. Continue for 3km to Audley then follow Bertram Stevens Drive southward for 10km then turn left and continue north-east a further 10km to Bundeena. Park near the corner of Brighton and Loftus Streets near the ferry jetty. An alternative is to park near Cronulla Railway Station and catch the ferry to Bundeena.

Public transport – from Sydney Central, trains operate on the 'Eastern Suburbs and Illawarra Line' to Cronulla – this may require a train change at Sutherland – refer www.cityrail.info for timetables. From Cronulla Railway Station head east to the wharf and catch the ferry to Bundeena – this leaves on the half hour each hour and the return ferry leaves Bundeena on the hour – refer www.cronullaferries.com.au for the current timetable.

Park entry gate

Coast near Marley Beach

Variation:

1. **The Waterrun**, 6.6km, return, 2 hours, Easy. Follow the first 3.3km of the walk to The Waterrun. After exploring the falls, reverse the outward track to Bundeena.

0.0km Start at the corner of Brighton and Loftus Streets near the ferry jetty. Follow Loftus Street east for 300m then turn right into Bournemouth Street. Follow it south for 600m then turn left into Reef Street then right into Beachcomber Avenue. Follow it south then south-east until it ends at the entrance to Royal National Park. Pass through the gate and follow the sealed, management road south-east for 100m to a track junction.

1.5km Ignore the track to the left and continue a further 50m to another track junction. Turn left onto Coast Track which heads towards Marley Beach. Follow the sandy track south-east rising gently onto a high ridge with views across the low heathland. Continue south-east to a track junction close to the coast. An optional, return sidetrack to the left leads to The Cobblers – 30 minutes return.

2.2km Continue on the right following open, rock slabs south-west above the coastal cliffs. There are excellent views of the coastline. Follow the cliff tops for 200m then pass through heathlands inland from the cliff top. Rise gently over a ridge then return to the cliff tops and descend into the gully of The Waterrun.

3.3km The Waterrun is a narrow gully and a short sidetrip scrambling down slabs beside the creek leads to a small waterfall tumbling into the ocean – take care near the cliff edge. Past The Waterrun the track rises over a high ridge then starts descending towards Marley Beach. A management track on the right parallels the

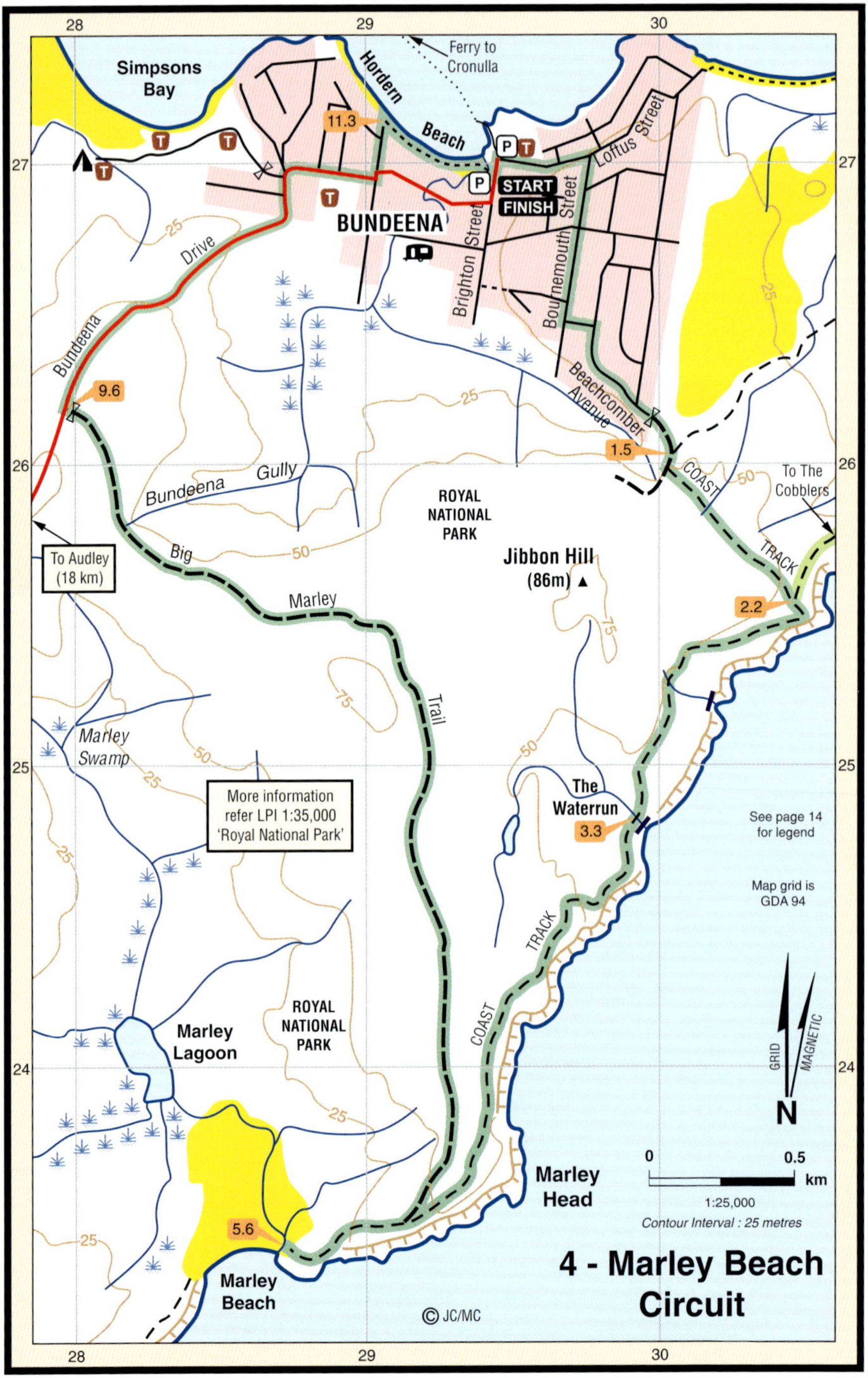
Simpsons Bay
Ferry to Cronulla
Hordern Beach
11.3
START
FINISH
BUNDEENA
Loftus Street
Brighton Street
Bournemouth Street
Beachcomber Avenue
Bundeena Drive
9.6
1.5
COAST TRACK
To The Cobblers
Bundeena Gully
ROYAL NATIONAL PARK
Jibbon Hill (86m)
To Audley (18 km)
Big Marley Trail
2.2
Marley Swamp
More information refer LPI 1:35,000 'Royal National Park'
The Waterrun
3.3
See page 14 for legend
Map grid is GDA 94
Marley Lagoon
ROYAL NATIONAL PARK
GRID
MAGNETIC
N
Marley Head
0
0.5
km
1:25,000
Contour Interval : 25 metres
5.6
Marley Beach
© JC/MC
4 - Marley Beach Circuit

Marley Beach

walking track for several hundred metres – the management track will be used for the return. Continue south-west following the cliff top with good views of Marley Beach. Descend to the sand.

5.6km Marley Beach is a broad expanse of sand surrounded by vegetated sand dunes – there is a lagoon behind the sandblow. After exploring the beach reverse the outward route for 400m then veer left onto the management road – Big Marley Trail. Follow this road north for 2.0km rising steadily onto a broad ridge where there are good views of the coast to the south. The track then swings west and views open up to the north of the Hacking River, Cronulla Peninsula and in the distance the tall buildings of Sydney. The track then swings north-west through tall heathland to pass through a locked gate to meet Bundeena Drive.

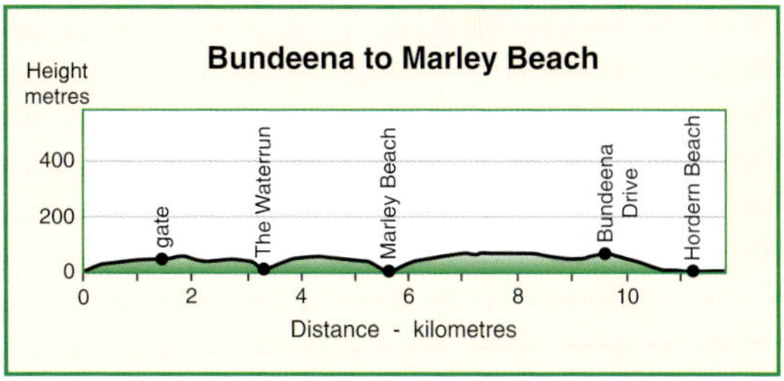

9.6km Turn right and walk beside the sealed road. The left side is generally easier to keep off the road surface – wait for any cars to pass before continuing. Head north-east for 1.2km into Bundeena. At the first sharp bend turn right following the main road east for 300m then at the kink in the road turn left and head north to a boat ramp and Hordern Beach.

11.3km Turn right and follow the sand south-east for 400m then cross the walking bridge and head up steps into the town centre. The jetty is to the left.

5 CURRA MOORS CIRCUIT

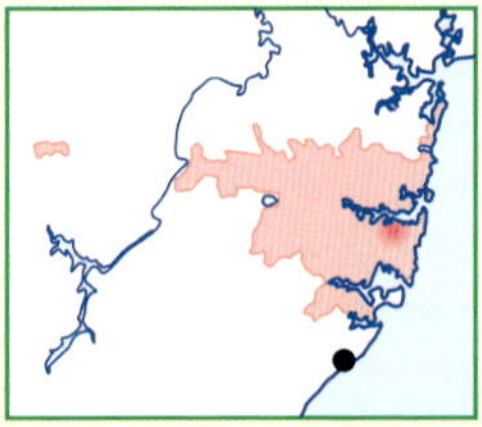

Length: 11.2 km, circuit
Time: 3½ hours
Grade: Medium
Total Climbing: 290m
Maximum Height: 190m
From Sydney: 47km
Closest Town: Sutherland 19km
Map: LPI 1:35,000 *Royal National Park*

The area of Curra Moors in Royal National Park is famous for its wildflower displays. While spring is the peak season, wildflowers can be found year round. There are more than 500 species on the moors. The track to the moors initially passes through light forest where trees such as native apples, peppermints and turpentines are passed. The moors are covered in heathland and needle-bush, grevilleas, banksias, tea-trees, honey-myrtles and sedges, such as purple-flags, are common. Near the drainage lines, christmas bells, broom, banksias and grass trees are readily seen. Clumps of the low growing mallees provide variety on the open moors. Most of the vegetation seen along this walk are species which recover well after fire. The moors have been burnt several times. The track across the moors and along the coast is at times eroded, but some raised, steel walkways have been constructed to help minimise further damage.

Access

From Sydney follow the Princes Highway south for 28km to Sutherland. Continue on the highway another 3km then turn left into Farnell Avenue to enter Royal National Park – an entry fee applies. Continue for 3km to Audley then follow Bertram Stevens Drive southward for 13km ignoring side roads to Curra Moors Car Park on the left. There is no public transport to the start.

0.0km From the north end of the car park follow the walking track north-east into light forest. It soon starts descending gently through open forest. The track is very eroded in places and leads to a crossing of a creek above a small waterfall. On the other side the track climbs gently as it widens into a sandy, management road. Follow it into tall heathland to an unmarked road junction. The return will be along the track to the right.

1.7km Continue straight ahead following the wide, management track north-east. The heathland becomes more open with alternating areas of grassland and scrub. Continue for 1.0km to a management road

Purple-flag

Curra Moors Track

Curracurrong Creek

junction. Ignore the road to the left and continue north-east through heathland for a further 600m to a ford crossing of Curra Brook.

3.3km The wide track rises eastwards then swings south-east descending gently and follows a ridge towards the ocean. There are views of an interesting cliff formation known as Eagle Rock ahead and soon after signposts indicate the junction with Coast Track. There are also good views of Eagle Rock from beside the track near the junction.

4.3km Turn left for a sidetrip to Curracurrong Creek. Follow the track for 200m to where it crosses the creek – the creek is very wide with many pools and rock slabs and some small falls just downstream. Do not go close to the edge of the last fall as this tumbles directly into the ocean. Return to the track junction.

4.9km Turn south-west towards Garie. Coast Track soon crosses Curra Brook then rises onto the high ridge above and parallel to the coast. Steel mesh has been used for much of the track to protect the vegetation and this makes it easy to walk. Follow the track along the ridge top for

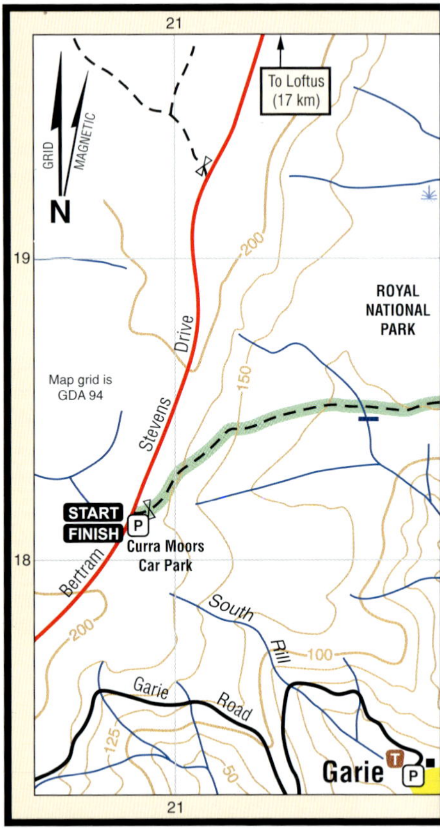

Garie Beach

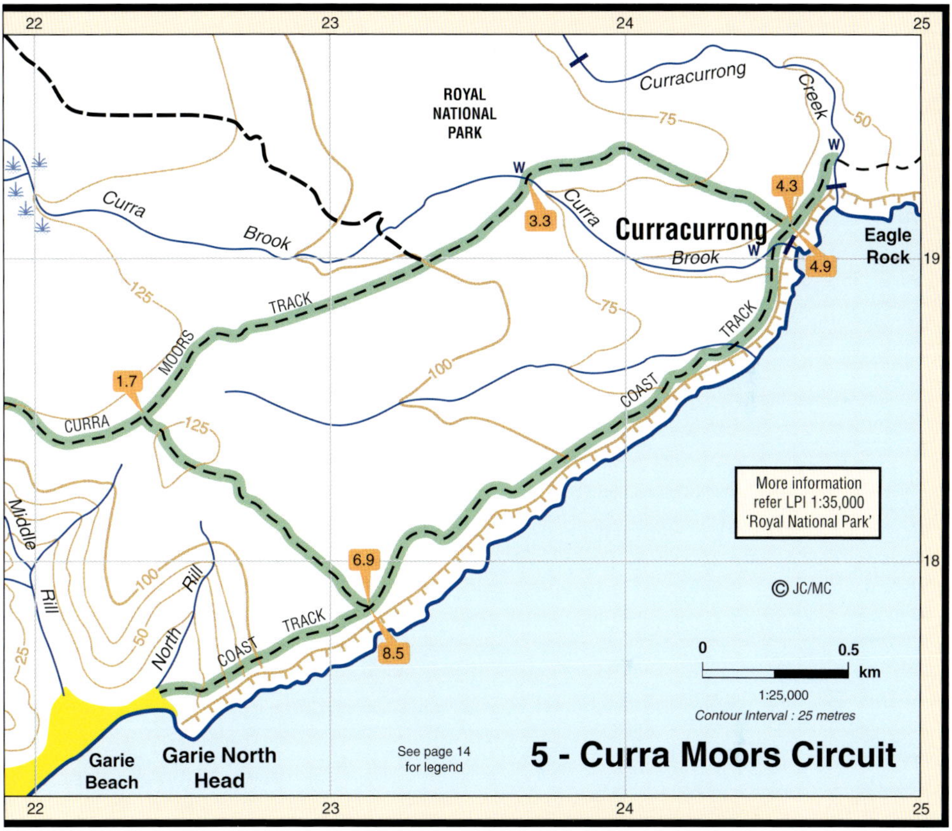

2.0km to a signpost on the left indicating Coast Track. This is very close to the cliff edge and marks a track junction. The track on the right is not marked and is easily missed – it will be used for the return.

6.9km Continue straight ahead on a sidetrip. Follow Coast Track for a further 400m until overlooking Garie Beach. A steep descent follows to the sand at Garie Beach. After exploring the beach return the same way to the track junction.

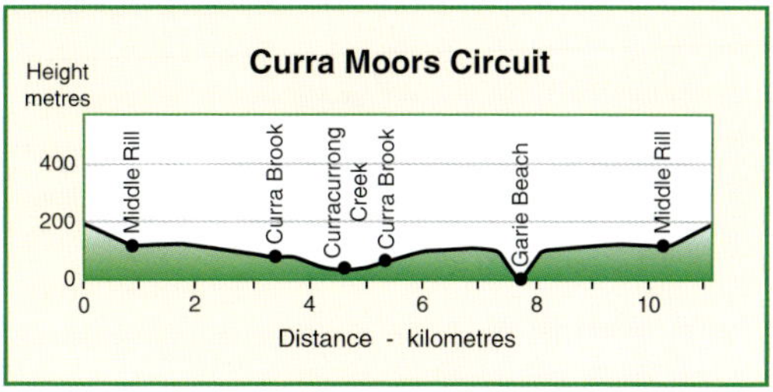

8.5km Turn left to head north-west away from the coast. The track is initially scrubby, but soon widens into another management road. Follow this north-west across the sometimes wet heathland for 1.0km to the first track junction met early on the walk. Turn left and head west to reverse the first 1.6km of the walk back to the car park.

6 OTFORD TO BURNING PALMS

Length: 12.3km, circuit
Time: 3½ hours
Grade: Medium-Hard
Total Climbing: 410m
Maximum Height: 290m
From Sydney: 56km
Closest Town: Otford 1km
Map: LPI 1:35,000 *Royal National Park*

Most of Royal National Park is underlaid with a thick bed of sandstone which produces poor soils and results in most of the park being covered with heathland. In the south the underlying rocks change to shales. As these rocks weather they create rich soils in which taller forest grows. In the more sheltered gullies and southern slopes rainforest has developed and this walk passes through a patch of forest known as Palm Jungle. Under the dense forest canopy are tangled vines and many distinctive Cabbage Tree Palms.

The remainder of the walk passes mainly through drier eucalypt forests. There are a number of clearings left from previous human activity and these, along with some natural outcrops, provide the occasional good view. The coastal edge is less spectacular than the sandstone coastal cliffs seen further north as shales weather more readily leaving behind steep slopes with only a few rocky outcrops.

Turnoff to Palm Jungle

Burning Palms

Access

From Sydney, follow the Princes Highway south for 42km to Waterfall. Continue south along the highway for another 8km then exit left onto Lawrence Hargrave Drive. Follow it for 4km then veer left onto Lady Wakehurst Drive and continue northwards for 2km to Otford. The ridge beside the road is a popular launch area for hang gliders. Park between the hang gliding platform and Otford Lookout.

Public transport – from Sydney Central trains operate on the 'Eastern Suburbs and Illawarra Line' to Otford Railway Station – refer www.cityrail.info for timetables. From the railway station climb steeply south-east for 100m to a gravel road and follow the road for 200m to meet the sealed Lady Wakehurst Drive. Turn left and follow the road 300m to Otford Lookout.

0.0km From Otford Lookout follow Lady Wakehurst Drive north-east for 300m to the start of Coast Track. Follow the walking track north-east up steps into coastal forest. This soon leads to a fence above bluffs where there are good views of the coast to the north-east. The track soon re-enters forest following the ridge crest for 100m to a track junction to Werrong Beach. Keep to the left and pass through forest for 1.0km to where the track widens into a sandy management road. Follow this north-east to a track junction. The walk will return from the left later in the day.

2.2km Turn right following Coast Track towards North Era. This is a well used, but slightly overgrown, walking track passing through tall heath and coastal forest. Continue south-east for 500m descending gently to an unmarked track junction. There is a lookout on Werrong Point 10m right of the track – this has good views of Werrong Beach and the coast to the south.

2.7km Continue on the walking track and 50m further on there is another similar lookout. The Coast Track then descends steps to cross a shallow gully and meets another unmarked track junction. Ignore the very steep, rough track to the right and continue east descending steadily into Palm Jungle. This is an area of rainforest that contains many Cabbage Tree Palms – the track is well defined, but does wind its way around fallen trees and vines. The track levels out and continues north-east through the forest for 900m to a clearing covered with coastal grasses where there is a poorly defined track junction.

Alternative Route to Burning Palms 30 minutes extra

This route involves a steep scramble and should not be attempted at high tide or in heavy seas. In the clearing follow the unmarked track to the south-east. This descends steeply through cliffs to a wave-cut platform which can then be followed north-east around a point to the Figure Eight Pool – this is a naturally formed rock pool. Continue north-east following rocky terraces beside the ocean to the sandy beach at Burning Palms. Rejoin Coast Track near Wren Rill.

4.1km The track is often wet and muddy across the grassland. Follow it north-east then north to descend briefly to pass a rangers' hut then enter the bay of Burning

Palm Jungle

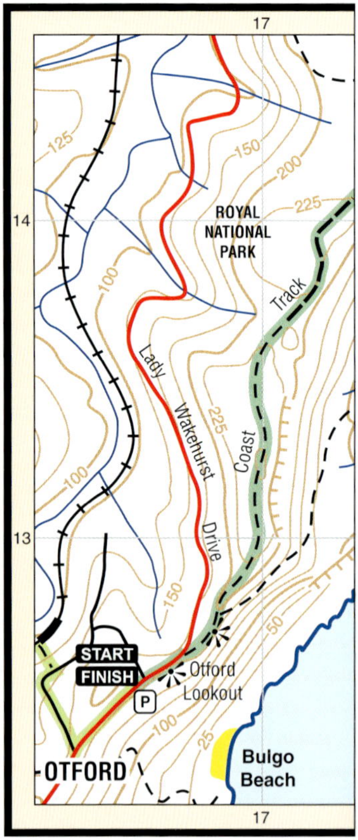

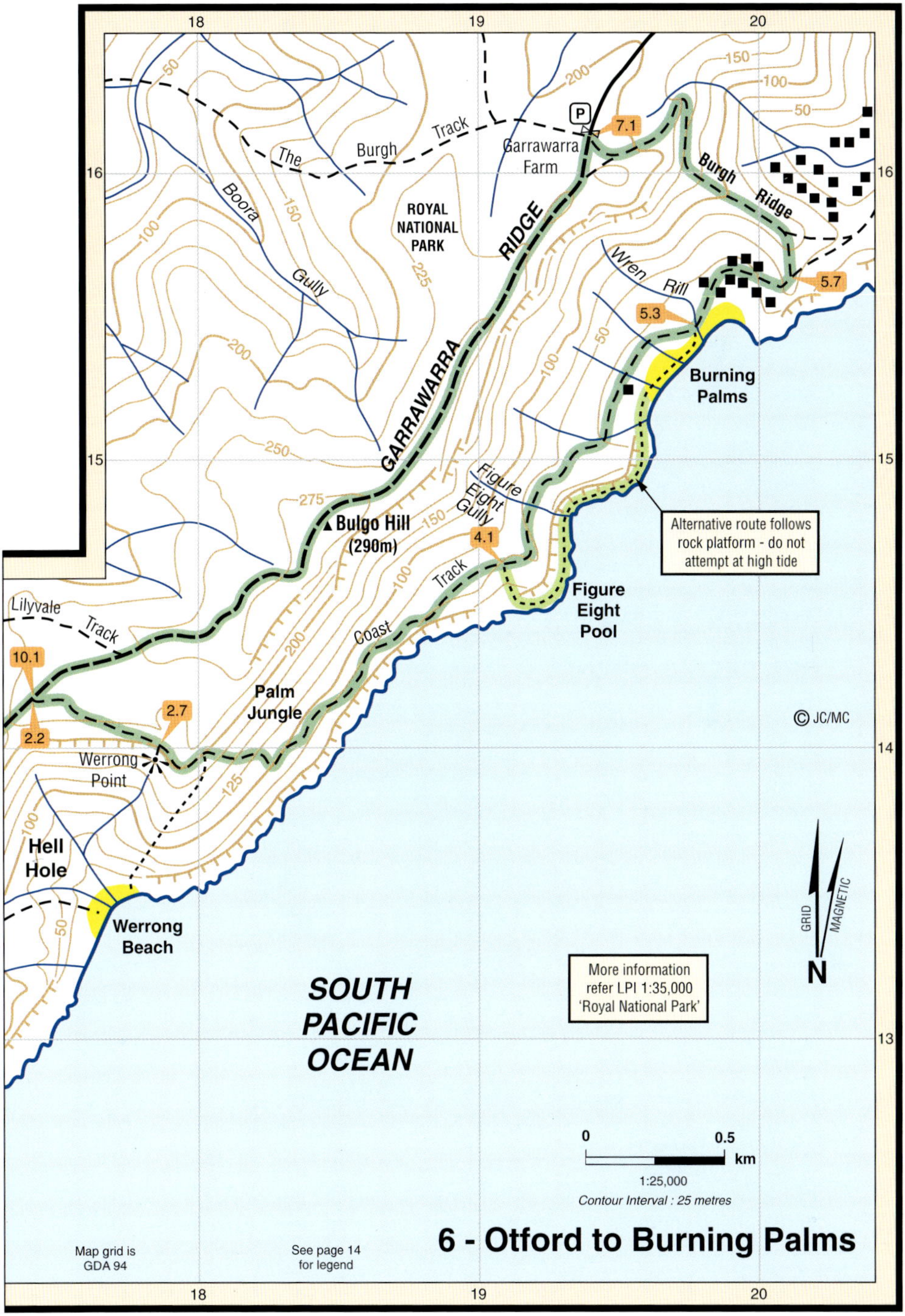

6 - Otford to Burning Palms

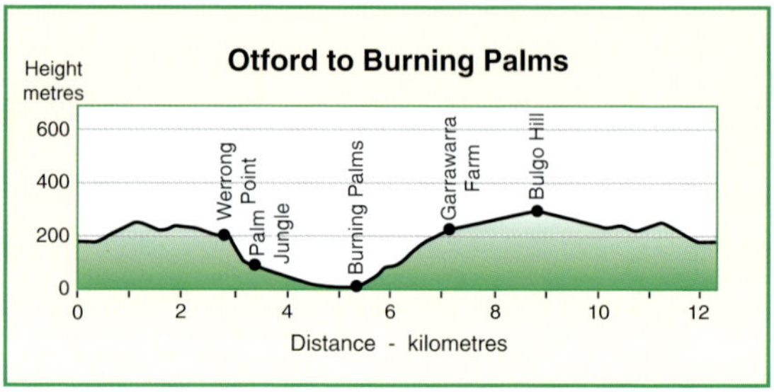

Palms. There are numerous tracks in this area and most of them have been closed to reduce erosion – keep to the signposted track. From the rangers' hut Coast Track initially climbs briefly then sidles the slopes 30m above the bay then descends to Wren Rill. A 10m long sidetrack on the right leads to the sandy beach.

5.3km Continue following Coast Track which crosses the creek via a steel bridge then a steel mesh track gradually climbs north-east. It passes the surf life saving club house then swings south-east climbing above the small village of holiday cabins to a signposted track junction on the ridge.

5.7km Leave Coast Track by turning left and head north-west towards Garrawarra Farm. This is a steep, open climb following the ridge to a knoll on Burgh Ridge where there is another track junction – ignore the track on the right to Era. Continue straight ahead following Burgh Ridge north-west. This is initially level and open, but soon starts climbing and enters dry, coastal forest. The track swings north and then swings back south-west to an unmarked track junction. Ignore the track to the left as it is overgrown. Keep to the right and a short climb leads to a track junction and car park at Garrawarra Farm.

Garrawarra Ridge

7.1km Turn left and follow the wide management track south-west towards Otford along the top of Garrawarra Ridge. While the track follows a high ridge top there are no scenic views from the track as it passes through dry forest that is dominated by eucalypts. The track now rises gently for 1.7km to cross Bulgo Hill then descends gradually for 1.0km to a track junction. Ignore Lilyvale Track on the right and continue straight ahead for 300m to the next track junction which was met earlier in the day.

10.1km Continue south-west reversing the first 2.2km of the walk to Otford Lookout.

HEATHCOTE AUDLEY CIRCUIT 7

The western section of Royal National Park is clothed by a mosaic of open woodland and heathland. Wildflowers are common with waratahs, grevilleas, heaths and boronias often found close to the tracks. On bare rocks near streams, water dragons are sometimes found soaking up the sun.

The landscape consists of a series of rocky ridges separated by deep gullies with rock-filled streams flowing through them. While most of the walking is through the woodland, some of the higher ridges and heathlands provide views of the tall buildings of central Sydney. The tracks are well used and generally signposted making them fairly easy to follow. Being very close to houses, there are a number of minor untracked pads and at unmarked intersections follow the more major track. To reduce erosion there are some steel staircases and timber steps, but in general the tracks are rough underfoot and at times quite narrow.

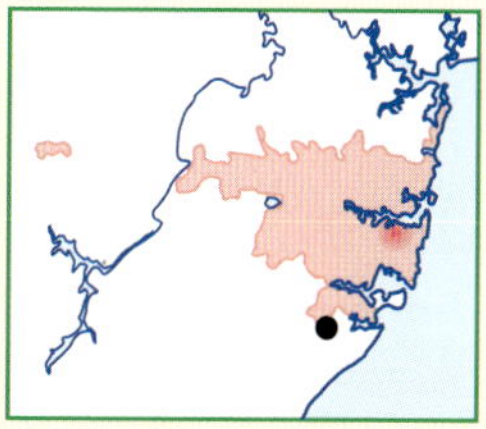

Length: 15.4km, circuit
Time: 5½ hours
Grade: Medium-Hard
Total Climbing: 490m
Maximum Height: 200m
From Sydney: 36km
Closest Town: Heathcote 0km
Map: LPI 1:35,000 *Royal National Park*

Karloo Pool

Access

From Sydney, follow the Princes Highway south for 36km to Heathcote. Parking is available on both sides of the railway station.

Public transport – from Sydney Central trains operate on the 'Eastern Suburbs and Illawarra Line' to Heathcote Railway station. Refer www.cityrail.info for timetables.

Variations:

1. **Heathcote to Karloo Pool**, 5.4km, return, 2 hours, Easy-Medium. Follow the first 2.7km of the described walk to the pool. After exploring the pool return along the same track to the start.
2. **Heathcote to Uloola Falls**, 10.0km, return, 4 hours, Medium. Follow the first 5.0km of the described walk to Uloola Falls. Return along the same track to the start.

0.0km From the east side of the railway station, cross Wilson Parade to the Emergency Services buildings. Turn right passing the Fire Brigade sheds to the signposted start of Karloo Track. Turn left and follow the track east for 400m passing behind the emergency services buildings to a track junction. The return will be on the fire trail on the left.

0.5km Turn right and follow Karloo Track descending steadily south-east for 900m to cross the headwaters of Heathcote Creek. Past the creek merge with another track and swing east rising gently onto a rock slab. Continue east following level sandstone terraces to the crest of Goondera Ridge. Descend north then east to a track junction beside Kangaroo Creek.

2.7km Turn right and head towards Uloola Falls skirting the edge of Karloo Pool which is a popular swimming spot. The track soon leaves the pool and climbs steadily

Uloola Brook

Waratah

passing many grass-trees as it rises onto a high ridge. Swing south-east crossing the open tops of the ridge from where there are views to the north of the tall buildings of Sydney. The track is fairly easy to follow except where it crosses bare rock slabs – painted white lines are provided as track markers. The track veers left through a band of rocks called the Uloola Turrets then descends gently to Uloola Falls. Cross Uloola Brook above the falls to a camping area, toilet and track junction.

5.0km Turn left towards Audley. The track climbs gently eastwards for 400m onto the top of a ridge where there are scratched directions to the south-east on a flat rock. Within 30m of the track are aboriginal sharpening grooves and some engravings on the largest rock slab.

5.4km Follow the walking track north along the ridge top for 400m to where the track divides. Veer left and a very gentle descent north following a long ridge for 1.0km leads to the 'Whaleback'. This is part of a series of large, rounded rocky ribs on top of Gurrumboola Ridge. The track follows the crest of the first rib then leaves it on the west side to round the base of the rib then continues north, passing other outcrops, onto the crest of the broad, heath-covered Gurrumboola Ridge. The low heath allows views of the surrounding ridges and Sydney is again visible in the distance. Continue to a saddle and track junction.

7.7km Turn right towards Audley and a gentle descent leads north-east through light forest to grassy flats and a car park beside Hacking River. This is Kookaburra Flat and there are toilets, a shelter hut and many picnic tables. In poor weather it is an ideal lunch site.

8.8km Walk northwards following the sealed road beside the Hacking River for 1.0km to the road bridge. Stay on the east side of the river for 100m to enter another car park and the start of the Engadine Track – signposted as Audley Heathcote Trail.

9.9km Follow the walking track up steps to a track junction. Turn right towards Kangaroo Creek and continue west for 300m to the next track junction. Again keep to the right and climb gently west onto a ridge where there are good views of Kangaroo Creek. Continue north-west descending steeply. There are several sets of steel stairs and they lead to a rock hop across Kangaroo Creek.

11.1km Continue following the signposted walking track towards Heathcote. The track initially climbs west to meet the gully of Tuckawa Rill. It then swings south-west

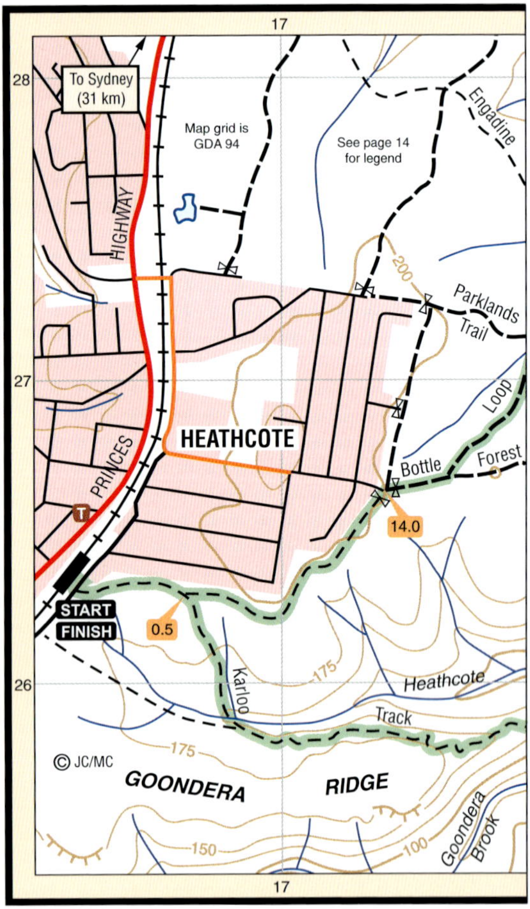

and climbs steadily following the gully upstream. After a long steady climb the track swings west to cross the now small gully. Past the gully ignore any unmarked, minor sidetracks to the left and continue climbing steadily onto a broad knoll to meet a fire trail. An alternative return route is to follow Bottle Forest Trail to the left.

12.6km Cross the firetrail and continue north-west for 300m towards Engadine to meet another fire-trail. Turn left and follow Loop Trail south-west towards Heathcote for 300m to where the fire trail divides. Veer left and continue south-west. In spring many waratahs can be seen flowering in the open forest. After 600m merge with Bottle Forest Trail and walk west for 200m to pass through a gate at the edge of the houses of Heathcote.

14.0km Turn left passing through another gate onto a fire trail that skirts south-west around the edge of the suburb. At the first division of the track take either track as they soon join. The track again divides as it swings west and the left track is more pleasant to walk along as it passes through bush away from the houses. The track soon merges again with the main fire trail and leads to the junction met near the start. To the left is Karloo Track, continue straight ahead and reverse the first 500m of the walk around the Emergency Services area back to Heathcote Railway Station to end the walk.

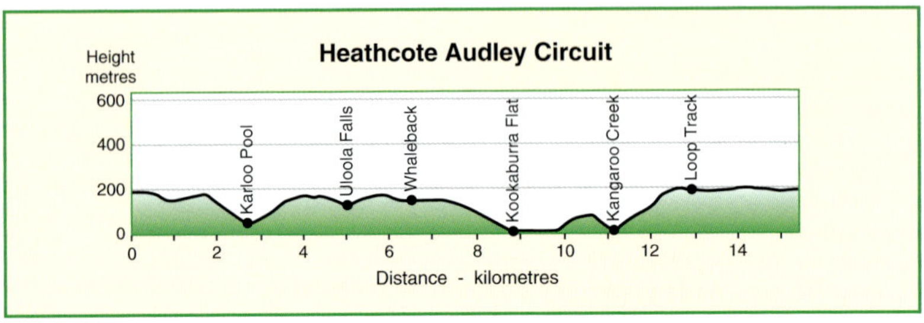

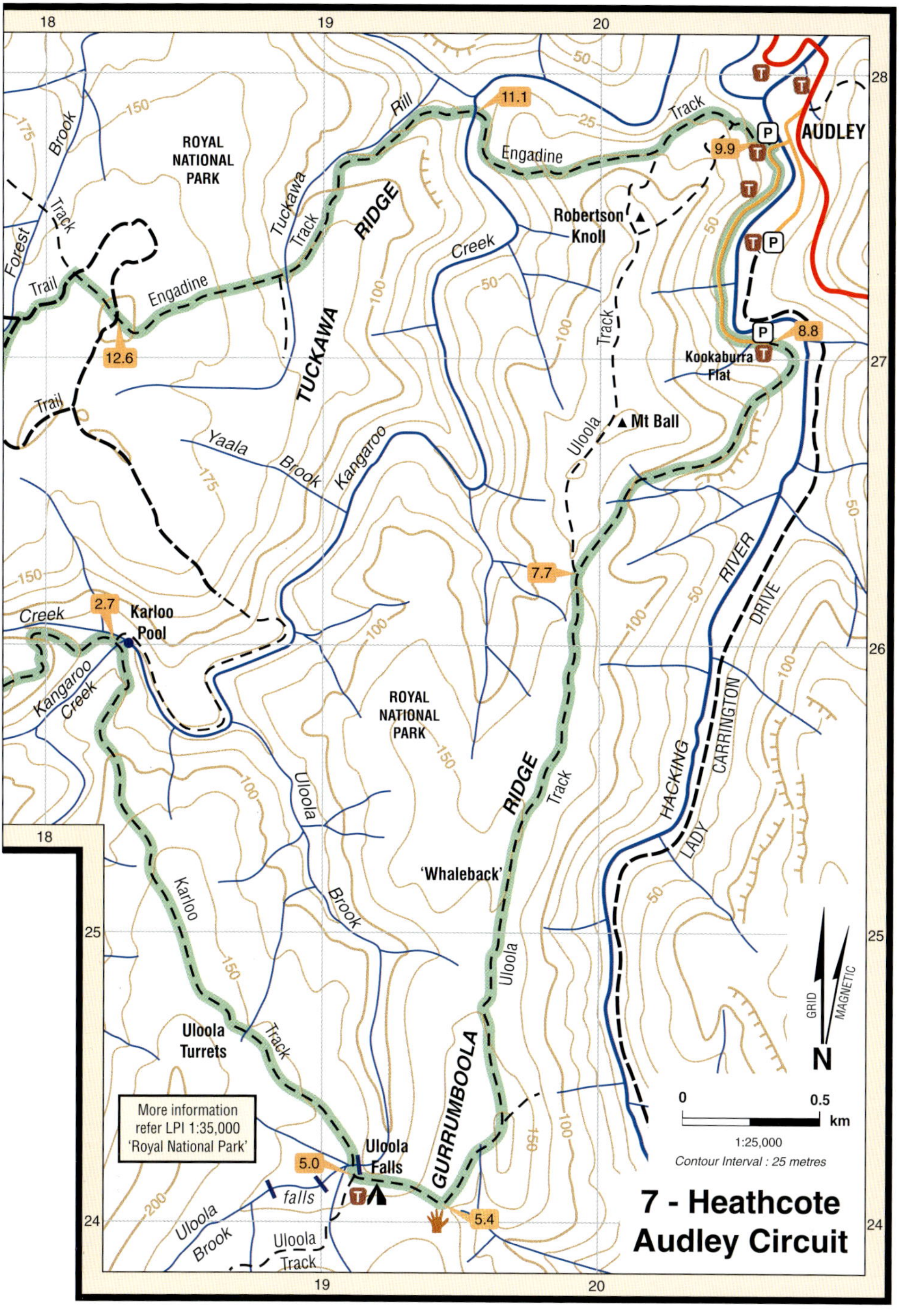
7 - Heathcote Audley Circuit
ROYAL NATIONAL PARK
AUDLEY
Robertson Knoll
Kookaburra Flat
Mt Ball
Karloo Pool
'Whaleback'
Uloola Turrets
Uloola Falls
TUCKAWA RIDGE
GURRUMBOOLA RIDGE
HACKING RIVER
LADY CARRINGTON DRIVE
Engadine Track
Engadine Trail
Tuckawa Track
Forest Track
Uloola Track
Karloo Track
Kangaroo Creek
Yaala Brook
Uloola Brook
Brook
Rill
Creek
falls
More information refer LPI 1:35,000 'Royal National Park'
GRID
MAGNETIC
N
0
0.5
km
1:25,000
Contour Interval : 25 metres
2.7
5.0
5.4
7.7
8.8
9.9
11.1
12.6

8 KANGAROO CREEK

Length: 14.8km, circuit
Time: 6 hours
Grade: Medium-Hard
Total Climbing: 490m
Maximum Height: 230m
From Sydney: 42km
Closest Town: Waterfall 0km
Map: LPI 1:35,000 *Royal National Park*

Kangaroo Creek is one of the major streams flowing through the bushland of Royal National Park. While there are no 'official' tracks along it, many walkers follow the creek and there is a well-used track through the valley. It starts at Waterfall Railway Station and is easy and well-defined until it reaches a 5m high waterfall. After the fall, the track becomes rougher as the valley narrows and the creek heads through small gorges to Karloo Pool. Kangaroo Creek is very scenic with several cascades and many quiet pools surrounded by light forest. Wildflowers abound in spring when the dry, sparse woodlands come to life with colourful heaths, wattles, tea-tree, boronias and banksias.

From Karloo Pool there are several options. This walk describes the return via the 15m high Uloola Falls and the Uloola Trail which follows a high sandstone ridge. Walk 7 provides details for walk variations to Heathcote Railway Station.

Waterfall, Kangaroo Creek

Kangaroo Creek

Access

From Sydney, follow the Princes Highway south for 42km to Waterfall. Parking is available on the east side of the railway station.

Public transport – from Sydney Central, trains operate on the 'Eastern Suburbs and Illawarra Line' to Waterfall Railway station. Refer www.cityrail.info for timetables.

Variations:

1. **Waterfall to Kangaroo Creek Falls**, 4.4km, return, 2½ hours, Easy-Medium. Follow the first 2.2km of the described walk to the falls then reverse the outward track back to Waterfall.
2. **Waterfall to Karloo Pool & Heathcote**, 9.2km, one-way, 4½ hours, Medium-Hard. Follow the first 6.5km of the described walk to Karloo Pool. After exploring the pool, reverse the first 2.7km of Walk 7 from Karloo Pool to Heathcote Railway Station. Use the train to complete a circuit.
3. **Waterfall to Audley & Heathcote,** 19.2km, one-way, 8 hours, Hard. Follow the first 8.8km of the described walk to Uloola Falls. From the falls follow the notes for Walk 7 from the 5.0km point to the end of the walk at Heathcote Railway Station. Use the train to complete a circuit.

0.0km At the car park on the east side of Waterfall Station there are two gates in the fence about 20m apart. The walk will return from the right hand gate. Pass through the left hand gate, follow the fence north for 20m then turn right and head north-east through bracken. The walking track is initially faint where it passes through the bracken, but soon becomes more clearly defined as it enters

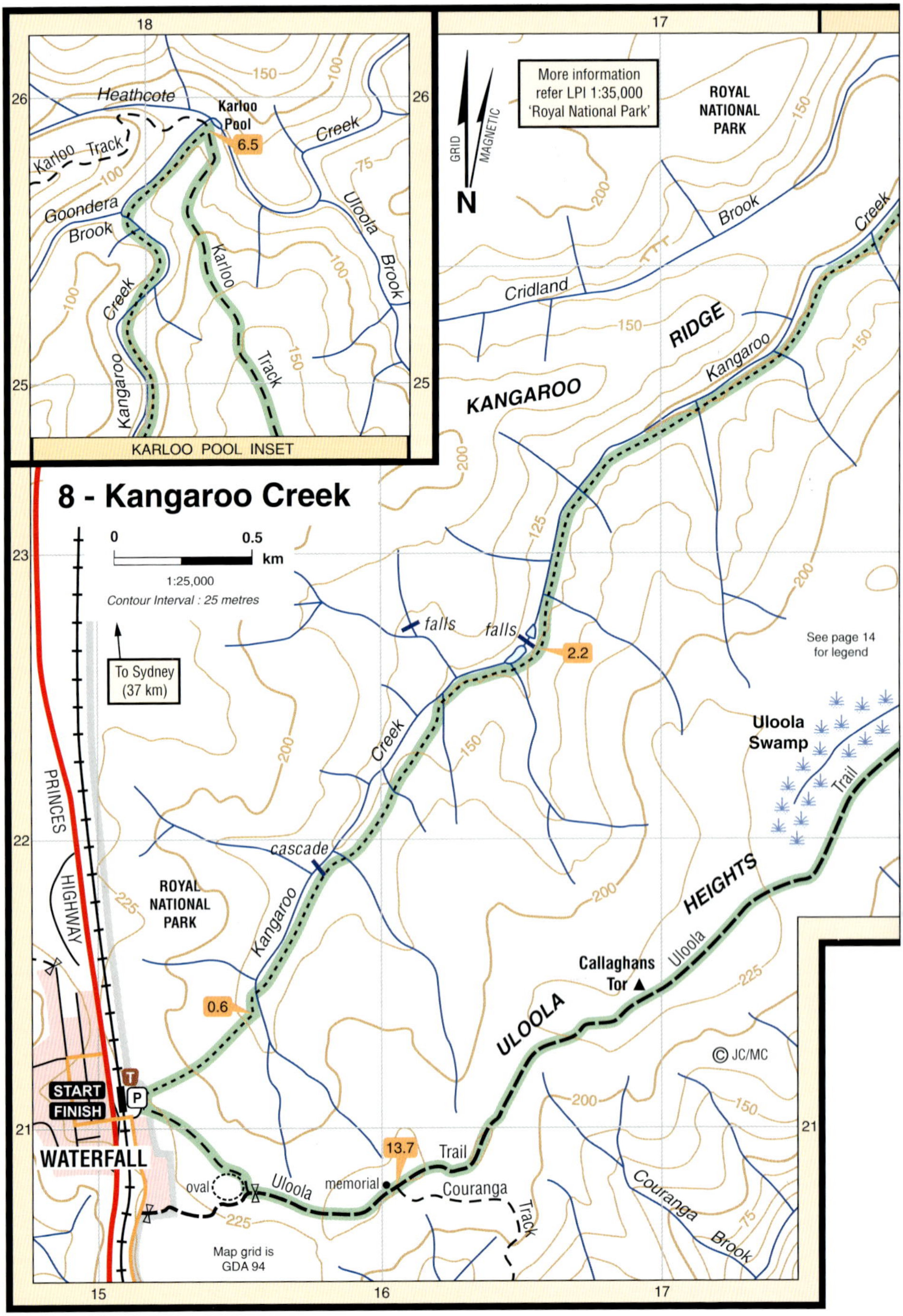
8 - Kangaroo Creek
KARLOO POOL INSET
Heathcote
Karloo Pool
6.5
Creek
Karloo Track
Goondera Brook
Kangaroo Creek
Karloo Track
Uloola Brook
More information refer LPI 1:35,000 'Royal National Park'
GRID
MAGNETIC
N
ROYAL NATIONAL PARK
Brook
Cridland
Creek
RIDGE
Kangaroo
KANGAROO
0
0.5
km
1:25,000
Contour Interval : 25 metres
To Sydney (37 km)
falls
falls
2.2
See page 14 for legend
Uloola Swamp
Creek
Trail
PRINCES
HIGHWAY
cascade
ROYAL NATIONAL PARK
Kangaroo
HEIGHTS
Callaghans Tor
Uloola
0.6
ULOOLA
© JC/MC
START
FINISH
WATERFALL
13.7
Trail
oval
Uloola
memorial
Couranga
Track
Couranga
Brook
Map grid is GDA 94

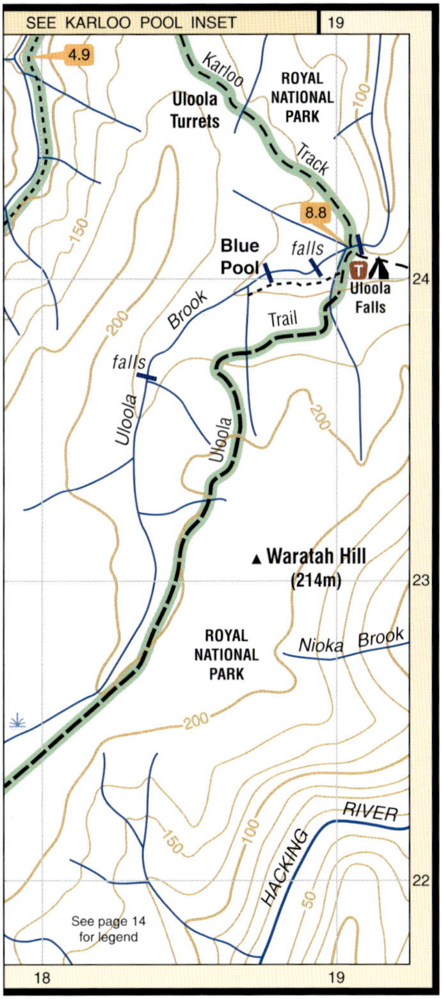

open forest. Continue north-east for 600m descending gently to meet Kangaroo Creek.

0.6km An unmarked, but generally well-defined, walking track follows the creek downstream. Follow it north-east and it soon crosses to the eastern bank. The track passes through mixed patches of tall heathland and open forest. Continue downstream for 500m to rock slabs above a small gorge where there are small cliffs on both sides. The track then leaves the creek and sidles the valley wall keeping above the cliff. It soon passes above cascades, crosses a side creek then sidles above the cliff line for a further 300m. Descend a spur to cross another side creek near its junction with Kangaroo Creek. From here follow rock slabs in the creek bed downstream to a long pool. Follow the eastern side of the pool to the top of a 5m waterfall. Continue past the fall then descend steeply to its base and the deep plunge pool.

2.2km The pool is a popular swimming spot and on the east side an overhang provides shelter in damp weather. From the pool, climb back to the track and continue following the creek downstream. The track becomes less obvious and deteriorates into a series of rough walking pads. Remain on the eastern bank close to Kangaroo Creek and follow a number of rock slabs then skirt past several, small cascades. Continue for 2.7km to enter a small gorge where Cridland Brook flows in from the west.

4.9km Beyond Cridland Brook the valley of Kangaroo Creek narrows as it passes through another small gorge. The walking pads become rougher and it is necessary to cross Kangaroo Creek several times to avoid cliffs on the outside of some sweeping bends. Cross to the east bank just before Goondera Brook from where a rough, rocky pad sidles north-east along the gorge wall to open slabs above Karloo Pool. The pool is a popular swimming spot and the well-marked Karloo Track is met here – this is about 3½ to 4 hours from Waterfall Railway Station.

6.5km Turn right and follow Karloo Track towards Uloola Falls following the edge of Karloo Pool. The track soon leaves the pool and climbs steadily passing many grass-trees as it rises onto a high ridge. Swing south-east crossing the open tops of the ridge from where there are views to the north of the tall buildings of Sydney. The track is fairly easy to follow except where it crosses bare, rock slabs – painted white lines are provided as track markers. The track veers left through a band of rocks called the Uloola Turrets then descends gently to Uloola Falls. Cross Uloola Brook above the falls to a camping area, toilet and track junction.

Uloola Trail

8.8km Turn right and follow the signposted walking track south-west towards Waterfall. The track climbs to an unmarked track junction – ignore the minor pad on the right which leads to Blue Pool on Uloola Brook. Continue following the main track on the left climbing up a small cliffline to meet Uloola Trail. Turn right onto this and follow it south – this wide fire trail provides easy walking. It soon rises onto the top of the ridge then remains fairly level as it follows the crest south-west onto Uloola Heights. Pass a number of clearings which are helicopter pads used for fire fighting operations. Continue onto the open rise of Callaghans Tor where there are views of the surrounding ridges. A gentle descent leads to a junction with Couranga Track.

13.7km Keep to the right and soon after the junction there is a Bushfire Volunteer Memorial to five fire-fighters who died near here in 1980. Continue a further 500m west following Uloola Trail to a gate. Pass though the gate and leave Uloola Trail veering right (north-west) towards Waterfall. Cross an old cricket oval covered in rough grass. The track is initially not obvious and after 100m signposts indicate where the walking track enters open forest. Continue for 500m to the car park and the end of the walk just east of Waterfall Railway Station.

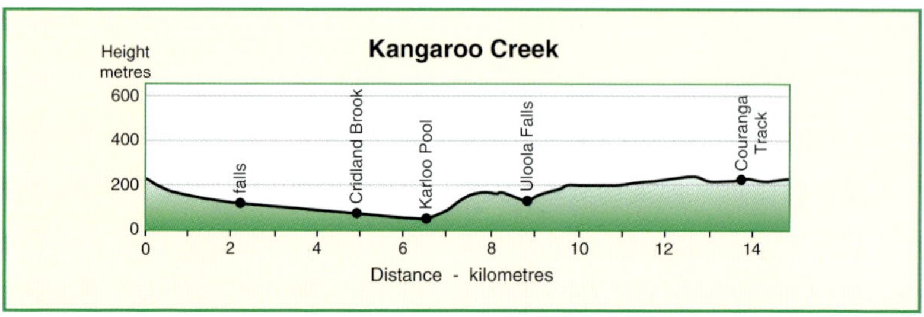

BULLAWARRING TRACK 9

West of Royal National Park is the much smaller Heathcote National Park. This little known park is wilder than its bigger neighbour with steeper gullies and no public roads dissecting it. The park consists of a series of sheltered gullies surrounding the headwaters of Heathcote Creek. The creek contains a number of deep, tranquil pools and in warm weather these are popular swimming spots.

The main track through the park is the Bullawarring Track. This is a pleasant walking track that follows Heathcote Creek. A train line runs along the eastern border of the park providing easy access to both ends of the track. A wide variety of plants are seen beside the track and common plants are kunzea, tea tree, causarina, angophera and bloodwoods. In spring and early summer the spectacular 2 to 3 metre tall flowers of the gymea lily can be seen from the rocky terraces. Lyrebirds are also sometimes seen close to the track.

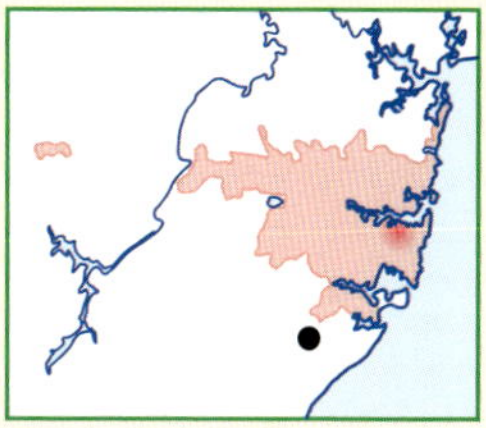

Length: 10.8km, one-way
Time: 3½ hours
Grade: Medium
Total Climbing: 250m
Total Descent: 285m
Maximum Height: 230m
From Sydney: 42km
Closest Town: Waterfall 0km
Map: LPI 1:35,000 *Royal National Park*

Access

From Sydney, follow the Princes Highway south for 36km to Heathcote. Parking is available on both sides of the railway station. To get to the start of the walk, catch a train from Heathcote Railway Station to Waterfall, which is the next station to the south.

Public transport – from Sydney Central, trains operate on the 'Eastern Suburbs and Illawarra Line' to Waterfall Railway Station. The return is from Heathcote Railway Station which is on the same line. Refer www.cityrail.info for timetables.

Variations:

1. **Kingfisher Pool**, 5.0km, return, 2 hours, Easy. Follow the first 2.5km of the described walk to Kingfisher Pool. Return along the same track to the start.
2. **Mooray Track**, 6.3km, circuit, 2½ hours, Medium. Follow the first 3.2km of the described walk then turn right and follow Mooray Track to return to Waterfall.

0.0km From Waterfall Railway Station head west crossing the bridge over the highway and 100m further west turn right into Warabin Street. Follow it north to the end then veer left onto a closed vehicle track. Follow the vehicle track for 50m and turn left onto the signposted Bullawarring Track. Follow the walking track south-west to the top of a small cliff where the track braids into multiple pads. Follow the cliff-top south for 50m then descend steeply through forest to meet a vehicle track. Turn right then within 10m turn left at a rock painted with 'Heath-

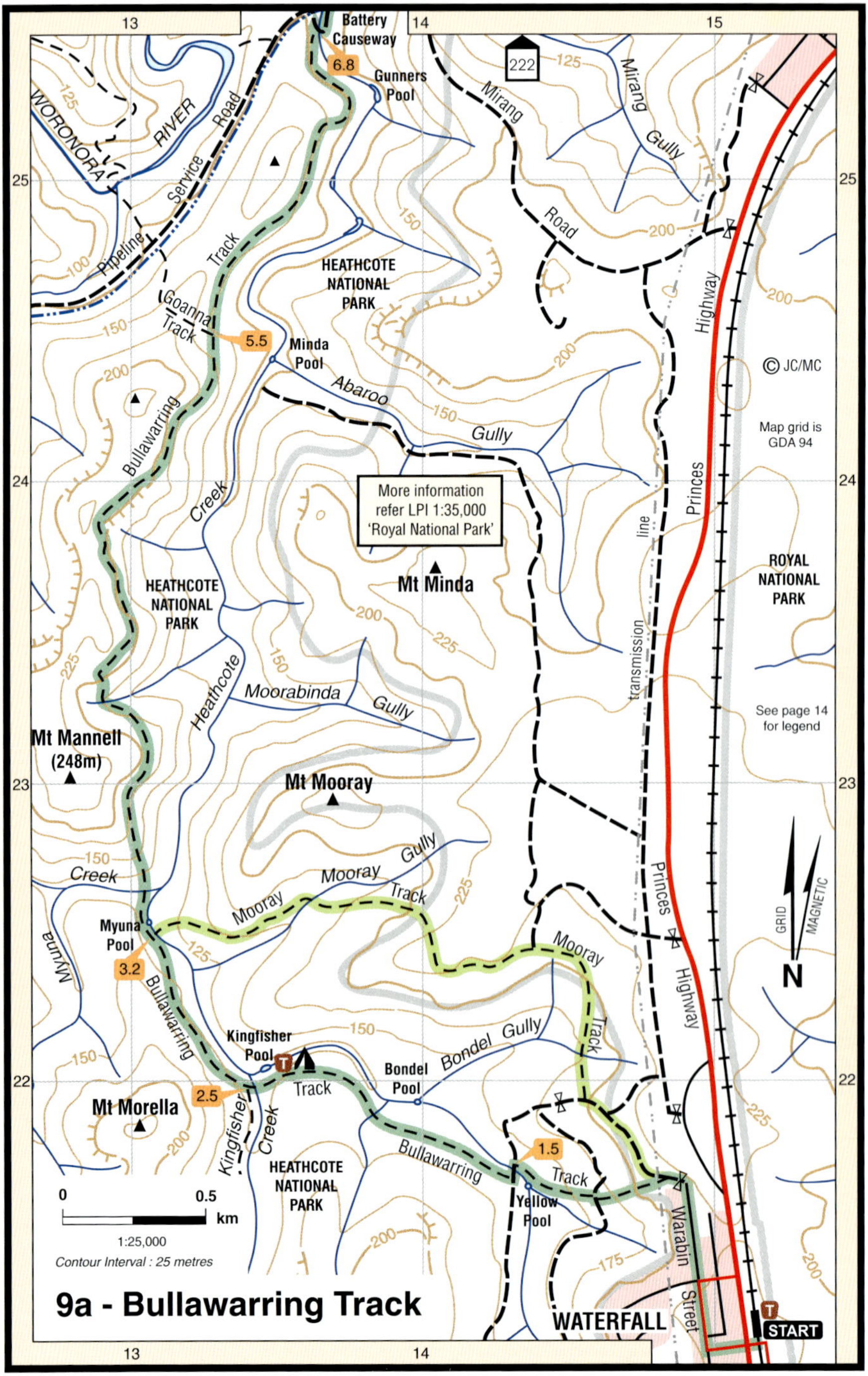
Battery Causeway
6.8
Gunners Pool
222
WORONORA RIVER
Pipeline Service Road
Mirang Road
Mirang Gully
Goanna Track
Track
5.5
Minda Pool
Abaroo Gully
HEATHCOTE NATIONAL PARK
© JC/MC
Map grid is GDA 94
Bullawarring
Creek
More information refer LPI 1:35,000 'Royal National Park'
Mt Minda
Princes Highway
transmission line
ROYAL NATIONAL PARK
Heathcote
Moorabinda Gully
See page 14 for legend
Mt Mannell (248m)
Mt Mooray
Creek
Mooray Gully
Mooray Track
Myuna Pool
3.2
Myuna
Bullawarring
GRID
MAGNETIC
N
Kingfisher Pool
Track
Bondel Pool
Bondel Gully
2.5
Mt Morella
Kingfisher Creek
HEATHCOTE NATIONAL PARK
Bullawarring Track
1.5
Yellow Pool
Warabin Street
0 0.5 km
1:25,000
Contour Interval : 25 metres
9a - Bullawarring Track
WATERFALL
START

Pool, Heathcote Creek

cote'. Follow the walking track descending north-west to meet a vehicle track near the creek.

1.5km Turn left, follow the vehicle track south across the creek then immediately turn right onto Bullawarring Track. Follow the walking track north-west through open forest close to the creek. Continue for 500m and cross a small, side creek then a further 400m leads to a clearing on the right. This is a campsite with a pit toilet and is close to Kingfisher Pool. Continue westwards on the walking track for 100m to cross the boulder-filled Kingfisher Creek.

2.5km Ignore a minor walking track to the south. Continue north-west following Bullawarring Track. The track is well above the creek and follows some rocky ledges passing below several overhangs. Continue for 700m to a signposted track junction.

Alternative track: Mooray Track 3.1km, 1 hour

This track can be used to complete a circuit walk returning to Waterfall.

0.0km From the track junction, descend eastwards to cross Heathcote Creek. Climb east to pass between some large boulders then cross the stream in Mooray Gully. The track continues climbing eastwards then swings south before again turning eastwards to meet a vehicle track. Turn right and Mooray Track heads southward rounding the head of some gullies to meet another vehicle track. Turn left and follow the vehicle track south-east ignoring side tracks to reach the end of Warabin Street in Waterfall. Follow Warrabin Street south then turn left into the second street to return to the railway station.

3.2km From the junction with Mooray Track continue north towards Battery Causeway. The track soon descends to cross Myuna Creek then climbs steeply north towards Mt Mannell. About two-thirds of the way up, the track swings right and sidles the east side of the mountain. It crosses the head of several gullies then follows a ridge north then north-east to another signposted track junction.

5.5km Ignore Goanna Track to the left. Continue north-east on Bullawarring Track to the end of the ridge then descend gently northwards through dry forest to meet a closed road at Battery Causeway.

Bullawarring Track sidling Mt Mannell

6.8km Turn right and cross Battery Causeway. The causeway is a concrete construction and there are pretty pools on both sides. Follow the narrow road north-east which soon changes to a gravel surface. The road follows a large, steel, water pipeline that has many repairs to try to stop it leaking. Follow the road for 1.0km to meet a vehicle track from the right.

7.8km Ignore the vehicle track on the right. Continue following the road beside the pipeline for 100m to cross Mirang Gully then pass above Mirang Pool. There are steps on the left leading down to the pool and a

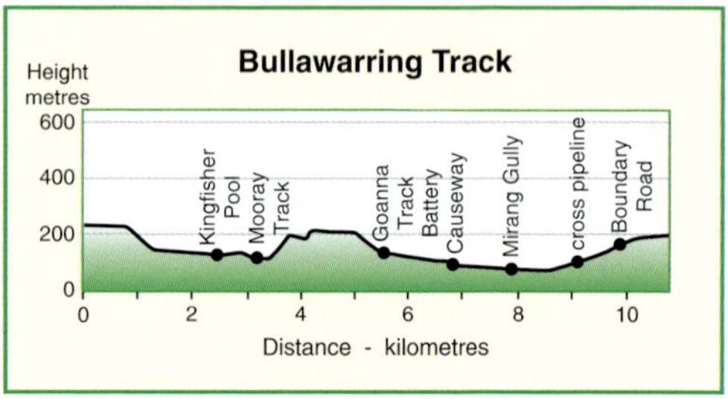

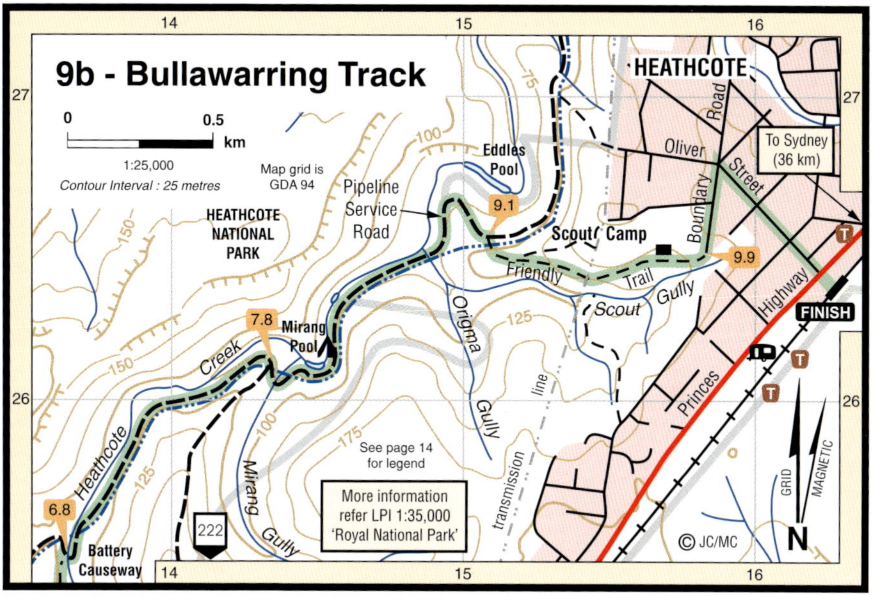

nearby campsite. The road continues north-east to cross Origma Gully. Here the pipeline is encased in concrete and heads steeply east over a spur. The road takes a more gentle ascent. It swings away from the pipeline heading north then south-east to meet the pipeline at a track junction.

9.1km Turn right to cross the pipeline and follow Friendly Trail eastwards for 500m to a track junction. Left leads into the Scout Camp – keep to the right and cross a minor gully and pass below a building. Friendly Track soon swings left and climbs to meet Boundary Road in Heathcote.

9.9km Follow Boundary Road north for 300m then turn right into Oliver Street and follow it south-east to the railway station.

Hairpin Banksia

Fuchsia Heath

Coral Heath

10 GLENBROOK TO RED HANDS CAVE

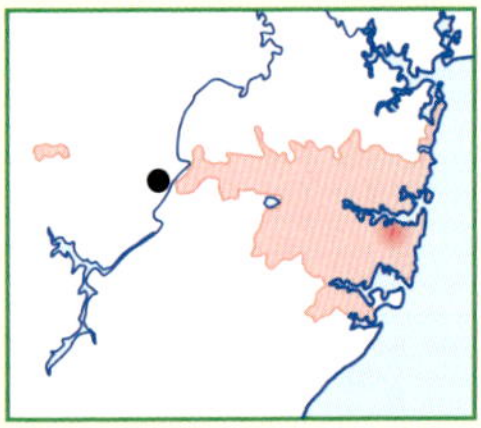

Length: 12.8km, circuit
Time: 5 hours
Grade: Medium
Total Climbing: 270m
Maximum Height: 205m
From Sydney: 63km
Closest Town: Glenbrook 0km
Map: LPI 1:25,000 *Penrith*

Glenbrook is the entrance to the Blue Mountains and provides some interesting walks. Close to the town, Glenbrook Creek has carved a gorge through the sandstone forming several deep pools. Unmarked, but well-used tracks lead to two, large pools close to Glenbrook Causeway. The area was also popular with aborigines and a well-marked track leads from Glenbrook Causeway to some aboriginal sites.

The most significant aboriginal site in this area is Red Hands Cave. This is a sandstone overhang containing many hand stencils which were left by the Daruk tribe. The stencils were made by spraying red ochre over a hand placed on the rock and the cave is one of the best examples of aboriginal art near Sydney. There are more than 60 stencils with some of them being made by children. In the same area there are a series of axe grinding grooves where the aborigines sharpened their weapons.

Red Hands Track

Glenbrook Creek

Access:

From Sydney follow the Great Western Highway west for 63km to Glenbrook. Turn left and head south for 500m to the railway station. Parking is available in Burfitt Parade east of the railway station.

Public transport – from Sydney Central, trains operate on the 'Blue Mountains Line' to Glenbrook. Refer www.cityrail.info for timetables.

Variations:

1. **Glenbrook Pools**, 4.7km, circuit, 2 hours, Medium. Follow the first 2.7km of the described walk to Glenbrook Causeway then continue from the 10.8km point of the notes via Jellybean Pool then the end of the walk.
2. **Red Hands Cave**, 8.1km, circuit, 3 hours, Easy-Medium. This walk starts from the car park just south of Glenbrook Causeway – an entrance fee applies for car entry to the national park. From the car park a walking track descends north to the track beside Camp Fire Creek. Follow the described walk from the 2.7km point to the 10.8km point and return to the car park.

0.0km From Glenbrook Railway Station, head westwards along Burfitt Parade and turn left to follow the road bridge over the railway. Veer left and cross the road to enter Memorial Park and follow the foot track south across the park. When it divides veer right to the south-western corner of the park. Turn right into Cox St and follow it to its end.

0.3km Turn right onto a vehicle track (left is a private property entrance) and 30m later turn left onto another vehicle track. Follow this south-west along the crest of the ridge. Keep right when it divides and follow the main track to the end of the

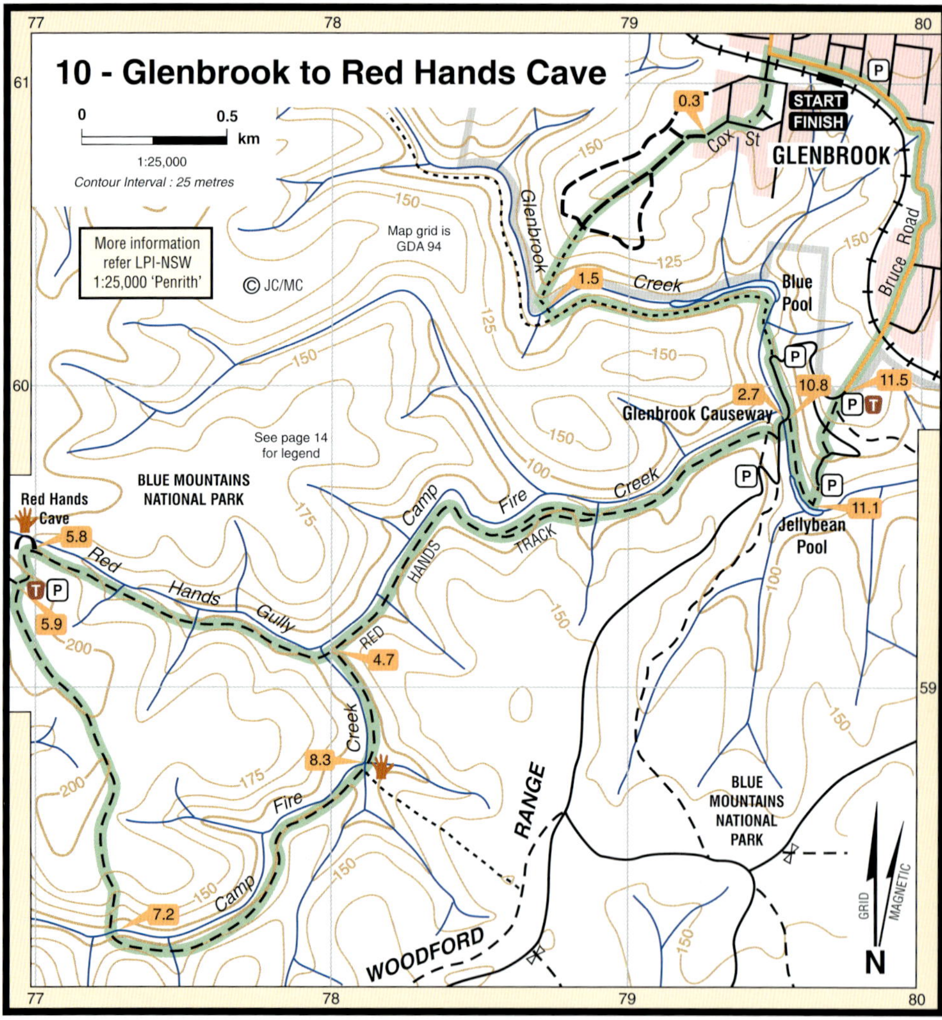

ridge. There are multiple tracks here – keep to the left and locate the unmarked start of a well-defined walking track. This heads south-west initially descending gently. It passes through a low cliff line via a narrow slot. At the next rocky slot, ignore a false track to the left, continue on the right for 30m then descend steeply 5m to a ledge. Head left passing under an overhang then easily down to the base of the cliff. Continue descending steeply south-west to the creek.

1.5km Cross the creek to the southern bank and head left following it downstream. There is no defined track, but many walkers have passed through and there are pads which can be followed. At times this requires scrambling over boulders. Continue to a sandy section of the creek bed. Just beyond is Blue Pool and rough tracks can be followed down either side of the pool. At the end of the pool cross to the northern bank to the start of a constructed walking track. This climbs to a

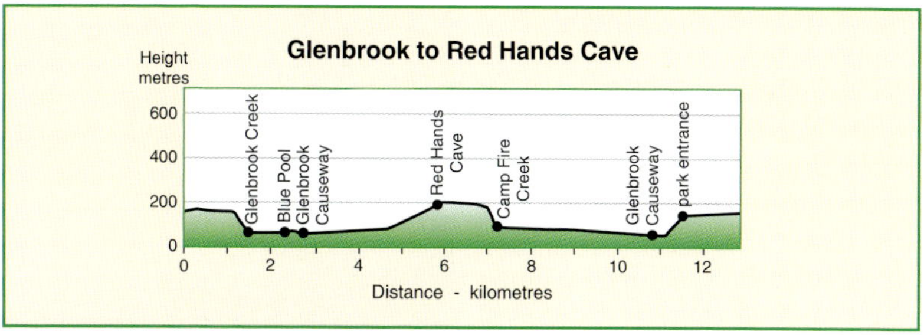

track junction just before the road. Left climbs to a small car park. Keep to the right and follow the public road 200m to Glenbrook Causeway.

2.7km Cross the concrete causeway to the south side then turn right towards Red Hands Cave. Head south-west following Camp Fire Creek upstream. Just past a signboard, ignore steps on the left that lead to a car park. The track passes through light, scrubby forest beside the creek. Follow it south-west for 700m to an unmarked track junction at a signboard that describes aboriginal life. Either track can be followed as they rejoin within 600m. Follow the right track to merge with the left track then continue a further 700m to a track junction beside a creek junction – the return will be from the left.

4.7km Keep to the right and cross Camp Fire Creek. The track now follows Red Hands Gully climbing steadily for 1.0km to a series of timber steps that lead to Red Hands Cave.

5.8km To prevent vandalism the cave is protected by a solid steel frame, mesh wire and perspex – views of the hand stencils made with ochre are good. Small hand stencils are on the left and some stencils overlap. From the cave the track rises south then swings west to a car park where there is a toilet.

Hand stencils

5.9km Turn left onto a walking track that heads south. This passes through open forest and is easy walking across a level plateau. The plateau ends and the track starts descending a gully towards Camp Fire Creek. The final descent follows a dry spur to the creek.

7.2km Cross the creek on rocky slabs which can be slippery after rain. The track then swings east and follows the creek downstream. It rises to pass below a sandstone overhang then descends gently to cross a large, side creek.

Axe grinding grooves

8.3km The creek junction is the site a series of aboriginal axe grinding grooves. There are about a dozen of these in the creek bed. From the creek junction follow the track beside Camp Fire Creek northwards for 500m to the track junction met earlier. Turn right and retrace the track down Camp Fire Creek. At the first track junction, turn right and follow the higher track down the creek. This is around 10m higher than the lower track and provides a slightly different perspective of the valley. Continue a further 700m to Glenbrook Causeway.

10.8km Cross the causeway and turn right to cross the old parking area then follow rough tracks downstream for 300m to the Jellybean Pool. The route is a mixture of well-defined pads and rough boulders.

11.1km On the north-east side of Jellybean Pool there is a set of steel stairs. Climb the stairs and follow the constructed track to a car park. At the car park entrance turn right onto a walking track and follow this uphill crossing the road twice to another car park beside some buildings at the entrance to the national park.

11.5km Follow the gravel-surfaced Bruce Road north-east. Take care with traffic as initially the road must be followed. Continue north-east then north-west following the footpath beside Burfitt Parade back to the railway station.

Jellybean Pool

WARRIMOO TO GLENBROOK 11

In the late 1800s and early 1900s each town in the Blue Mountains cut walking tracks to nearby features. These were aimed at attracting visitors and for most towns this was successful with many travelling to the Blue Mountains for health and recreation. The increase in private, motorised transport enabled visitors to travel further and some of the smaller towns that were initially popular were bypassed as people headed to the larger towns. Warrimoo is one of the smaller, less popular towns with a good walking track. This is known as Florabella Pass which descends into the gorge of Glenbrook Creek providing some enjoyable walking. From Glenbrook Creek, Pippas Pass provides an easy walking track that ends in the small town of Blaxland. For the more adventurous, continue downstream through the untracked Glenbrook Gorge to the medium-sized town of Glenbrook. This walk features many large quiet pools and swimming holes, numerous caves and a variety of wildflowers.

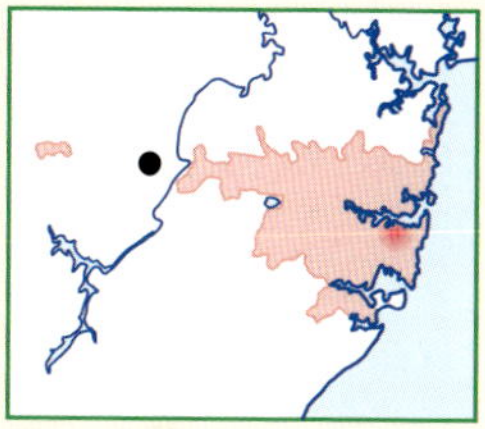

Length: 9.3km, one-way
Time: 5 hours
Grade: Hard
Total Climbing: 220m
Total Descent: 340m
Maximum Height: 280m
From Sydney: 69km
Closest Town: Warrimoo 0km
Map: LPI 1:25,000 *Springwood, Penrith*

Access

From Sydney, follow the Great Western Highway west for 63km to Glenbrook. Turn left and head south for 500m to the railway station. Parking is available in Burfitt Parade east of Glenbrook Railway Station. To get to the start of the walk, catch a train from the railway station to Warrimoo, which is the second station towards Katoomba. Parking is also available on the east side of Warrimoo Railway Station – follow the Great Western Highway a further 6km from Glenbrook to Warrimoo.

Public transport – from Sydney Central, trains operate on the 'Blue Mountains Line' to Warrimoo Railway Station – refer www.cityrail.info for timetables. The return is from Glenbrook Railway Station which is on the same line.

Variations:

1. **Warrimoo to Blaxland**, 6.0km, one-way, 3 hours, Easy-Medium. Follow the first 4.3km of the described walk then follow the alternative exit via Pippas Pass to Blaxland Railway Station.
2. **Blaxland to Glenbrook**, 6.7km, one-way, 4 hours, Medium-Hard. Start from Blaxland Railway Station and reverse the Pippas Pass track notes then follow the described walk from the 4.3km point to the end of the walk.

0.0km From Warrimoo Railway Station cross the foot bridge over the highway and descend to road level. Walk west following the service lane for 150m then turn left into the first street, The Boulevarde. Follow this street south to a T-intersection,

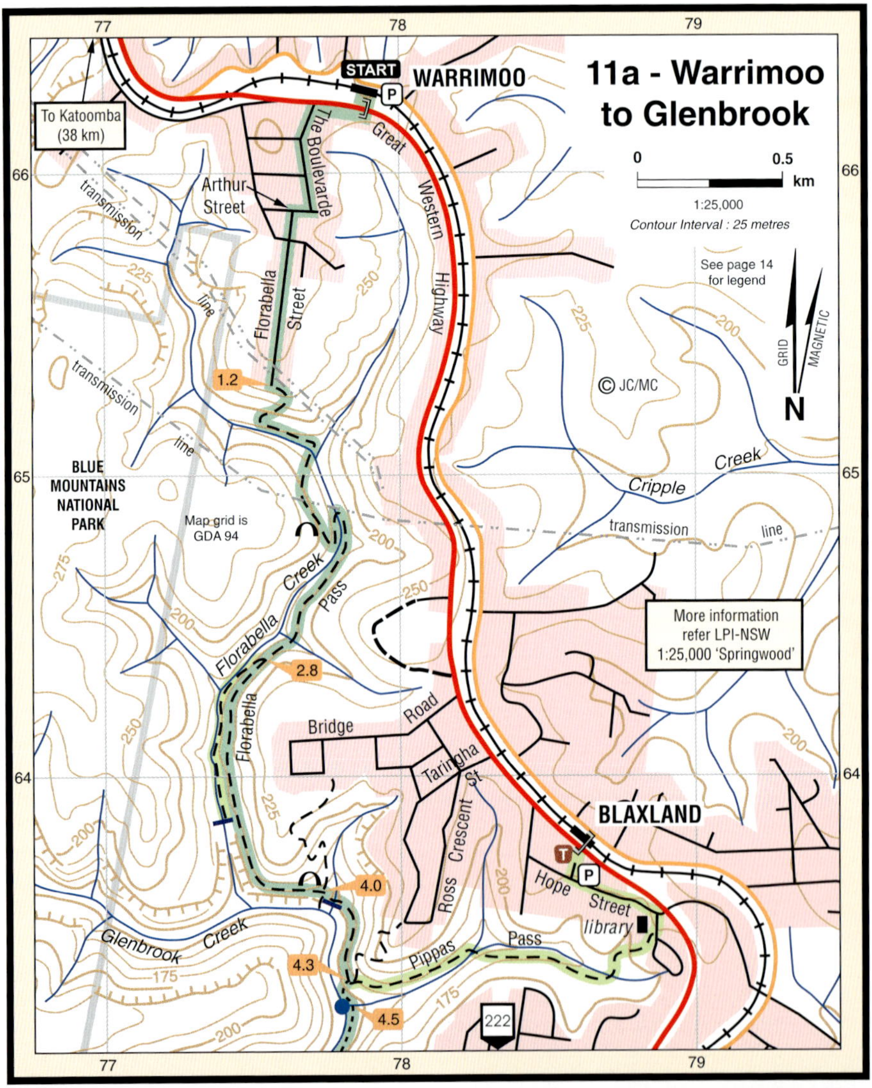

Doubletail orchid

Dusky Coral-pea

Bush-pea

turn right into Arthur Street then left into Florabella Street. Follow the street to its end and a walking track starts just left of the Florabella Pass sign.

Florabella Pass

1.2km The track is rough at first, but soon improves and becomes better defined. Steps lead down a gully in a cliff then the track zigzags down through open forest to the gully below. The track initially follows the creek south-east for 250m then crosses it and starts climbing steeply above the creek. It soon descends again and close to the creek it swings north for 200m, crosses Florabella Creek, then heads south-west along the eastern side of the valley. Cross a minor side creek via a timber bridge and 200m further on there is a track junction.

Sidetrip: Florabella Falls 1.0km, 1 hour return

Turn right towards Florabella Creek. This is marked as having 'No Exit'. Follow the rough, little-used track descending to the creek below. The track ends near a small waterfall, return from here. Ignore the poorly-defined pad that continues downstream through the canyon for 700m to Glenbrook Creek – this section is very poor and not recommended.

2.8km Continue following the main track southwards as it sidles the slopes above the canyon on Glenbrook Creek. Continue for 1.2km to a track junction. The track on the left climbs into an overhang with honeycomb weathering then continues climbing to the end of Bridge Road in Blaxland.

4.0km Follow the main track to the right descending to cross a creek. Ignore a rough track on the right that leads to a muddy terrace and chained, steel ladder. This provides an access to Glenbrook Creek, but there is an easier track. Continue following the main track (signposted to Ross Crescent) which climbs steadily for 250m to a track junction beside a large, red-coloured rock. This junction is not ob-

Glenbrook Creek

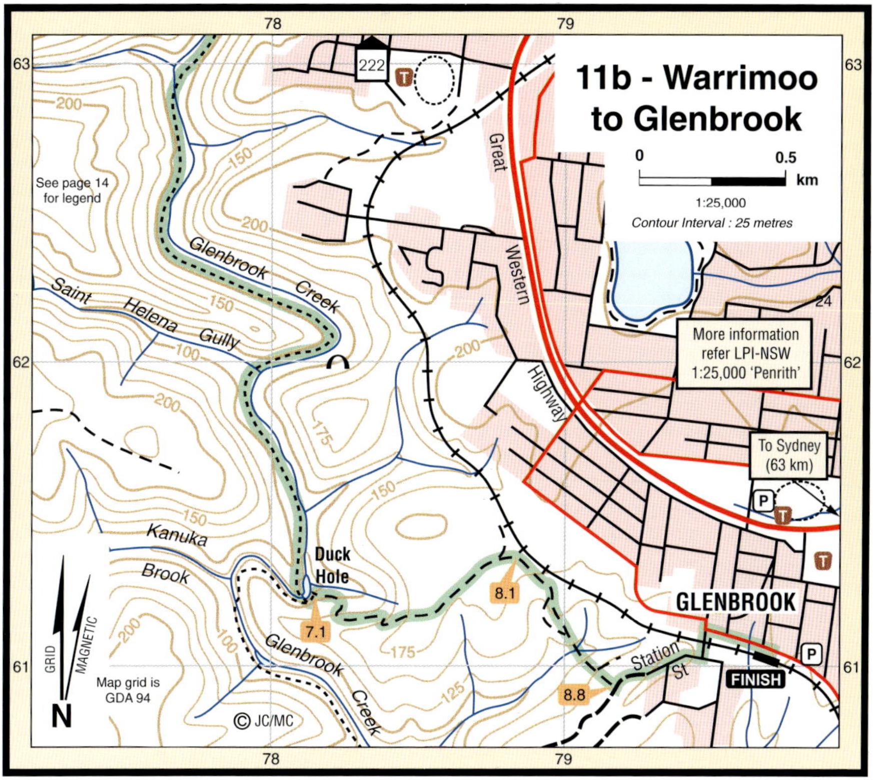

vious. (If you reach another track junction with steps leading up to the left then reverse 50m back down the track to the red rock.)

Alternative exit track: Pippas Pass 1.7km, 40 minutes

From the red rock, follow the major track on the left for 50m to another track junction. Ignore the steps on the left – they climb steeply to Ross Crescent. Continue on the right following Pippas Pass. The track climbs gently eastwards through rainforest following the creek. After 1.0km the track leaves the creek and rises north to end at the car park beside the Blaxland Library. Turn left and follow Hope Street north-west for 300m to Blaxland Railway Station.

4.3km Turn right onto an unmarked, but well-worn track. This descends steeply – it has some steps and was once constructed, but is now badly eroded in places so care is needed. Follow it down to the stony bank of Glenbrook Creek. Turn left and follow the creek downstream to a large pool at the base of a side gully – this is a popular swimming hole. From here to Duck Pool there is no track and this is the hardest section of this walk.

4.5km Initially follow the untracked, eastern bank of Glenbrook Creek, but soon cross over to the western bank. The walking is at times rough crossing boulders and

Duck Hole

fallen trees. A faint pad exists for much of the way on the western bank and it is generally about 10m above the creek. Continue steadily downstream for 2.6km (about 2 hours) to Duck Hole. Approaching Duck Hole, scramble along the cliff base on the western bank onto the sandy edge of the large waterhole. Cross to the eastern bank by wading across at the bend or at the rapids 50m downstream then head upstream to the gully that enters Duck Hole from the east.

7.1km Locate an unmarked walking track that starts just south of the gully. This rough track heads south-eastwards zigzagging onto the spur above. It soon widens into an old road formation and this is followed east then north-east. Ignore any minor pads and when the main track divides keep right and follow it to the top of a deep railway cutting.

8.1km Turn right and follow the cutting south-east descending to a fence beside the rail line. Do not cross the railway, instead head south for 30m then veer left onto a minor walking track. Other tracks soon join and the well-defined pad heads south-east to cross a gully then rises to an unmarked track junction. Keep to the right climbing towards a house, pass it on the right and continue up to the end of Station Street.

8.8km Turn left into Station Street, follow it north-east for 200m then turn left to cross the road bridge over the railway line. Turn right and follow the footpath south-east to Glenbrook Railway Station.

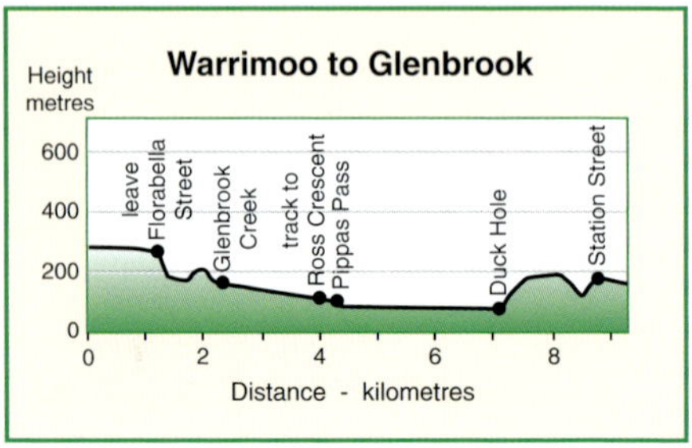

SASSAFRAS GULLY & MAGDALA CREEK 12

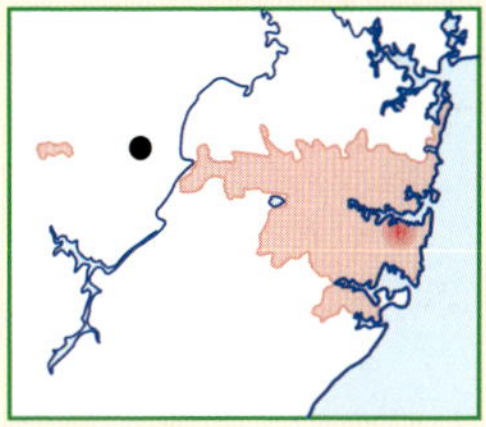

Length: 10.2km, circuit
Time: 3½ hours
Grade: Medium
Total Climbing: 270m
Maximum Height: 370m
From Sydney: 75km
Closest Town: Springwood 0km
Map: LPI 1:25,000 *Springwood*

The Blue Mountains township of Springwood is the starting point for this enjoyable circuit walk. Commencing with a short walk through the town, Sassafras Gully Track then descends quickly into open forest in a deep gully. It continues following the valley downstream entering patches of rainforest and passing several large, blue-green coloured pools. The colour is due to very fine clay particles suspended in the water.

The return walk follows a walking track along the valley of Magdala Creek. This creek has two, wispy waterfalls and numerous overhanging cliffs in its lower reaches. The upper part of the creek is an easy walk along a broad gully leading into the centre of Springwood. The tracks pass through mixed forest that includes stringybark, coachwood and sassafras. In spring a wide variety of wildflowers can be found including orchids, waratah and banksia.

Access

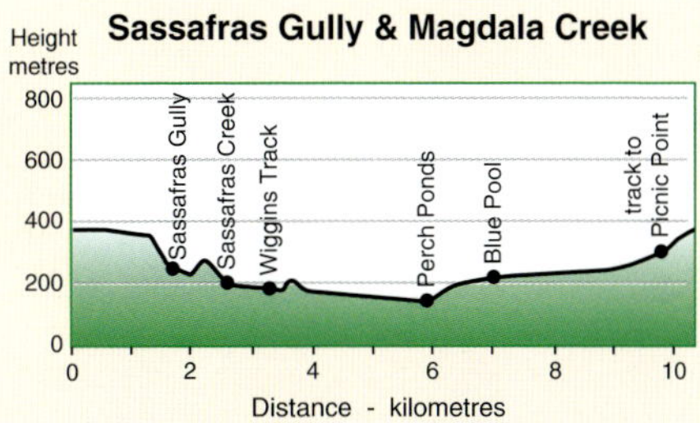

From Sydney, follow the Great Western Highway west for 75km to Springwood. Leave the highway and follow Macquarie Road into the town. Turn left at the second roundabout into Raymond Road then right at the next roundabout into Springwood Avenue. Continue 200m to locate car parking areas on the north side of the street.

Public transport – from Sydney Central, trains operate on the 'Blue Mountains Line' to Springwood Railway Station – refer www.cityrail.info for timetables. From the railway station walk south to cross Macquarie Road then pass between shops to the car parking area on Springwood Avenue.

Variation:

1. **Sassafras Gully & Wiggins Track**, 5.9km, circuit, 2 hours, Easy-Medium. Follow the first 3.3km of the walk then turn left and follow Wiggins Track, Yondell Avenue and Bee Farm Road back into Springwood.

One of the many overhanging cliffs

0.0km Walk west then south-west following Springwood Avenue to a T-intersection. Turn left then right at the next corner into Valley Road. Turn left at the second corner into Sassafras Gully Road. Walk to its end then follow the signposted Sassafras Gully Walking Track south. This soon becomes well defined and a zigzagging descent leads into the gully below.

1.6km Cross the creek and head south-west following the valley downstream. Pass below overhanging cliffs (a feature of this walk) and soon cross the main gully and a side creek. The track then zigzags climbing high above the main gully before heading south passing below an often dry waterfall. Descend to the junction of Sassafras Gully Track and Sassafras Creek. Ignore the walking track that heads west following Sassafras Creek – this is Victory Track and leads to Faulconbridge.

2.6km Cross Sassafras Gully and follow the eastern bank of Sassafras Creek downstream. The track is not well defined in this section of open forest, but usually stays close to the creek. Continue for 700m to a timber post marking a track junction. The track on the left is Wiggins Track which can be used for a shorter return.

Alternative exit: Wiggins Track 2.6km, 50 minutes

Wiggins Track follows a gully and heads north-east climbing quickly. The zigzagging track has many stone steps and high up, crosses the gully on a sturdy bridge. Continue climbing to meet a track on top of the ridge. Turn left and follow Yondell Avenue north then turn right and follow Bee Farm Road northwards to Valley Road in Springwood. Retrace steps along Valley Road and Springwood Avenue to the car parking areas or railway station.

3.3km Keep to the right and head south to cross a gully then 100m further on cross Sassafras Creek. The crossing has slippery rocks and a rough bridge spanning a gap between two boulders. The track then climbs to a track junction marked by old signs. Ignore the track to the right and continue to the left downstream towards Perch Ponds. The track follows the western slopes above Sassafras Creek and undulating walking leads downstream for 700m to a large campsite clearing above the junction of Sassafras and Glenbrook Creeks. Glenbrook Creek is interesting with a potholed stream base.

4.2km Cross the clearing and veer left to cross Sassafras Creek just above the creek junction. Head east sidling around the edge of the large waterhole. The track then rises eastwards to sidle the valley wall well above Glenbrook Creek. Pass above a rocky gorge then descend south-east to Perch Ponds. This is a popular swimming hole.

5.9km Continue downstream a further 100m rising gently to a small clearing on a spur. This is a signposted track junction with the track to the right leading to Martins Lookout. There is also another large pool further downstream. From the track junction turn left and climb the spur north-east. The track soon swings right and sidles into the valley of Magdala Creek. It climbs gently to the base of a cliff then follows this north-east to Martins Falls. A sidetrack on the right leads to an outcrop with a view of the falls. Another sidetrack directly ahead follows a ledge just under the overhang to the back of the falls.

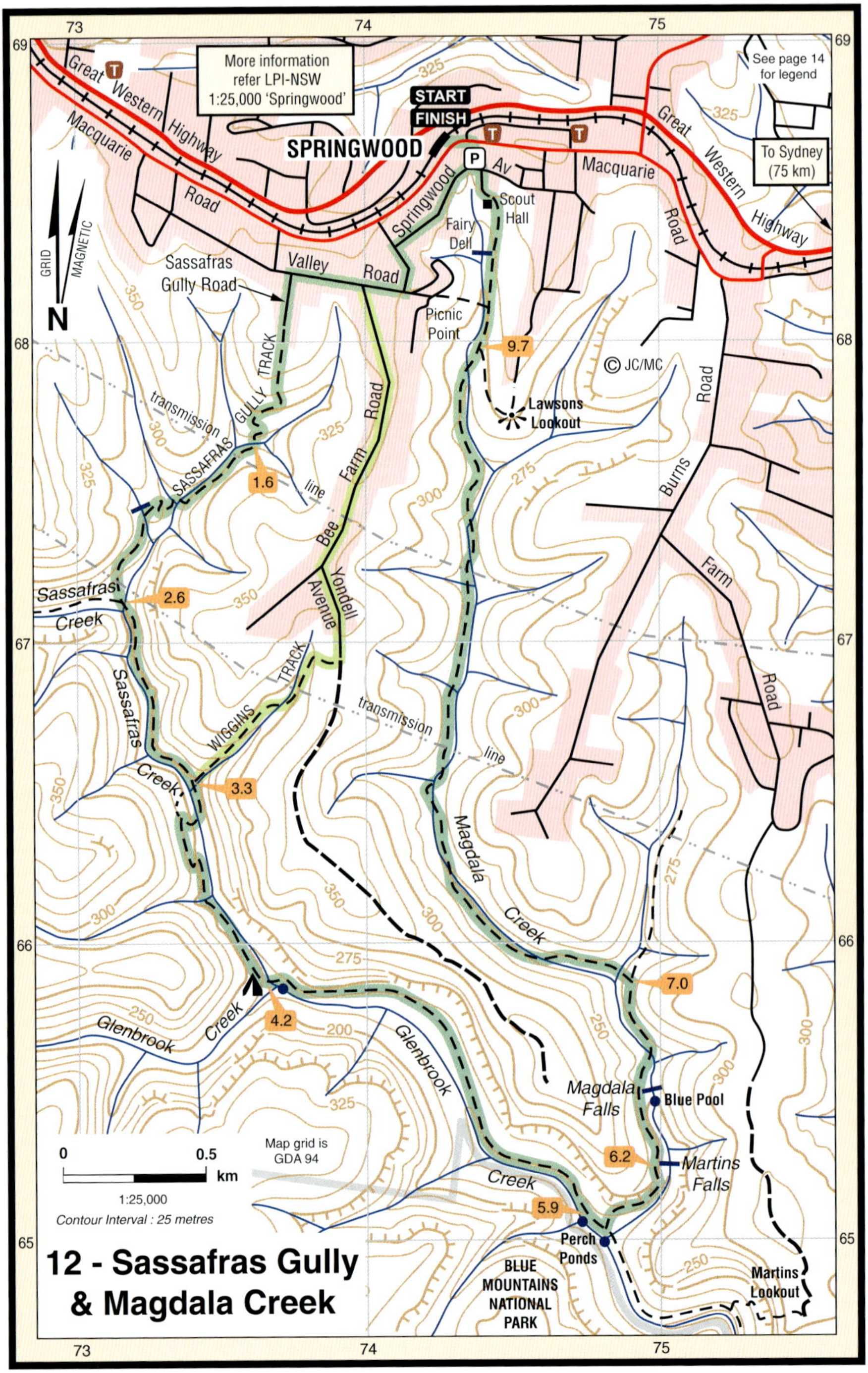
12 - Sassafras Gully
& Magdala Creek
More information
refer LPI-NSW
1:25,000 'Springwood'
See page 14
for legend
To Sydney
(75 km)
START
FINISH
SPRINGWOOD
Great Western Highway
Macquarie Road
Springwood Av
Scout Hall
Fairy Dell
Sassafras Gully Road
Valley Road
Picnic Point
Lawsons Lookout
© JC/MC
Burns Road
Bee Farm Road
Yondell Avenue
SASSAFRAS GULLY TRACK
WIGGINS TRACK
transmission line
Sassafras Creek
Magdala Creek
Glenbrook Creek
Magdala Falls
Blue Pool
Martins Falls
Perch Ponds
Martins Lookout
BLUE MOUNTAINS NATIONAL PARK
1.6
2.6
3.3
4.2
5.9
6.2
7.0
9.7
GRID
MAGNETIC
N
Map grid is
GDA 94
0
0.5
km
1:25,000
Contour Interval : 25 metres

Track at Perch Ponds

6.2km Follow the main track to the left climbing to the top of the falls. The track then closely follows the western bank of the creek climbing to the base of more overhanging cliffs. Magdala Falls cannot be seen from the track – the only view is from a dangerously sloping boulder. Continue climbing to more overhangs then descend gently to cross Magdala Creek at a set of rocky slabs – take care if wet. Follow the right hand side of the creek northwards underneath more overhangs to a track junction. Ignore the dead end track to the right.

7.0km Turn left and descend north-west to cross a side creek and 100m further on cross Magdala Creek again to its western bank. The track remains close to the creek then soon crosses Magdala Creek four more times. From there it continues northwards up the western side of the valley through dry, open forest with a bracken understorey. Waratahs are common here in spring. Upon entering rainforest the creek is again crossed several times as the track passes below more overhangs. A scramble up the right hand side of a cascade leads to a signposted track junction. Ignore the track on the right leading to Lawsons Lookout.

9.7km Continue following the valley north for 200m to the next track junction on the left – ignore the stepped track leading to Picnic Point. Keep following the gully north through Fairy Dell. The track passes a 3m high waterfall then climbs to pass east of the scout hall. Follow the track into a picnic area, keep to the right passing more picnic tables and follow the walking track to meet a sealed road. Follow the short road north to Springwood Avenue. Cross the avenue to the car parking areas. The station is a further 100m north-west.

13 LAWSON & HAZELBROOK WATERFALLS

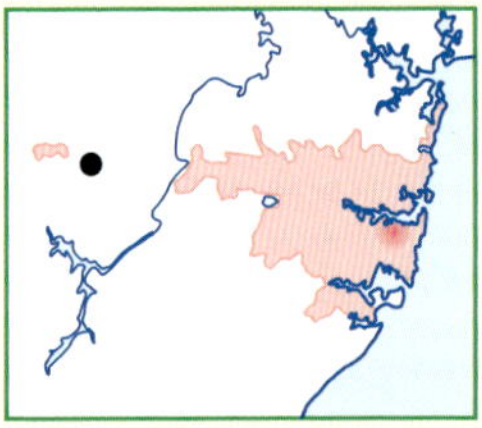

Length: 9.9km, circuit
Time: 4 hours
Grade: Medium
Total Climbing: 370m
Maximum Height: 690m
From Sydney: 91km
Closest Town: Lawson 1km
Map: LPI 1:25,000 *Katoomba*

Two of the larger concentrations of waterfalls in the Blue Mountains are located in the gullies close to the township of Lawson and deep in gullies south of Hazelbrook. While never very tall, the falls are pretty with many terraces and surrounded by lush vegetation. Some falls also have rock slabs or sandy banks below them.

Early European settlers recognised the beauty of the area and they created the first reserves around the falls in 1876. To attract visitors, an extensive network of tracks was established. These had substantial bridges over the streams, but most of these were destroyed in fires or floods. Bolts and bridge remnants can be found near some of the creek crossings. The walk is composed of two short circuits linked by a stroll along a quiet, gravel road. It passes through mixed forests with a wide variety of wildflowers and visits one lookout.

Access

From Sydney, follow the Great Western Highway west for 90km to Lawson. Opposite the railway station, turn left into Honour Avenue and follow it south-east for 1.1km to a car park opposite Livingstone Street.

Federal Falls

Public transport – from Sydney Central, trains operate on the 'Blue Mountains Line' to Lawson Railway Station – refer www.cityrail.info for timetables. From the railway station cross the highway with care and follow Honour Avenue south-east for 1.1km to the car park on the right at the start of the walk. Using the train adds 2.2km to the walk.

Variation:

1. **Lawson Waterfalls**, 2.5km, circuit, 1 hour, Easy-Medium. Follow the first.1.6km of the walk to the track junction above Cataract Falls. Turn left and follow the notes from the 9.0km point to the end of the walk.

0.0km Start 10m north-west of the car park and follow the walking track south to a track junction. The return will be from the left. Ignore a track to the right and continue straight ahead to a view of Adelina Falls. Descend to a fenced lookout (no views) then steps lead down to a track junction. The short sidetrack on the right leads to the base of Adelina Falls. Continue south on the main track for 500m towards Junction Falls. Ignore an unmarked pad on the left to the top of falls – follow the main track which swings south-west to cross Ridge Creek then zigzags descending to a bridge over Lawson Creek close to the bottom of Junction Falls.

Junction Falls

0.9km Continue downstream on the eastern bank to the next track junction. The main track climbs steps to the left. Continue straight ahead on a sidetrack which curves left along the base of a cliff to a sandy beach at the bottom of Federal Falls. Return to the main track.

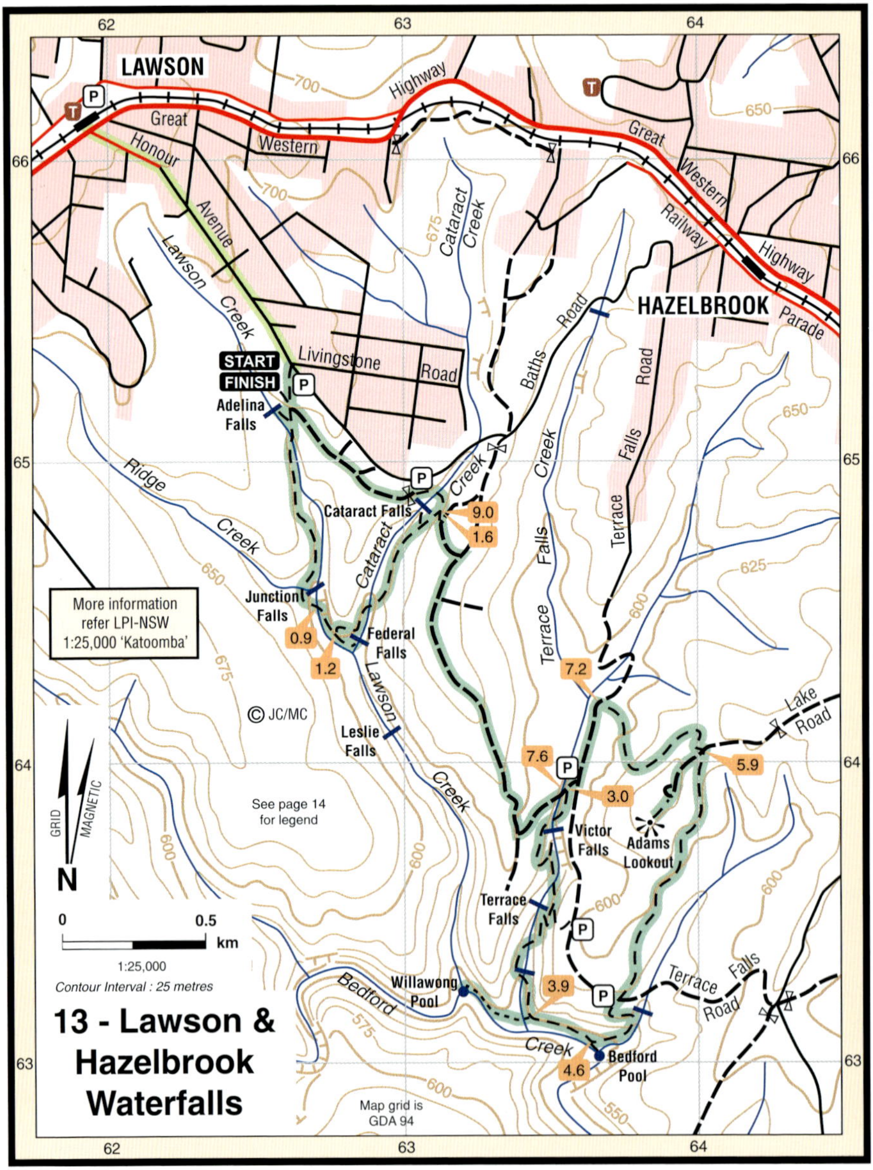

1.2km Climb the steps to the east, then above Federal Falls cross Cataract Creek to the eastern bank. Head north-east for 300m to a track junction. Follow the sidetrack on the left passing under an overhang to the base of Cataract Falls. Return to the main track and continue north-east following zigzags to the next sidetrack to the left. This leads to the centre of this multilevel fall – do not venture onto the slippery slabs. Return to the main track and continue to the next track junction above Cataract Falls. The return walk will follow the track to the left.

Terrace Falls

1.6km Turn right onto a vehicle track and follow it 150m south-east climbing to meet a gravel road on top of the ridge. Turn right and follow the road southward. After 150m ignore the vehicle track on the left as it descends into private land. Continue following the vehicle track southward a further 1.0km rising over a knoll then descending to a track junction. Turn left and descend north-east to a ford over Terrace Falls Creek.

3.0km Turn right and follow a walking track southward following the east bank of Terrace Falls Creek. The track soon crosses to the west bank then zigzags descending to a track junction near the bottom of Victor Falls. A short sidetrack on the left leads to the sandy beach at the base of the falls. Continue following the main track south descending gradually to a slippery creek crossing above Terrace Falls. On the east side of the creek head south to the next track junction – left climbs to a car park on the road above. Keep to the right and descend to the base of Terrace Falls. Continue following the main track downstream crossing the creek then crossing back below a cascade. Continue downstream to a track junction close to the junction of Bedford and Terrace Falls Creeks.

3.9km Turn right for a sidetrip to Willawong Pool. Cross Terrace Falls Creek then follow Bedford Creek north-west. Ignore an old track heading north and scramble along the base of a high cliff to a sandy bank beside Willawong Pool. Return the same way to the main track then head downstream along Bedford Creek. Follow the base of another cliff passing some stone seats and soon after reach another track junction.

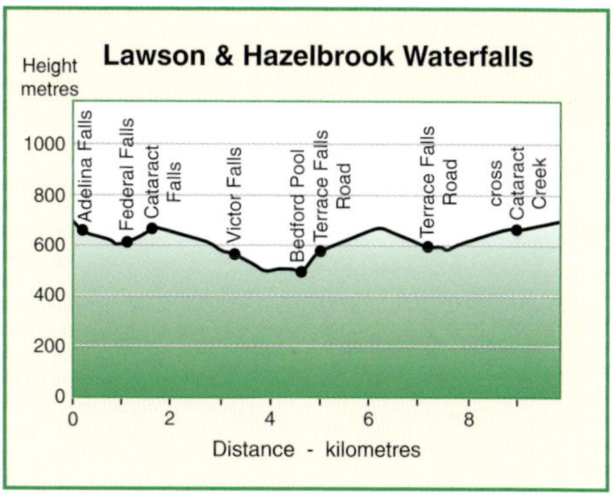

4.6km The 100m long sidetrack on the right leads to Bedford Pool. Continue east on the main track as it climbs steadily, zigzagging its way uphill to a car parking area beside Terrace Falls Road. Cross the road and follow a walking track north-east. This is an old road formation and varies from a wide, rocky surface to a sandy walking track. Follow it for 900m to a four-way track junction.

5.9km Turn left for a return sidetrip to Adams Lookout. Follow the old vehicle track south-west for 200m to a turning circle then follow the foot track on the left for 100m. Turn left again for 30m to the lookout where there is a good view to the south-west. Return to the four-way track junction then turn left to follow an old vehicle track north. This rough track soon starts zigzagging westward to meet Terrace Falls Road.

7.2km Turn left and follow the gravel road south-west for 300m then turn right and follow a vehicle track to meet the outward track at the ford over Terrace Falls Creek.

7.6km The next 1.4km of the walk reverses part of the walk. Follow the vehicle track south-west climbing steeply to meet a road. Turn right and follow the road northward for 1.1km then turn left onto a vehicle track and follow this for 150m then turn left again onto a walking track to a track junction above Cataract Falls.

Cataract Falls

9.0km Leave the outward track by turning right and follow a fenced lookout to a bridge over Cataract Creek. Continue west climbing briefly to a car parking area on Honour Avenue. Do not enter the car park, instead keep to the left and pass through a locked gate to continue west then north-west following a fire track. Ignore all the minor sidetracks and an easy walk through dry forest leads to a track junction near the start of the walk. Turn right and climb to the car park beside Honour Avenue.

NATIONAL PASS & NATURE WALK 14

Some of the best scenery in the Blue Mountains is near the township of Wentworth Falls. Tall cliffs, waterfalls, cascades and lookouts abound. The best known feature is Wentworth Falls an impressive, double-tiered waterfall. Some spectacular tracks have been created around the falls enabling walkers to descend the precipitous cliffs and view the falls close up.

From the centre of the falls, National Pass walking track follows a narrow terrace between the tiers of a long cliffline. This is a very popular track as it has great views of the towering cliffs and into the depths of the Jamison Valley below. The track leads into the deep gully of Valley of Waters Creek and follows this upstream passing many cascades and waterfalls. The described walk ends by passing through heathland on a circuit of Nature Walk. This skirts the valley above the main cliffs and while the views are not as spectacular, it is the best track for discovering the many wildflowers.

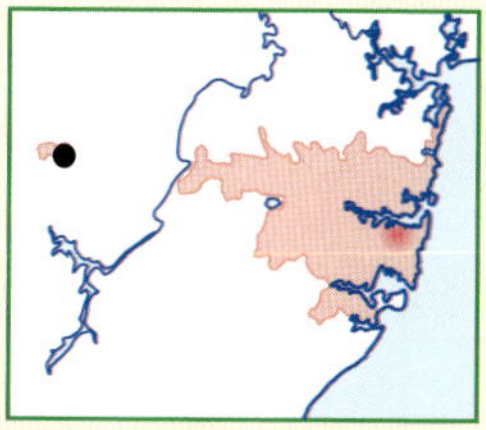

Length: 6.7km, circuit
Time: 4½ hours
Grade: Medium
Total Climbing: 280m
Maximum Height: 900m
From Sydney: 102km
Closest Town: Wentworth Falls 2km
Map: LPI 1:25,000 *Katoomba*

Access

From Sydney, follow the Great Western Highway west for 100km to Wentworth Falls. Leave the highway and follow Falls Road south for 1.3km then turn right into Fletcher Street. Continue west for 500m and when the street divides continue straight ahead to car parking areas near Conservation Hut. The hut contains the visitor centre and a café.

Public transport – from Sydney Central, trains operate on the 'Blue Mountains Line' to Wentworth Falls Railway Station – refer www.cityrail.info for timetables. From the station, Blue Mountain Bus www.bmbc.com.au operate a regular weekday bus service on Route 685 from the station to Valley of Waters stop which is in Fletcher Street 100m from the car park entrance. Weekend services are infrequent with four bus services on Saturdays and only two on Sundays.

Variations:

1. **Nature Walk**, 1.9km, circuit, 1 hour, Easy. From Conservation Hut follow the first 200m then keep right and continue for 300m passing Queen Victoria Lookout. Descend to the next junction, turn right and follow the notes from the 4.3km point to the end of the walk.
2. **National Pass**, 4.6km, circuit, 3½ hours, Medium. Follow the first 4.3km of the walk then turn right and follow the track past Queen Victoria Lookout to Conservation Hut.

0.0km On the south side of Conservation Hut, at the junction with Short Cut Track, turn right. Continue west for 150m to another track junction – the return will be from the right.

Jamison Valley from Overcliff Track

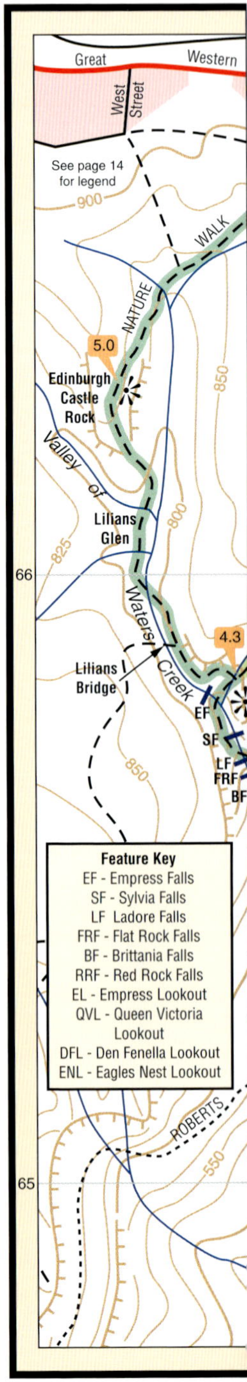

0.2km Turn left onto Overcliff Track and follow it south-east through scrub and heathland to Lyrebird Lookout which has good views of the Jamison Valley and the deep ravine of Valley of Waters. Continue south-east along the clifftops passing through heathland – there are many views along the way. Cross the head of a shallow, damp gully and pass below a rocky outcrop to a track junction. A short sidetrip to the right leads to Breakfast Point Lookout. Take care as is has low stone walls. Return to the main track, turn right and zigzag eastward into Den Fenella Creek.

Sidetrip: Den Fenella Lookout 15 minutes return

Follow the gully south then cross the creek on stepping stones, descend steeply on steps then cross the creek on a bridge. The track continues to a lookout on a ledge in the cliff face. Return to the main track.

1.2km From Den Fenella Creek climb east to a track junction. Left leads to the picnic area. Turn right onto Undercliff Track and continue eastward. This track follows the base of a low, upper cliffline hence its name. Continue to an unmarked, four-way track junction.

1.7km A steep, short sidetrack to the right zigzags down to Eagles Nest Lookout which has good views of all the tiers of Wentworth Falls. Return to Undercliff Track and continue east-

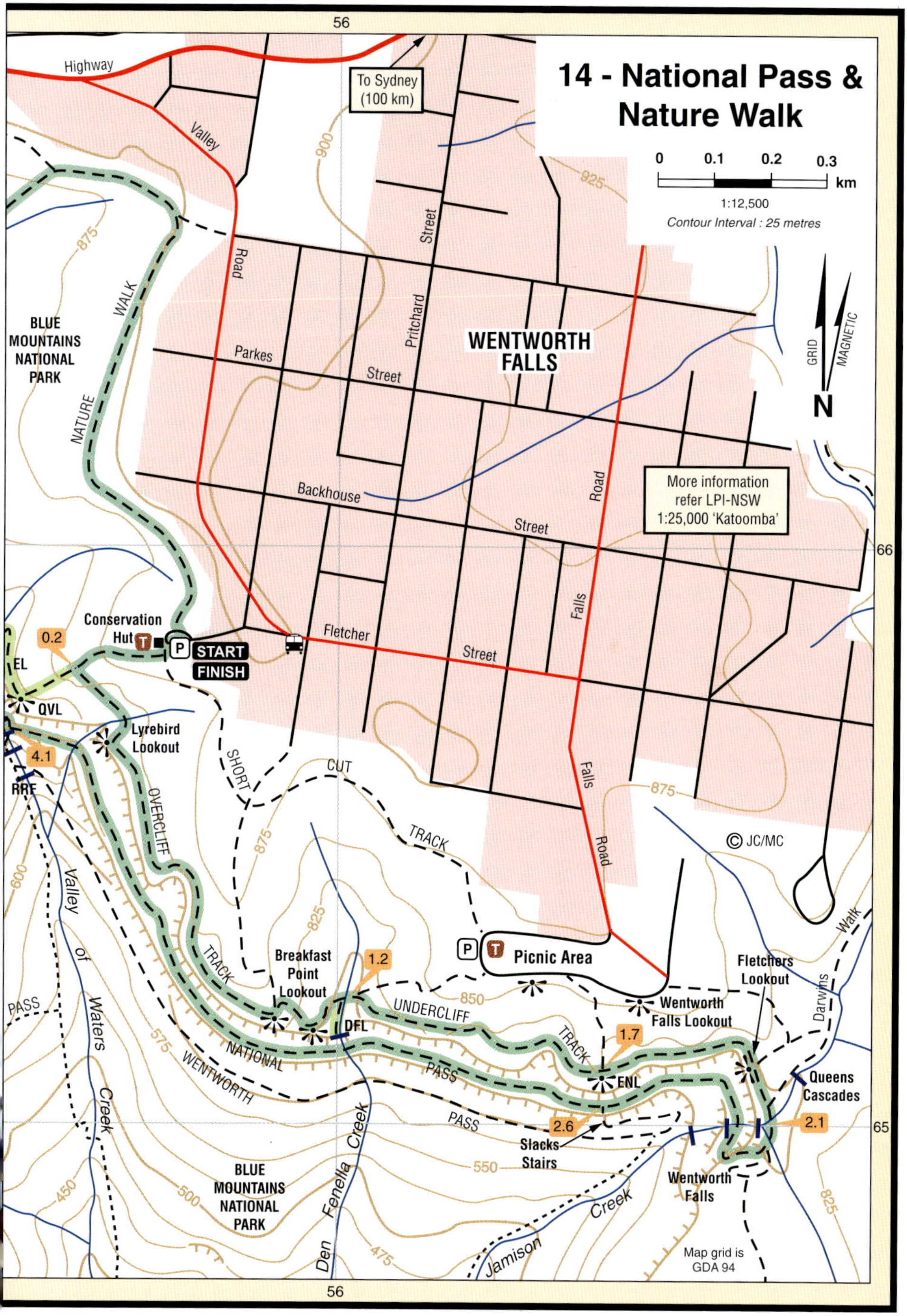
14 - National Pass & Nature Walk
0 0.1 0.2 0.3 km
1:12,500
Contour Interval : 25 metres
To Sydney (100 km)
Highway
Valley
Road
Parkes
Street
Pritchard
Street
WENTWORTH FALLS
Backhouse
Street
Falls
Road
Fletcher
Street
More information refer LPI-NSW 1:25,000 'Katoomba'
GRID
MAGNETIC
N
BLUE MOUNTAINS NATIONAL PARK
NATURE WALK
Conservation Hut
START
FINISH
0.2
EL
QVL
Lyrebird Lookout
4.1
RRF
SHORT CUT TRACK
OVERCLIFF TRACK
Valley of Waters Creek
Breakfast Point Lookout
1.2
DFL
Picnic Area
UNDERCLIFF TRACK
NATIONAL PASS
WENTWORTH PASS
PASS
Wentworth Falls Lookout
Fletchers Lookout
1.7
ENL
Darwins Walk
Queens Cascades
2.1
2.6
Slacks Stairs
Wentworth Falls
Den Fenella Creek
Jamison Creek
BLUE MOUNTAINS NATIONAL PARK
© JC/MC
Map grid is GDA 94
56
66
65

wards for 300m to another four-way track junction. Turn right again for another short sidetrip to reach the three-tiered Fletchers Lookout where there are fine views of the top of Wentworth Falls. Return to the main track and turn right to head south-east to a junction with Darwins Walk and shortly after cross Jamison Creek via concrete stepping stones.

The ledge near Wentworth Falls

2.1km Continue south entering light forest and at the next junction turn right. Steps descend steeply to a narrow, natural ledge jutting out from the cliff. The position here is spectacular. Follow the ledge around the corner then descend very steeply on more steps to the base of the cliff where the track swings north-east into rain forest. It soon meets Jamison Creek. Follow it downstream 30m then cross the creek. This is underneath the top fall of Wentworth Falls. The track then follows a terrace in the middle of cliffs. Initially it heads north then swings west passing underneath a low overhang to a track junction. Ignore the track on the left to Slacks Stairs.

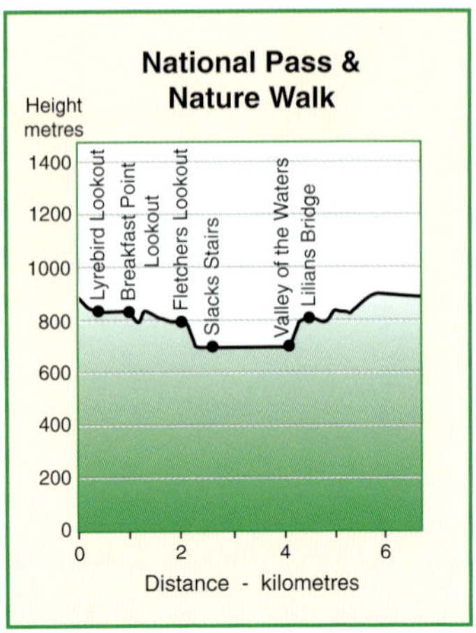

2.6km Continue on the right following National Pass. This undulating track follows a narrow terrace in the middle of a long cliff and provides spectacular views. Follow the track westward to some bridges below the wispy waterfall of Den Fenella Creek. The track rises into a saddle and the rocks on the left provide good views. From here National Pass swings north-west and continues along the terrace. Pass below an amphitheatre then descend into the valley of Valley of Waters to a track junction.

National Pass cliffs from Valley Of Waters

4.1km Turn right and follow the walking track climbing up the narrow valley. Cross the creek below Sylvias Falls to the western bank and continue climbing to the base of Empress Falls. These falls tumble into an overhanging amphitheatre and a set of timber stairs on the right climbs through the cliffs. Continue up some short zigzags to a track junction.

Alternative finish: Queen Victoria Lookout to Conservation Hut

500m, 15 minutes return

Turn right and climb to a ledge. Follow this north-east under an overhang then climb steel steps to Empress Lookout. Continue south-east to Queen Victoria Lookout then climb north-east and keep left at the next two track junctions to return to Conservation Hut.

4.3km Turn left onto Nature Walk. Climb over a ridge and descend briefly to the next track junction. A short sidetrip to the left onto Lilians Bridge provides a view of the canyon below. Return to the main track and continue north-west to a creek crossing and 100m further on cross the creek again at Lilians Glen. Continue north using a side creek to bypass cliffs then climb north-west towards Edinburgh Castle Rock. Pass an unfenced lookout then follow a ledge under an overhang to an easy climb along a cliff. This leads to open heathland where there are views near the top of Edinburgh Castle Rock.

5.0km A short descent north-east leads into a broad gully. Continue climbing up steps to a track junction. Keep to the right and climb to meet an old pipeline vehicle track. Turn right passing below private property following the vehicle track. Turn right at the next junction and head south ignoring all side tracks to return to the car park near Conservation Hut.

15 VERA FALLS

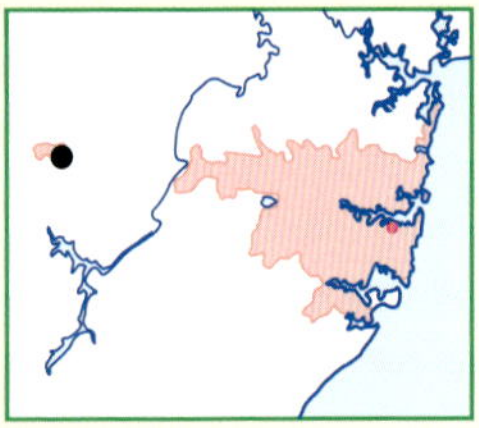

Length: 6.2km, circuit
Time: 5 hours
Grade: Hard
Total Climbing: 580m
Maximum Height: 890m
From Sydney: 102km
Closest Town: Wentworth Falls 2km
Map: LPI 1:25,000 *Katoomba*

The township of Wentworth Falls in the Blue Mountains has a maze of walking tracks, most of which were cut more than a hundred years ago. The great majority of these are still in use today, but a few are no longer maintained by the local council or the Department of Environment and Conservation. One such abandoned track follows Valley of Waters Creek deep into the valley to Vera Falls and returns to Wentworth Falls by following Jamison Creek past Hippocrene Falls. This track is now a rough, historic route along which are remnants of cut steps and benching.

Care is needed to follow the track as markers are often scarce and there are no signposts along it. It is only suitable for walkers with good navigation ability. The track visits many cascades and waterfalls, passes through a wide variety of forest types and has some excellent views. The ascent from the valley is via a series of ladders and very steep stairs.

Access

From Sydney, head west on the Great Western Highway for 100km to Wentworth Falls. Leave the highway and follow Falls Road south for 1.3km then turn right into Fletcher Street. Continue west for 500m and when the street divides continue straight ahead to car parking areas near Conservation Hut. The hut contains the visitor centre and a café.

Public transport – from Sydney Central, trains operate on the 'Blue Mountains Line' to Wentworth Falls Railway Station – refer www.cityrail.info for timetables. From the station, Blue Mountain Bus www.bmbc.com.au operate a regular weekday bus service on Route 685 to Valley of Waters stop which is in Fletcher Street 100m from the car park entrance. Weekend services are infrequent with four bus services on Saturdays and only two on Sundays.

0.0km On the south side of Conservation Hut, there is a track junction – the return will be on Short Cut Track from the left. Turn right and continue west 150m to meet Overcliff Track. Keep to the right and descend south-west to Queen Victoria Lookout. The lookout provides a great view of the cleft the walk descends as well as a sweeping view over the Jamison Valley. Head northward to Empress Lookout which provides a glimpse of Empress Falls. Continue north to descend steel steps then follow a ledge under an overhang descending south-west to a track junction. Right leads to Nature Trail.

0.5km Turn left and descend a zigzag track then timber steps to the base of Empress Falls. Cross the creek and head southward down the valley. Cross the creek

Vera Falls

again below Sylvia Falls and continue 50m to a major track junction. Left is National Pass. Keep to the right and follow a zigzagging track passing Flat Rock Falls then cross the creek on boulders – take care as they can be slippery. Follow the western bank of the creek passing more cascades to another junction. Ignore Wentworth Pass track to the left.

Valley Of Waters

0.8km Continue southward following the rough track for 300m to the junction on the right to Roberts Pass. Continue straight ahead following the unmarked foot pad through tall forest passing an isolated boulder on its left. Descend south-east following a series of short zigzags to the boulder-filled creek and cross it with care.

1.5km The track then follows a benched terrace and is soon high above Valley of Waters Creek. Continue for 300m to where the valley starts to widen and where there are views of the cliffs on Kings Tableland. Zigzag down to an unmarked track junction.

1.9km Turn right for a sidetrip to the top of Vera Falls. The narrow track sidles west for 150m to open, slippery slabs above the falls where there are good views of surrounding cliffs – take care particularly when the rock slabs are wet. Return to the track along the same path. Turn right and descend more zigzags for 100m to the next, unmarked junction. Turn right for the short sidetrip to the base of Vera Falls – there is a good view of the falls and a dry cave on its right. Return to the main track.

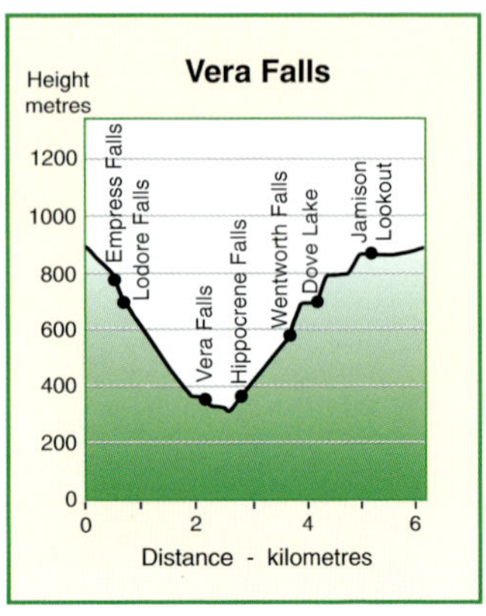

2.4km Follow the track downstream to an unmarked track junction – ignore the pad to the right that leads to a campsite at the creek junction. Keep to the left following yellow markers – they range from tapes to painted blazes on trees and painted rocks. Continue south-east for 50m until just above the junction of Den Fenella and Jamison Creeks. Do not cross either creek – instead follow the track as it veers

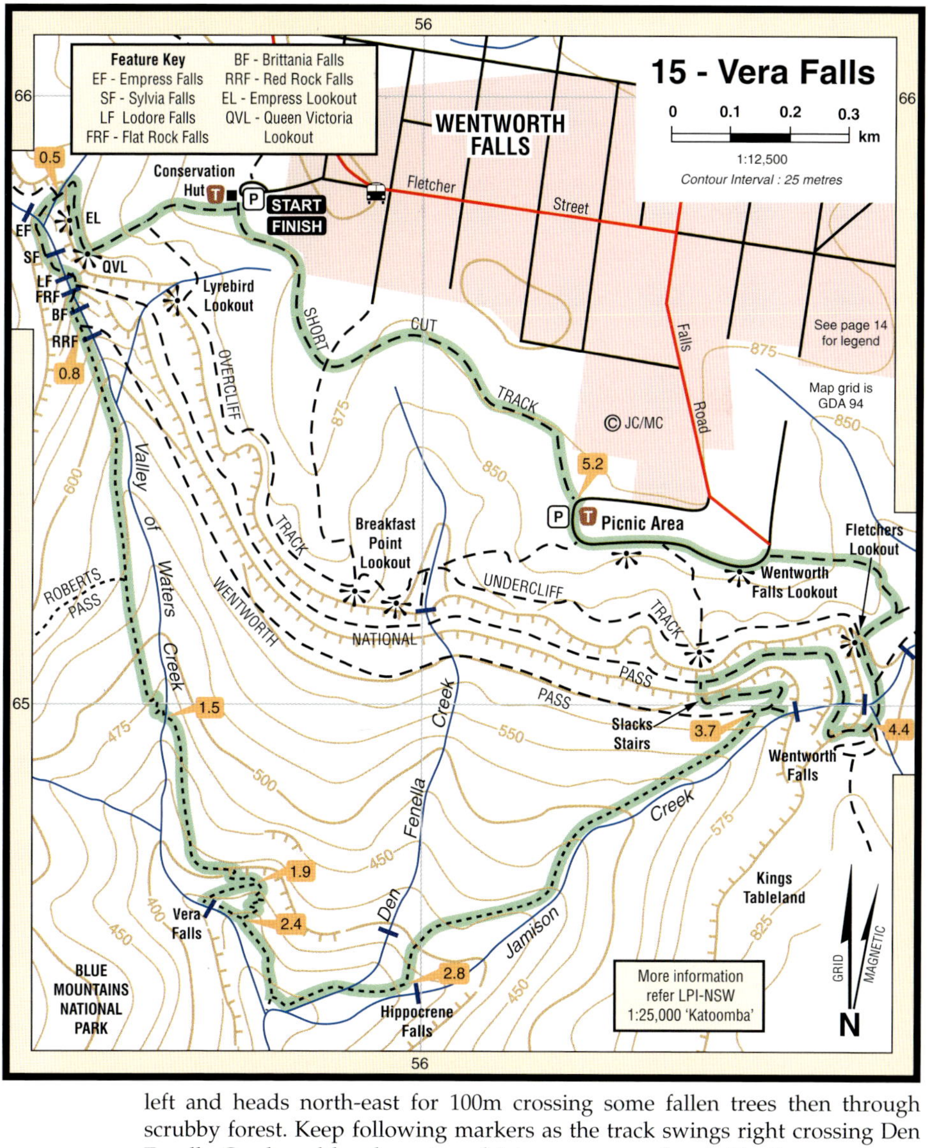

left and heads north-east for 100m crossing some fallen trees then through scrubby forest. Keep following markers as the track swings right crossing Den Fenella Creek and heads eastward into more open forest. Continue upstream through scrub to the base of Hippocrene Falls.

2.8km On the northern side of the falls climb steeply north. Old steps and track benching are remains of the original track construction. Climb the spur between Den Fenella and Jamison Creeks passing a cascade on Den Fenella Creek then veering north-east towards Jamison Creek. The track follows the creek north-east and remains 10m to 30m above the creek as it heads upstream. Ignore any false leads to the left and continue a further 600m to meet Wentworth Pass.

Slacks Stairs

3.7km Turn right and immediately to the right there is an unmarked track junction to the base of the lower tier of Wentworth Falls. The sandy pool below the falls is worth the short sidetrip. Return to the main track and continue following the eroded track north-east. This soon turns west and climbs steeply rising to the base of cliffs. Slacks Stairs ascends the cliffs via a series of very steep, enclosed, steel ladders. Take care, particularly at the top where the track passes through a narrow, rocky slot. Here there is a good view of the lower tier of Wentworth Falls. Turn right onto Federal Pass and continue under a low overhang then descend gently to the wide terrace between the upper and lower sections of Wentworth Falls. Cross the creek then follow it upstream 30m for a good view of the upper tier of Wentworth Falls. The track heads south into forest then steps climb very steeply up an almost vertical cliff. An exposed walk north-east along a spectacular ledge leads to an easier climb to a track junction.

Cascade above Wentworth Falls

4.4km Turn left and cross the creek above Wentworth Falls to another track junction. Ignore the track on the right to Darwins Walk. Keep left and head north to a four-way track junction. Before turning right, turn left for a short sidetrip to Fletchers Lookout – this is posied above Wentworth Falls and worth visiting. Back at the four-way track junction head north-east then north-west towards Wentworth Falls Lookout. Climb steadily ignoring minor side tracks to the right. Upon meeting the road turn left and follow the footpath west for 300m ignoring walking tracks to the left and passing two lookouts, then swing north to enter a large car park. Head to the north end where Short Cut Track starts on the left.

5.2km Follow Short Cut Track north-west. The almost level track passes through low, scrubby forest. Continue 600m then cross the track to Breakfast Point. Continue north-west for a further 400m to the first track junction met earlier in the day. Turn right to Conservation Hut.

KATOOMBA CLIFF WALK 16

Katoomba is famous for the views from its many lookouts poised high above sheer cliffs. While most visitors come to Echo Point to see The Three Sisters, there are a dozen other lookouts near the town and the Prince Henry Cliff Walk links most of them. Completed in 1931, the track follows the top edge of the cliff – it is very scenic and forms the first part of this walk. To gain a better perspective of the cliffs, the walk descends a steep, rainforest gully passing Linda Falls to the valley below. The return follows Federal Pass through dry forest below the cliffs. Seen from below, the height and vertical nature of the sandstone cliffs is apparent. The walk ends with a steep climb up Furber Steps – these are a long set of steps cut into the cliff face and they pass several waterfalls to return to the start. The steep climb can be avoided by using either the Sceniscender, a very steep, cable car or the Scenic Railway, a very steep, inclined railway.

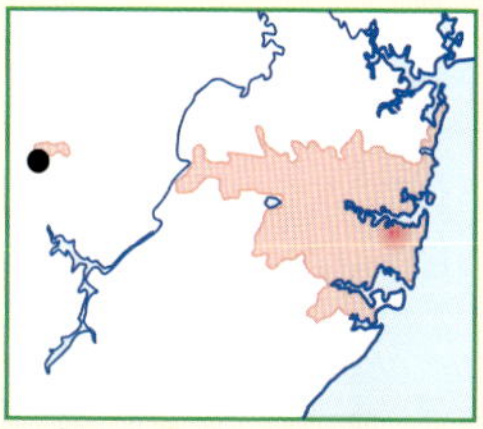

Length: 11.3km, circuit
Time: 5 hours
Grade: Medium-Hard
Total Climbing: 480m
Maximum Height: 980m
From Sydney: 109km
Closest Town: Katoomba 2km
Map: LPI 1:25,000 *Katoomba*

Access

From Sydney follow the Great Western Highway west for 107km to Katoomba. Turn left crossing the railway, left at the first roundabout then right at the next roundabout and follow Katoomba Street south for 1.3km. Turn right onto Cliff Drive and follow it for 400m then turn left into a car park at Cascades Picnic Area. Alternatively the walk can be started at Scenic World or Echo Point (parking fees apply).

Public transport – from Sydney Central, trains operate on the 'Blue Mountains Line' to Katoomba Railway Station – refer www.cityrail.info for timetables. From the station three different companies operate bus services to Cascades Picnic Area. Blue Mountain Bus www.bmbc.com.au operate several buses each hour on Route 686. Blue Mountains Explorer, www.explorerbus.com.au and Trolley Tours www.trolleytours.com.au operate at least one service each hour between 9am and 5pm.

Linda Falls

The Three Sisters

Variations:

1. **Prince Henry Cliff Walk**, 4.0km, one-way, 2 hours, Easy. Follow the first 4.0km of the described walk then turn left to Kiah Lookout and use one of the shuttle buses to complete the walk.
2. **Echo Point & Giants Staircase**, 6.8km, circuit, 3 hours, Medium-Hard. Follow the first 1.8km of the walk to Lady Game Lookout then descend Giants Staircase. Turn right onto Dardenelles Track then follow the notes from the 7.0km point to the end of the walk.
3. **Echo Point & Leura Forest**, 7.1km, circuit, 3 hours, Medium. Start from the 1.2km point and follow the notes to the 7.0km point, turn right and reverse the notes for Giants Staircase then reverse the notes from 1.8km to 1.2km to return to Echo Point.
4. **Katoomba Cliffs & Scenic Railway**, 9.6km, circuit, 4 hours, Medium. Follow the first 8.9km of the described walk then use either the railway or Sceniscender to Scenic World on top of the cliffs. From the front of Scenic World, follow the Prince Henry Cliff Walk north-east for 400m to the four-way junction then follow the notes from the 11.0km point to the end of the walk.

0.0km Head south following Prince Henry Cliff Walk for 300m to Cliff View Lookout. The lookout is the first of many that provide extensive views over the Jamison Valley. From the lookout the track heads south-east close to the cliff-top passing through eucalypt forest and fern-filled gullies. It also passes two lookouts – both with great views. Climb steeply up a ladder and a long set of stairs to Lady Darleys Lookout. From there a gentle climb leads to the massive, tourist car park and lookout at Echo Point.

1.2km Echo Point is the most popular tourist destination in the Blue Mountains and provides a classic view of The Three Sisters, Mount Solitary and the extensive cliff lines on either side of the Jamison Valley. There is an information centre and toilets. It is worth visiting the often crowded lookout as it extends 2m beyond the cliff edge. After enjoying the dramatic views, return to the visitor centre and follow the walking track east towards The Three Sisters. Ignore two sidetracks to Spooners Lookout and continue to a signposted junction with Prince Henry Cliff Walk. Keep to the right and follow the main track for 130m to Lady Game Lookout where there is an excellent view looking down onto the First Sister. A staircase leads down to the top of Giants Staircase and a bridge crosses the void to a ledge and cave on the First Sister.

Alternative track: Giants Staircase 700m, 30 minutes

Giants Staircase can be used to shorten the walk. From the First Sister, descend the steep staircase to Dardenelles Pass. Turn right and follow the track for 500m to meet Federal Pass at the 7.0km point of the walk.

1.8km Return to Lady Game Lookout and continue 30m further up the track then turn right onto a minor, unmarked track. This follows a spur crest and within 100m meets Prince Henry Cliff Walk. Turn right and follow the walking track north for 300m where a short track to the right leads to Lady Carrington Lookout on top of two, large rocks.

2.3km From Lady Carrington Lookout continue northwards through forest passing Millamurra and Tallawalla Lookouts. Cross the head of a gully and continue north to Honeymoon Lookout. The lookout is 15m below the track and poised on a very narrow outcrop.

2.8km From Honeymoon Lookout continue on the main track crossing several gullies and passing a further two, old, unnamed lookouts. At a signposted junction to Burrabarroo Lookout turn right for the 80m sidetrip. The track rises onto a rock which is not the lookout. Cross the rock then follow carved rock steps descending to the fenced lookout. Return the same way to the main track.

3.5km The walking track continues northward crossing a steep slope above a broad, rainforest-filled gully. The gully is the first, large break in the cliffs and the walk will follow this gully into the valley below. Continue to a track junction close to the junction of Cliff Drive and Merriwa Street. Turn right descending gently south-east for 200m to the next track junction. The left track leads 30m to Kiah Lookout.

4.0km Turn right towards Federal Pass. Descend west for 50m and a short track on the left leads out onto the large, rock platform of Jamison Lookout. Return to the track to Federal Pass and descend steeply following a zigzag track into the gully. The steep descent has many stairs that were rebuilt in 2001-2002. The gully floor is met at the start of Fern Bower which is dominated by sassafras and coachwood trees. A large number of steps and stairs enable the track to follow the steep gully south-east. Another signpost marks the end of Fern Bower and soon after the junction with Amphitheatre Track is met.

4.3km Turn right descending a steep and narrow staircase then cross Linda Creek on a bridge. The track winds

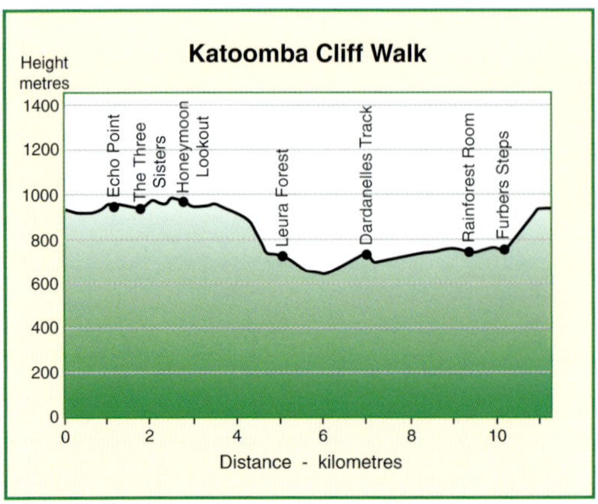

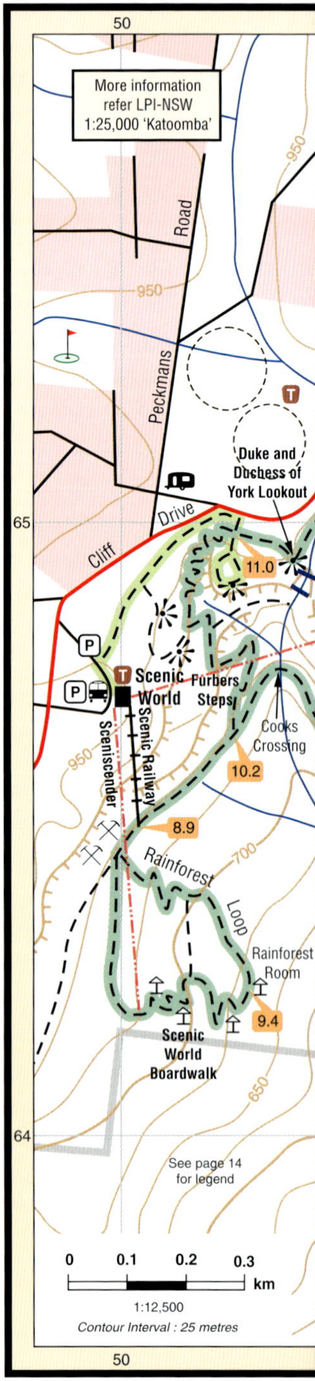

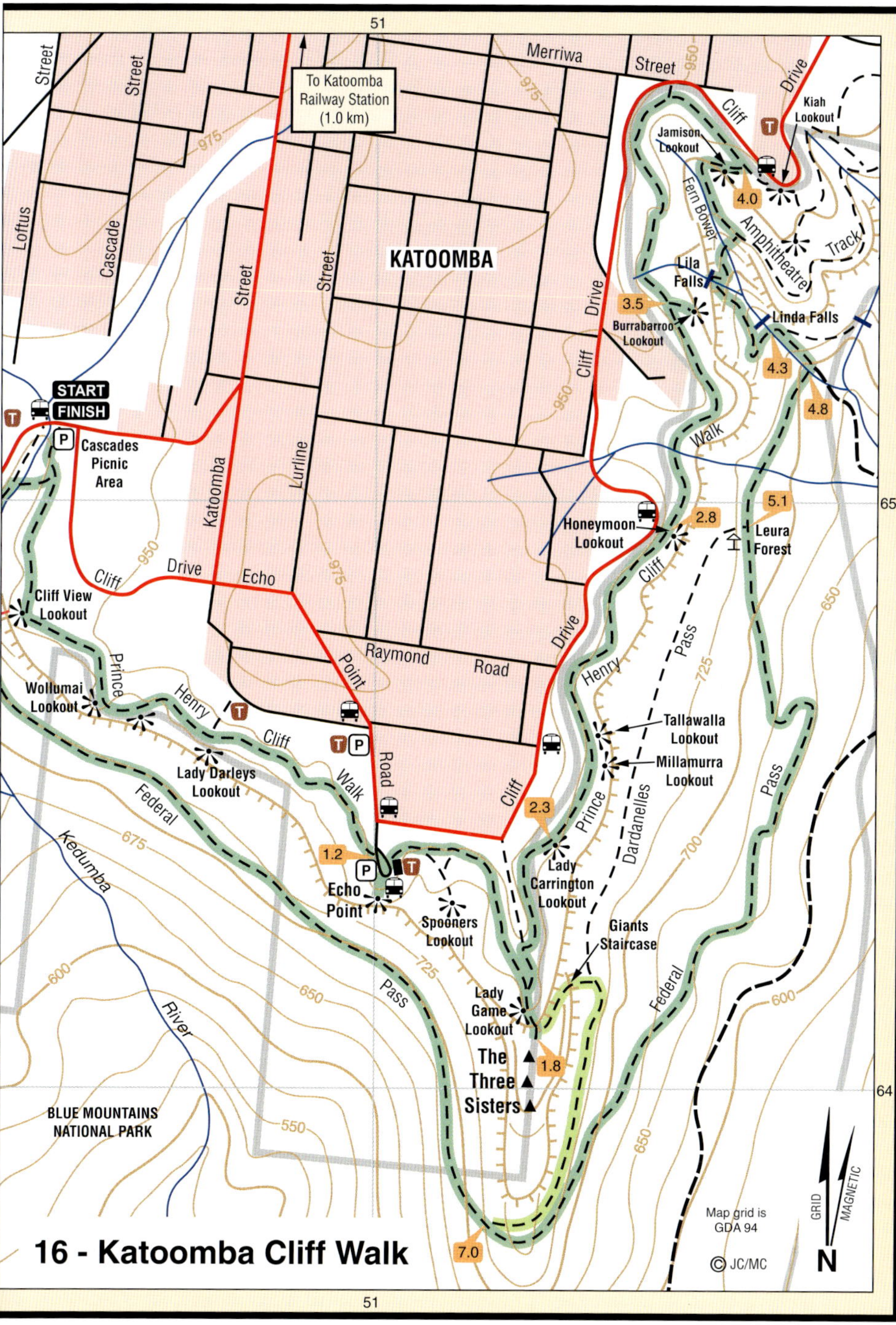

16 - Katoomba Cliff Walk
To Katoomba Railway Station (1.0 km)
KATOOMBA
START
FINISH
Cascades Picnic Area
Merriwa Street
Loftus Street
Cascade Street
Katoomba Street
Lurline Street
Cliff Drive
Echo Point Road
Raymond Road
Jamison Lookout
Kiah Lookout
Fern Bower
Amphitheatre Track
Lila Falls
Linda Falls
Burrabarroo Lookout
Cliff Walk
Honeymoon Lookout
Leura Forest
Henry Cliff
Prince Henry Cliff Walk
Tallawalla Lookout
Millamurra Lookout
Dardanelles Pass
Federal Pass
Lady Carrington Lookout
Giants Staircase
Echo Point
Spooners Lookout
Lady Game Lookout
The Three Sisters
Cliff View Lookout
Wollumai Lookout
Lady Darleys Lookout
Kedumba River
BLUE MOUNTAINS NATIONAL PARK
1.2
1.8
2.3
2.8
3.5
4.0
4.3
4.8
5.1
7.0
51
64
65
Map grid is GDA 94
© JC/MC
GRID
MAGNETIC
N

Marguerite Cascades, Linda Creek

its way down more stairs and under rock ledges and crosses a small side creek under Lila Falls before zigzagging down to cross Linda Creek again below Linda Falls. The track continues downstream passing a cascade then a short descent leads to the final crossing of Linda Creek. Ignore old, closed tracks to the left and cross the bridge.

4.8km From Linda Creek an easy, level walk south leads into the open, flat-floored Leura Forest. Beneath the very tall trees are the first of several picnic tables and a roofed shelter is found 50m further on. The shelter is located at the junction of the Federal Pass and Dardenelles Track.

5.1km Continue left along Federal Pass descending steadily under tall forest. Bellbirds are often heard and in wet weather leaches might be encountered. Lyrebirds are also sometimes seen in this area. The track descends until close to a management road which can be seen through the trees. The track now rises gradually as it approaches The Three Sisters. There are occasional views of the cliffs of The Three Sisters above. When the track swings to the west there are views across the valley of Mount Solitary. Continue along the undulating track to meet the other end of the Dardenelles Track where there are several seats.

7.0km Continue following Federal Pass north, then north-west below the cliffs of The Three Sisters and Echo Point. The lookout platform at Echo Point can be seen jutting out from the cliff above. The undulating track passes through turpentine and eucalypt forest to reach a bridge over the Kedumba River at Cooks Crossing. From the bridge there is a view of Katoomba Falls high above. A few metres up the track a very short sidetrack leads to the base of a large turpentine tree. Continue following Federal Pass rising to a track junction at the base of Furbers Steps. The steps provide the exit from the valley and will be followed later. Continue on the left to enter the Scenic World property and meet the bottom station of the Scenic Railway.

8.9km From the Scenic Railway follow Federal Pass south-west to some old mining tunnels. Recordings and information displays tell the story of how the coal and shale was mined until the early 1930s. At the next track junction, turn left onto the Rainforest Loop. Descend following the wide, suspended boardwalk keeping left at the next junction. Pass some abandoned buckets which are the remains of an aerial cableway. Continue through the rainforest to the Rainforest Room. This is a large shelter on a short sidetrack.

Waratah

9.4km From the Rainforest Room follow the winding boardwalk climbing steadily passing some small shelters. Keep left at junctions and rise to the terminus for the Sceniscender, a cable car that can be used to exit the valley – fees apply. Continue along the boardwalk rising to meet Federal Pass. Turn right passing the entrance to the Rainforest Loop and return to the Scenic Railway – the railway provides another alternative exit to the town above – fees also apply. Continue along Federal Pass for 200m to the track junction to Furbers Steps.

10.2km There is a lot to see on the steep climb up Furber Steps with numerous lookouts close to the track. The track has many rock steps carved into the cliff and was built in 1908. Climb steeply passing several, small lookouts and waterfalls. Continue to a signposted sidetrack to Underfalls Walk. An optional, 10 minute return sidetrip to the right leads to the base of Katoomba Falls. Continue following the main track climbing past Rainforest Lookout to a track junction. Turn right and follow Round Walk northwards past Witches Leap rising to a four-way track junction.

Sidetrip: Reids Plateau 200m, 15 minutes

From the four-way junction follow the track south climbing steps onto Reids Plateau. When the track divides veer left and follow a circular track passing several lookouts. There are very good views of Mount Solitary, Orphan Rock and the gully of Witches Leap. Continue around to the track junction and head north to the four-way track junction.

11.0km Continue straight ahead following Prince Henry Cliff Walk. Ignore minor tracks on the right to an old lookout and continue to the Duke and Duchess of York Lookout directly above Katoomba Falls. This provides an awesome view of the falls below. The track leaves the cliff heading upstream along the western side of the creek. When the track divides, veer right and cross the creek on stepping blocks below a cascade. Climb steps, then turn left to the Cascades Picnic Area and car park.

17 RUINED CASTLE

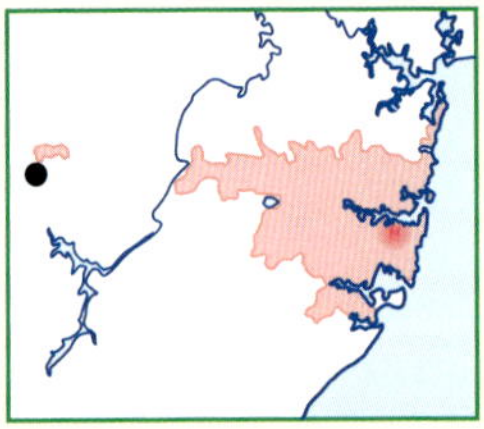

Length: 15.0km, return
Time: 5 hours
Grade: Medium-Hard
Total Climbing: 530m
Maximum Height: 940m
From Sydney: 109km
Closest Town: Katoomba 2km
Map: LPI 1:25,000 *Katoomba, Jamison*

The Ruined Castle is a small peak crowning a long ridge to the south of Katoomba. The summit is a pile of eroded, rocky outcrops that resemble a collapsed castle, hence the name. In the 1890s the mountain was the site of a rich, shale mine and a small village was built. The shale was dug up, moved by horse along a tramway to an inclined railway where it was carried up to Katoomba. Kerosene was extracted from the shale. The inclined railway is claimed to be the world's steepest railway and it now provides tourist access into the valley.

A walking track starts from the top of the Scenic Railway following a steep gully with many steps, into the valley. From the Scenic Railway, the old tramways provide easy walking to the base of the Ruined Castle. The summit provides magnificent views of the rugged cliff line edging the Katoomba escarpment and into the deep, secluded valleys below.

Access

From Sydney follow the Great Western Highway west for 107km to Katoomba. Turn left crossing the railway then left at the first roundabout and right at the next roundabout to follow Katoomba Street south for 1.3km. Turn right onto Cliff Drive and follow it for 1km to Scenic World. Parking is available in either the multi-storey car park or in the overflow car park on the west side of Cliff Drive.

Public transport – from Sydney Central, trains operate on the 'Blue Mountains Line' to Katoomba Railway Station – refer www.cityrail.info for timetables. From the station three different companies operate bus services to Scenic World. Blue Mountain Bus www.bmbc.com.au operate several buses each hour on Route 686. Blue Mountains Explorer, www.explorerbus.com.au and Trolley Tours www.trolleytours.com.au operate at least one service each hour between 9am and 5pm.

Variations:

1. **Scenic Railway to Ruined Castle**, 12.8km, return, 4 hours, Medium. An easier walk as it avoids the steep descent to Federal Pass and return ascent. Use the Scenic Railway or the Sceniscender cable car (fees apply) and start walking at the 1.1km point in the notes. Follow the return walk to the Ruined Castle and use either the Scenic Railway or Sceniscender to return to the top of the cliffs.
2. **Golden Stairs**, 7.8km, return, 3 hours, Medium. Follow the first 3.9km of the described walk to the base of Golden Stairs then return either along the same track or the alternative route via Golden Stairs to the start.

Cyclorama Point with The Landslide below

0.0km Start 20m left of the entrance to Scenic World and follow the walking track north-east towards Prince Henry Cliff Walk. Follow it for 50m and turn right to Vanimans Lookout. This provides the first view of the gulf below into which the track descends. There is a lot to see on the steep descent with numerous lookouts close to the track. Continue down steel stairs to the next lookout on the right, known as Juliets Balcony. Soon after, descend below an overhang to a track junction – left climbs north towards Prince Henry Cliff Walk and Cliff Drive. Turn right and descend passing Rainforest Lookout to a junction with Underfalls Walk. An optional 10 minute sidetrip to the left leads to the base of Katoomba Falls. Continue following the main track passing several lookouts and some short sidetracks to waterfalls. The numerous steps carved into the cliffs are known as Furbers Steps and were built in 1908. Continue down to a track junction with Federal Pass, then turn right and head south-west for 200m to the bottom of the Scenic Railway.

1.1km The inclined railway was originally built for shale mining and it provides an alternative start or exit from the walk – fees apply for use. Continue south-west along the boardwalk. Pass the Katoomba Coal Mine entrance where a video display and recorded commentary tells the story of the mine. Continue south-west to leave the boardwalk and veer right following Federal Pass. This follows an old tramline that was used to move coal and shale to the railway and is generally level except where tree fall or landslides cause deviations. The track passes under some impressive cliffs and heads towards The Landslide. Ignore a steep, minor track on the left that leads into the valley – this follows the route of an old, collapsed aerial cableway. Just before the first landslide the track divides – keep to the left track and follow steel poles. The Landslide is a huge jumble of boul-

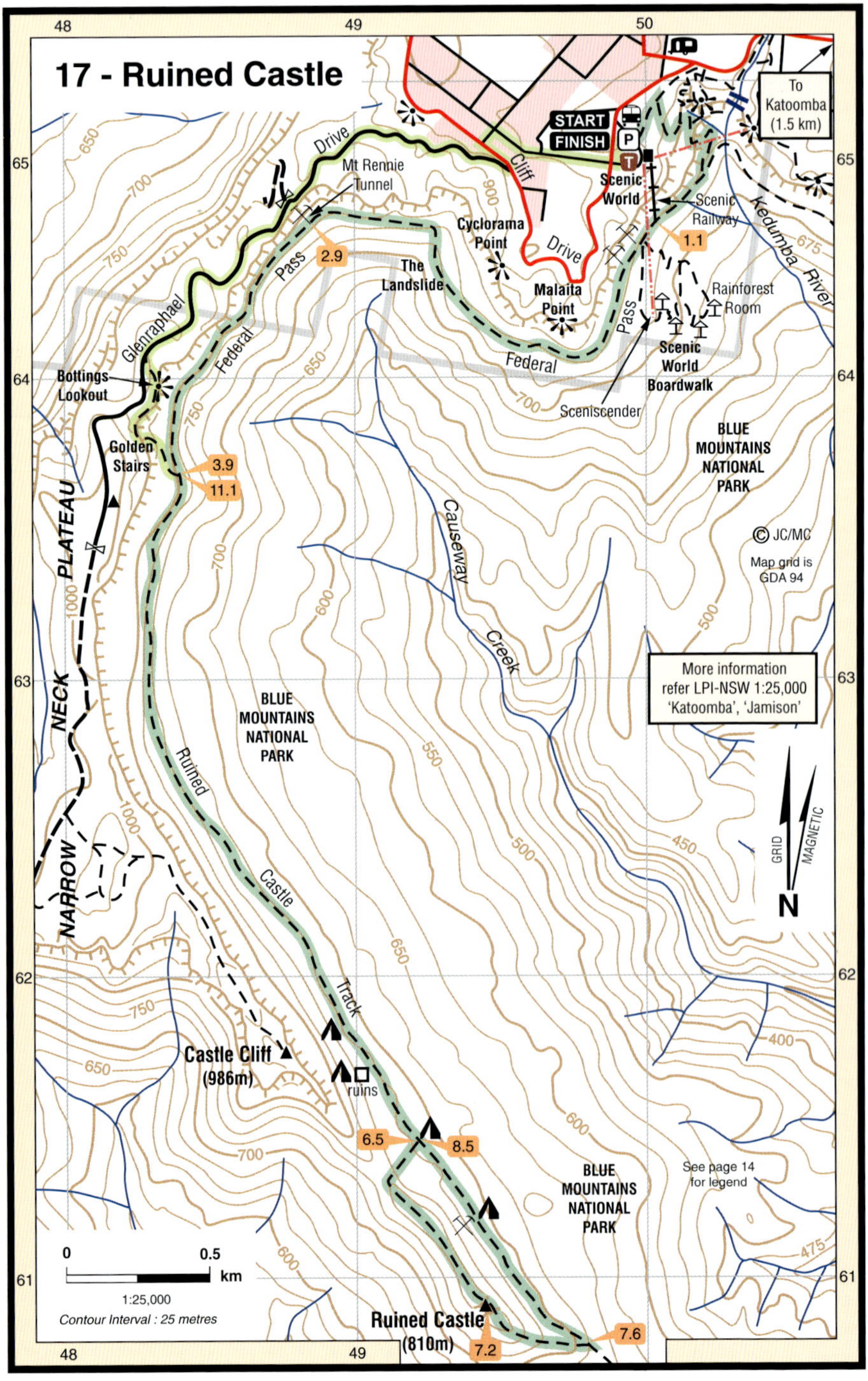
17 - Ruined Castle
START
FINISH
Scenic World
Cliff Drive
Mt Rennie Tunnel
Cyclorama Point
Malaita Point
Scenic Railway
To Katoomba (1.5 km)
Kedumba River
Rainforest Room
Scenic World Boardwalk
Sceniscender
The Landslide
Federal Pass
Glenraphael Drive
Bottings Lookout
Golden Stairs
NARROW NECK PLATEAU
BLUE MOUNTAINS NATIONAL PARK
Causeway Creek
Ruined Castle Track
© JC/MC
Map grid is GDA 94
More information refer LPI-NSW 1:25,000 'Katoomba', 'Jamison'
GRID
MAGNETIC
N
Castle Cliff (986m)
ruins
Ruined Castle (810m)
See page 14 for legend
0
0.5
km
1:25,000
Contour Interval : 25 metres
1.1
2.9
3.9
11.1
6.5
8.5
7.2
7.6

Castle Cliff from The Landslide

ders and scree. Follow the markers carefully as the track rises and falls quite sharply as it works its way across The Landslide area. The huge cliff above was created in 1931 – the coal seam under the hill had been extensively mined and this undercutting of the cliff led to its collapse. Rockclimbers call this cliff Dog Face. A 400m scramble across rocks leads to the end of The Landslide where the tramway formation is rejoined. Follow this southwards into forest – fallen trees and minor rockslides create small undulations along this section. Continue to the entrance to the Mt Rennie Tunnel under Narrow Neck – this was used to transport shale from Megalong Valley to the inclined railway.

2.9km Continue south-west following an old tramway formation through open forest. In the mining era, this area was denuded as the trees were cut for mine props. Most of the forest has since regrown. Continue for 1.0km to a track junction near the base of Golden Stairs.

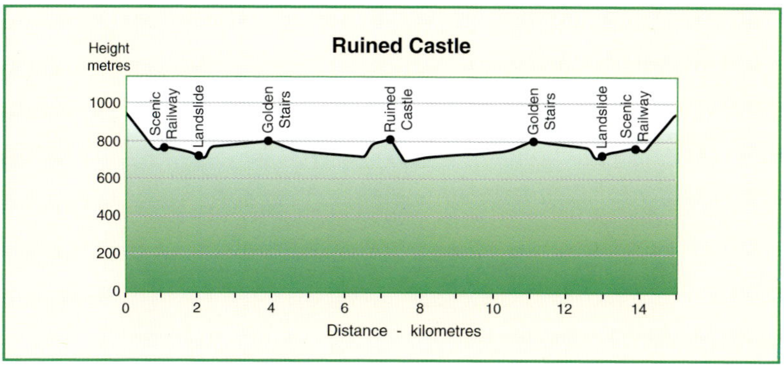

Old stone walls

3.9km Keep left and head southwards following the level track through more rainforest. Below the track is a series of very tall tree ferns. The forest canopy gradually becomes more open and the understorey changes to bracken as the forest floor becomes drier. Pass a campsite on the right and soon after a series of low, stone walls on the right mark the site of another campsite. The wall ruins are the remains of some huts built in the 1890s by shale miners. Continue south-east following the track a further 300m to another campsite at a signposted track junction.

6.5km Turn right towards Ruined Castle – the return will be from the left. Climb steeply south-west following an eroded track onto the ridge above. On the ridge the track swings south-east and follows the ridge crest to an isolated boulder where an overhang provides some shelter. Continue along the ridge to the summit rocks. They can be climbed in several places – the easiest is a scramble from the south-east side.

7.2km The summit of Ruined Castle provides a panoramic view of deep valleys crowned by sheer, vertical cliffs for which the Blue Mountains are famous. Birdlife is friendly, but beware as the currawongs are adept at stealing food. From the summit rocks follow a well-defined pad south-east along the ridge top towards its end – take care to find the correct track as there are several pads around the summit. The correct track initially descends gently south-east to a rocky area and then descends steeply to a track junction. Take care on the slippery track.

Currawong

View south-east from Ruined Castle

7.6km Turn left and follow Federal Pass through dry forest along the north-east slopes of the Ruined Castle. Continue for 500m to a tunnel entrance just above the track. The flats below the track are the former site of a mining village and are now often used for camping. From the tunnel continue north-west along the track a further 400m to the track junction to the Ruined Castle that was met earlier.

8.5km Continue straight ahead heading north-west reversing the walk along the old tramway to the base of Golden Stairs.

Alternative Return: Golden Stairs 1.0km shorter

Golden Stairs provide good views and an interesting exit from the valley. The negative of this route is that most of this alternative return walk is along roads and suburban streets.

0.0km Turn left and follow the steep track north-west to the base of the lower cliff. Steel stairs then carved steps provide a way up the cliff. The track traverses right across a gully then follows a ledge around the cliff where there are good views, but there are even better ones above. Climb to Bottings Lookout for the best views. The track then heads into scrub and soon ends at a car park beside Glenraphael Drive on Narrow Neck. Turn right and follow the road north-east to meet Cliff Road. Turn sharp left and after 150m turn right onto a quiet, suburban street then right at the next corner and follow another street east to Scenic World. Do not follow Cliff Drive as the narrow road is dangerous for pedestrians.

11.1km Continue northwards reversing the walk across The Landslide then past the Scenic Railway and up Furbers Steps to the start. Furbers Steps can be avoided by using the Scenic Railway or Sceniscender – the last daily ride is at 4:50pm (fees apply).

18 DEVILS HOLE

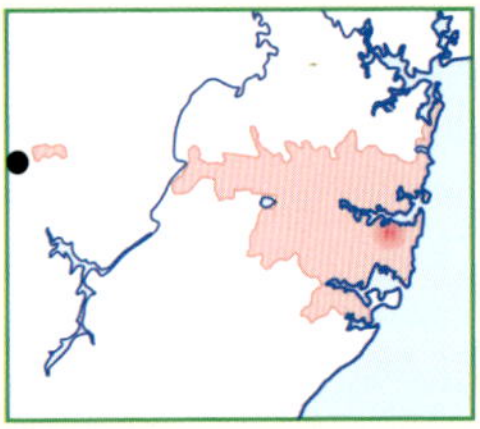

Length: 8.7km, circuit
Time: 3½ hours
Grade: Medium-Hard
Total Climbing: 500m
Maximum Height: 1010m
From Sydney: 110km
Closest Town: Katoomba 3km
Map: LPI 1:25,000 *Katoomba, Jamison*

West of Katoomba, the high sandstone plateau of the Blue Mountains ends dramatically with vertical cliffs plunging into Megalong Valley. The valley is the route for the Six Foot Track which runs from Katoomba to Jenolan Caves. The track was built in 1884 for horse drawn traffic and descended into the valley through the narrow gully of Nellies Glen. The Six Foot Track was abandoned in the 1930s, was remarked in 1985 and is now a pleasant walking track. An interesting circuit walk is completed with a return to the plateau via Devils Hole. This is a very narrow chasm that splits the huge cliffline near Katoomba. Devils Hole varies from 3m to 6m in width and from a distance looks impassable. While steep, a well-defined track passes through the chasm providing access from the valley to the cliff-tops. The walk passes through a wide variety of forest types and wildflowers can be found in most months.

Boars Head Rock from Six Foot Track

Access

From Sydney follow the Great Western Highway west for 107km to Katoomba. Continue 1km further on the Great Western Highway then exit the highway onto Bathurst Road. Turn right into Bathurst Road then immediately left onto Valley Road. Follow Valley Road then Narrow Neck Road south for 1.8km then turn right onto Cliff Drive. There is a car park at the junction and more parking places 100m further west along Cliff Drive.

Public transport – from Sydney Central, trains operate on the 'Blue Mountains Line' to Katoomba, refer www.cityrail.info for timetables. From the railway Blue Mountains Bus www.bmbc.com.au operate a very limited service on Route 686 to Cliff Drive. There are three services on weekdays and none on weekends and public holidays.

Six Foot Track

0.0km Follow Narrow Neck Road north-east for 800m to Stuarts Road. Turn left and descend steadily north-west for 500m to a T-intersection. Turn left and after 20m turn right onto Cliff Walk.

1.3km Follow the walking track north-west through light, dry forest for 200m to an unmarked track junction. Turn left for a return 300m sidetrip to Therabulat Lookout which has good views of Nellies Glen and the surrounding cliffs. Return to the main track and continue north. Descend into a gully and cross a small creek. Climb over a low ridge and cross another creek, then sidle slopes to a third small creek. Climb south-west onto an open, rocky ridge and a 50m side-track to the left leads to Norths Lookout. Follow the main track north along the ridge crest to pass through a gate to meet a fire trail – this is the Six Foot Track.

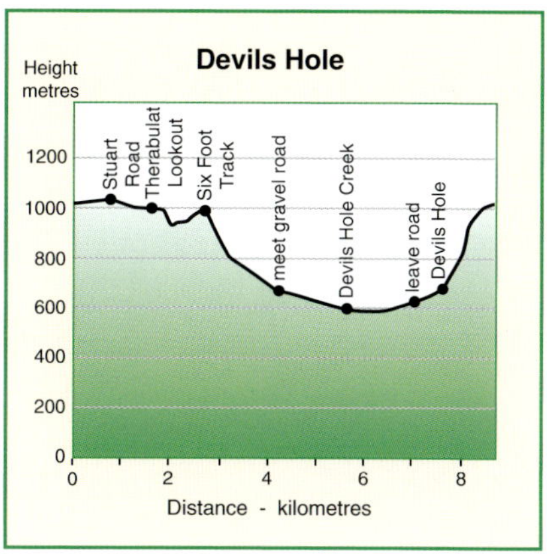

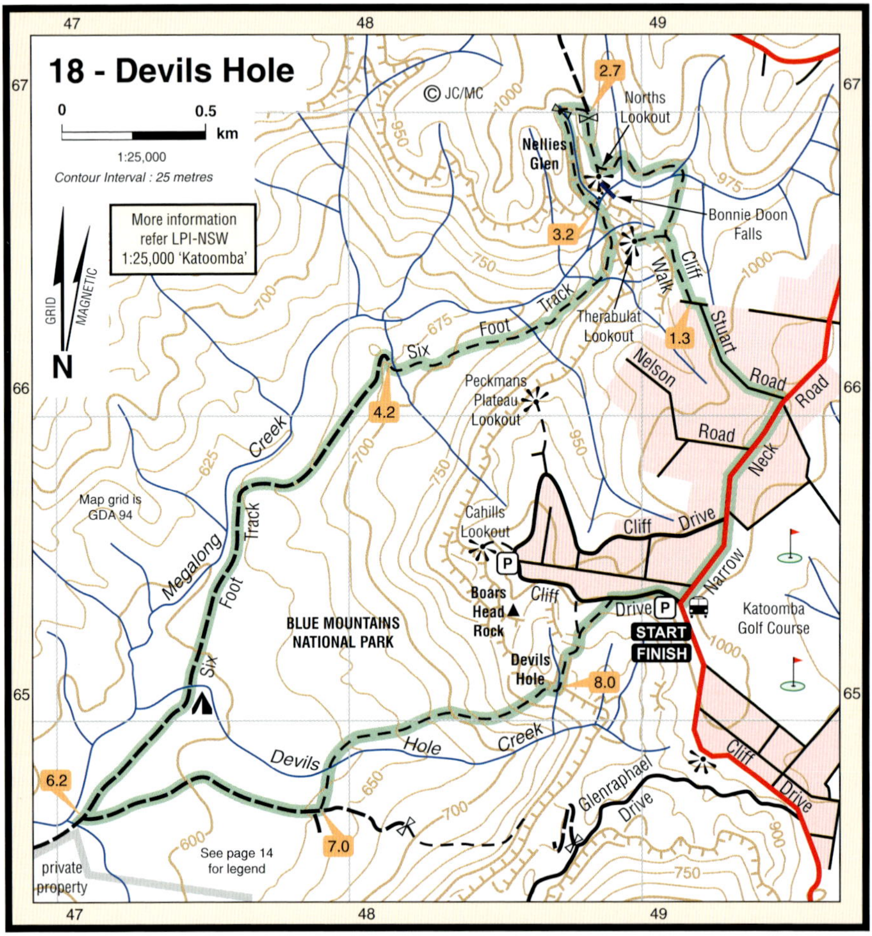

2.7km Turn left and follow the Six Foot Track 50m west descending to a bend and gate. After the gate descend south-south-east on a long line of steps into Nellies Glen. The track passes between two cliffs following a small creek. When the track crosses the main creek a short, untracked sidetrip leads upstream for 50m to the base of Bonnie Doon Falls. This wispy waterfall tumbles from up high and gets blown around in the wind.

3.2km From the creek crossing the Six Foot Track heads downstream. It remains on the southern side and descends gently. Continue for 250m to a signpost on the left that marks the site of a culvert over a gully which was part of the original track formation. Continue south-west still descending gently as the track gradually widens. Views of the surrounding cliffs are available from the rocks on the north side of the track. Continue westwards to circle left then right around a gully to meet a gravel road.

4.2km Follow the quiet fire road south-west for 1.4km to a bridge crossing Devils Hole Creek – a campsite is found on the southern bank. Continue south-west a further 600m to a road junction just before a creek crossing. The open land to the south-west is the site of historic Megalong Village – it is private property.

6.2km Turn left onto the minor, gravel road – this has a signpost indicating that ladders have been removed. This applies to ladders that once provided access onto Narrow Neck Plateau and the 'No Access' sign applies to that exit only. Continue eastward along the road – initially this follows a fenceline. There are good views of the surrounding cliffs from this track particularly of the Narrow Neck cliffs. Follow the road for 800m across a flat plain, up one rise, then continue level again to where the track begins climbing. A minor side-road to the south leads to a clearing. A walking track starts on the other side 20m further on – this is normally marked by a cairn.

7.0km Leave the road and follow the walking track north-east to cross Devils Hole Creek – there are some track markers around the creek. The poorly marked, but fairly well-defined track rises north-east following the crest of a spur. Climb steadily and when the spur begins to steepen the track veers right climbing to meet the base of a rocky outcrop. Pass to its right following a benched track then climb steeply up the gully south of the rock outcrop. Follow track markers as there are a number of confusing tracks in this gully. Nearing the base of the main cliff the track veers right and rises into the bottom of the narrow gully of Devils Hole.

8.0km The track uses ledges and has some zigzags as it climbs north-east through Devils Hole. The cliffs quickly close in and a steep, but easy climb leads up the narrow slot. Pass beneath an overhang then underneath the jammed block. Continue past a cave on the west side then exit out of Devils Hole into the gully above. When the track divides veer right and climb the spur. A final, steady climb follows an eroded section of walking track to meet Cliff Drive. Turn right and follow Cliff Drive 100m east to the car park at the junction with Narrow Neck Road.

Devils Hole

19 CENTENNIAL GLEN

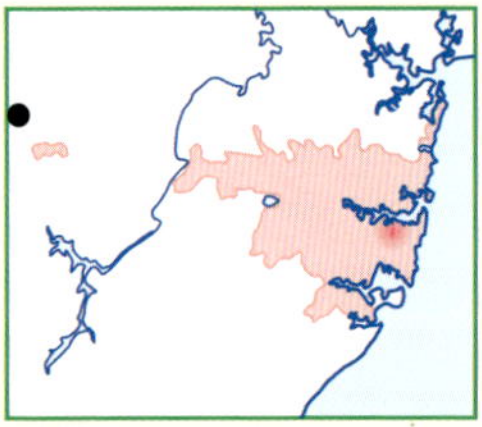

Length: 6.7km, circuit
Time: 3½ hours
Grade: Easy-Medium
Total Climbing: 290m
Maximum Height: 1070m
From Sydney: 118km
Closest Town: Blackheath 0km
Map: LPI 1:25,000 *Katoomba*

Sun Orchid

One of the oldest walking tracks in the Blue Mountains is located west of the small town of Blackheath. The track through Porters Pass and Centennial Glen was opened in 1888 for the centenary of European settlement in Australia. It has been used continuously for 130 years and has some eroded, rocky sections.

This varied walk passes through two small canyons, underneath numerous overhangs and close to some small waterfalls. The track makes extensive use of natural ledges in the cliffs. There are also many good views over the Kanimbla Valley and in spring plenty of wildflowers can be found in the heathland. While popular with walkers, the area is also extremely popular with rockclimbers and on most days climbers will be seen on the sheer cliff faces. There are numerous, minor sidetracks to the most popular climbs and walkers should ignore these are they are dead-ends.

Access

From Sydney, follow the Great Western Highway west for 118km to Blackheath. Just before the railway station, turn left into Bundarra Street, cross the railway line then turn right and park in Station Street.

Public transport – from Sydney Central, trains operate on the 'Blue Mountains Line' to Blackheath Railway Station – refer www.cityrail.info for timetables.

Variations:

1. **Porters Pass**, 5.1km, circuit, 3 hours, Easy-Medium. Follow the first 3.3km of the walk to the first track junction in Centennial Glen. Turn left and follow the notes from the 4.9km point to the end of the walk.

0.0km From the railway station follow Station Street north along the railway line for 500m. Just past the road bridge on the right, turn left into Wombat Street. Follow the street west for

Heading towards Porters Pass

400m, turn right then left into Burton Street. Continue west to the end of the street.

1.2km Follow the walking track west for 150m to a track junction. Keep to the left descending gently through light, scrubby forest and heath. When the track divides, take either as they soon rejoin. Continue for 400m to the edge of the plateau to an unmarked track junction. The 30m long sidetrack on the left leads onto a rock outcrop where there are good views to the west. Return to the main track and descend north into the cliff-lined gully. Follow the gully south-west for 80m then swing right following a ledge into the next gully. The stepped track then descends steeply through Porters Pass to the base of the cliff.

1.9km Turn south to pass under a cascade then follow the cliff base. The track passes through light scrub and is well defined, but rocky underfoot. Continue southward for 300m to pass below a high, wispy waterfall then rise gently onto an open ledge underneath the cliff. The ledge is known as Colliers Causeway and it provides views west over the valley. Continue south-east along the cliff base to cross a creek then veer north-east to cross the creek again. Ignore a minor dead-end track to the right and veer left climbing steps into the gully above. The track is right beside the cascading creek and the steps and handrail are often wet so take care on the climb. Just past the steps there is a track junction and a Porters Pass signpost. The left track is a 40m sidetrack into The Grotto – take care when wet. Back on the main track turn right and climb steeply up more steps to another track junction. Either track can be followed – the right track has views so turn right and follow it for 50m to another track junction at a painted rock. The walk will return to this junction after a circular sidetrip.

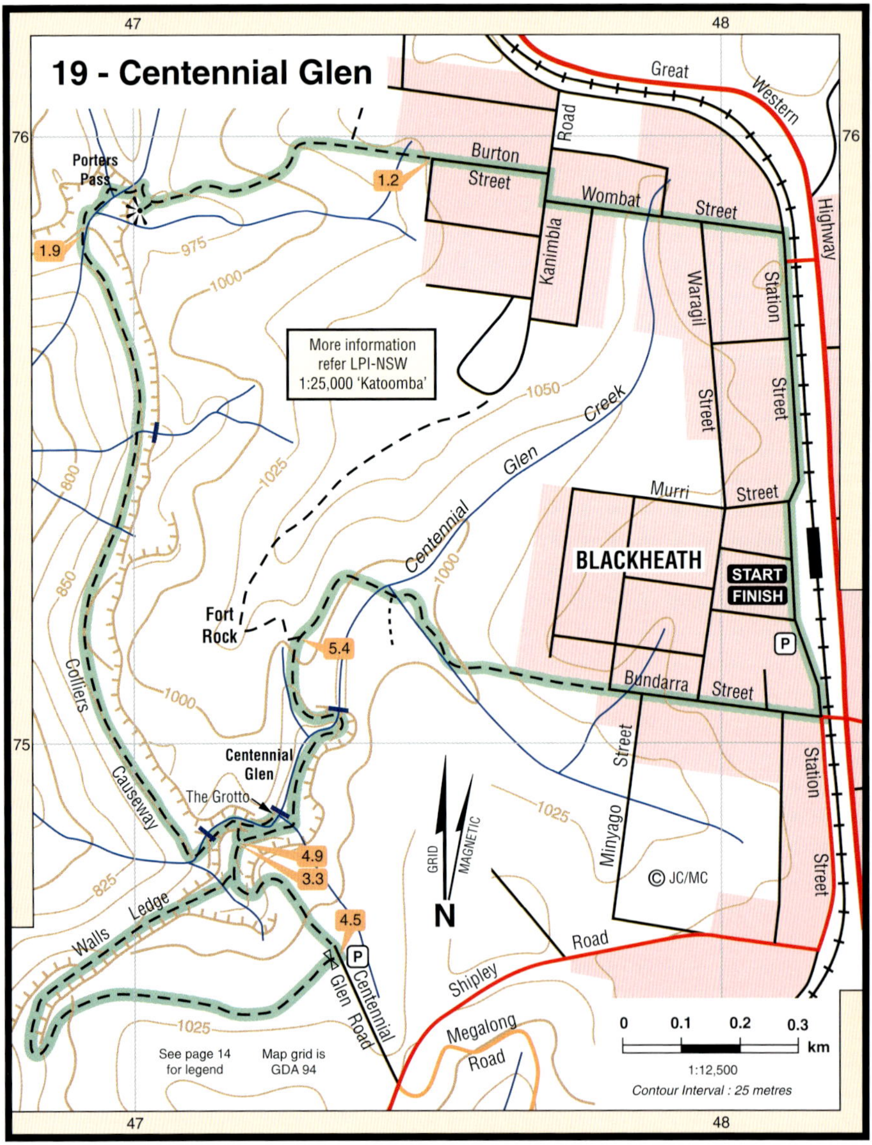

3.3km Turn right and continue 50m to the next track junction. The return from the loop will be from the left. Turn right and pass through a small grotto with a bath-like trough. The track then follows Walls Ledge south-west. This is a narrow ledge in the centre of a double cliff line and the area is popular with rockclimbers. Follow the ledge south-west until the upper cliff ends. The track then swings left and climbs north-east onto the plateau above. This is covered with low heath. Follow the track eastwards to a gate and carpark at the northern end of Centennial Glen Road.

Walls Ledge

4.5km Turn left and locate the track to Centennial Glen at the end of the carpark. Follow the track northwest through dense heath. Cross an open rock with views and descend briefly to the track junction at the end of the loop to Walls Ledge. Turn right and walk 50m to the next junction at the painted rock.

4.9km Turn right and follow a ledge under a high overhang ignoring minor side tracks on the left that lead down into the gully below. Stay on the east side of the gully following a series of ledges under cliffs and pass behind a waterfall on Centennial Glen Creek. Continue following more ledges then rock steps leading up a narrow gully to the top of the cliffs.

5.4km A poorly-defined track junction to Fort Rock is located on an open rock slab. Keep to the right heading north-east sidling the hillside and descend gently to meet Centennial Glen Creek. Cross the creek to a track junction and follow the more major track to the left. This rises east winding through dense heaths to a street junction. Continue straight ahead and walk east following Bundarra Street over a hill to meet the railway line. Turn left to the railway station.

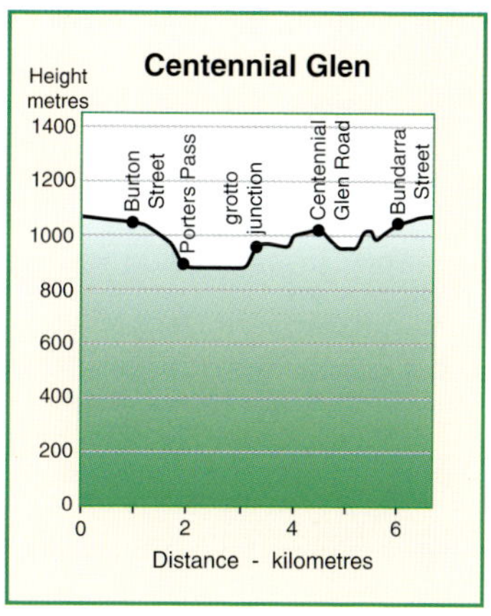

20 GRAND CANYON

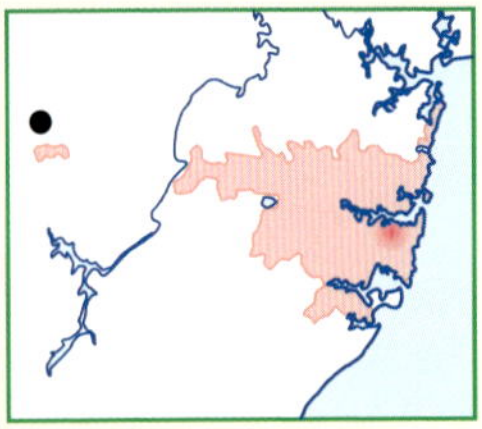

Length: 5.4km, circuit
Time: 3 hours
Grade: Medium
Total Climbing: 250m
Maximum Height: 1000m
From Sydney: 118km
Closest Town: Blackheath 5km
Map: LPI 1:25,000 *Katoomba*

Grand Canyon is one of the most popular walks in the Blue Mountains. The track was opened in 1907 and it is unique as it is the only constructed walking track that passes through a slot canyon. There are many other canyons throughout the Blue Mountains, but they are difficult to explore easily with most requiring skill with ropes. The track through Grand Canyon follows natural and man-made ledges in the cliff walls and provides views into the narrow slot. In places, the track is poised above big drops with simple hand rails and care is needed.

A worthwhile, optional sidetrip is to scramble and wade upstream into the bottom section of the main canyon. Grand Canyon also features many large, sandstone overhangs. This walk passes through a wide variety of plant habitats with the canyon containing many delicate ferns while the plateau above supports dry, eucalypt forest where wildflowers abound in spring.

Access

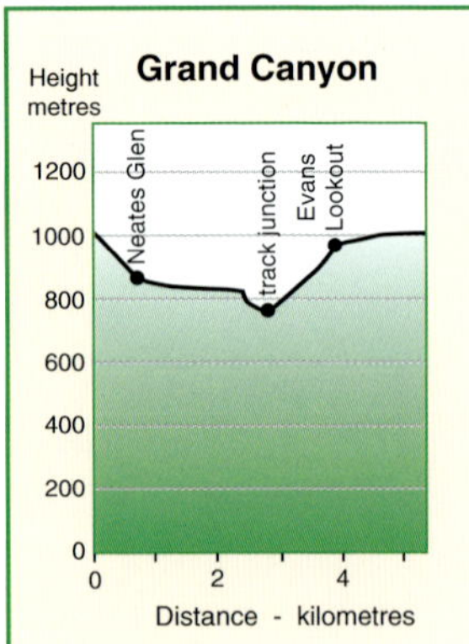

From Sydney, follow the Great Western Highway west for 107km to Katoomba. Continue following the highway a further 10km to the outskirts of Blackheath and turn right onto Evans Lookout Road. Follow the road eastwards for 2.7km to the Neates Glen car park on the right.

Public transport – from Sydney Central, trains operate on the 'Blue Mountains Line' to Katoomba and Blackheath Railway Stations – refer www.cityrail.info for timetables. Blue Mountains Bus www.bmbc.com.au operate a bus on route 698 between Katoomba and Blackheath stopping in Evans Lookout Road at the junction with St Andrews Avenue. This leaves a 1.0km walk to the start.

0.0km Follow the track south-west towards Grand Canyon. The track zigzags as it descends steeply into the cool gully of Neates Glen then swings south-east to follow the gully downstream to meet Greaves Creek near a large overhang. The track crosses the creek then follows the southern bank downstream to a tunnel.

1.3km The tunnel was formed by a rockfall. Pass through the tunnel to a sandy beach near overhangs – this is a popular stop. Continue following a rocky ledge passing below a waterfall. This is where the canyon begins with Greaves Creek fal-

Grand Canyon

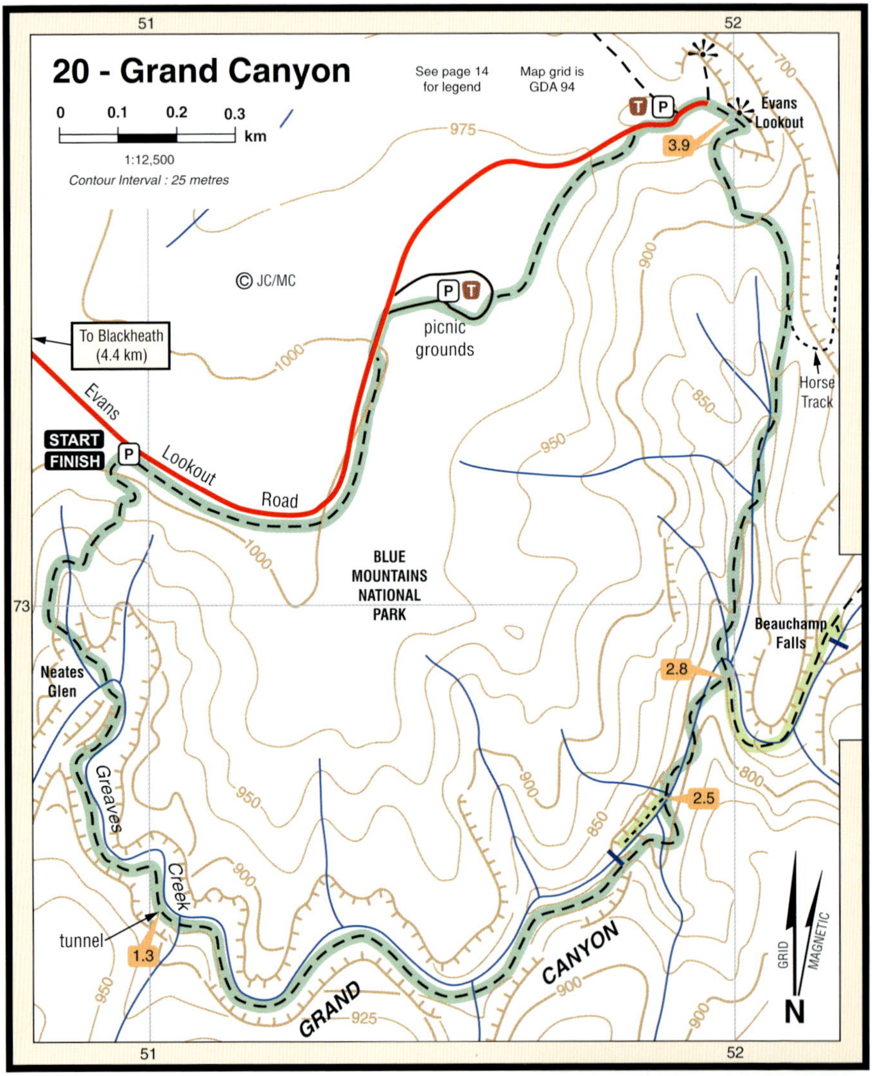

ling steeply into a narrow chasm. Continue along the narrow ledge crossing a side creek on a bridge. The canyon below gets deeper as the creek descends while the track continues using the narrow ledge in the cliff. The track leaves the canyon by swinging right around a spur and descends steps into a side creek then down the gully to cross Greaves Creek at the base of Grand Canyon.

Broad-leaf Drumstick

Sidetrip: Grand Canyon 300m return, 20 minutes

Turn left and head upstream into Grand Canyon. There is no track so take care as the rocks are slippery and wet feet can be expected. The tall cliffs on both sides close in and the level floor of the canyon ends in a waterfall. Return the same way to the main track.

2.5km Follow the creek to the north-east crossing it four times to reach a track junction.

Sidetrip: Beauchamp Falls 800m return, 20 minutes

Turn right and follow the walking track south through forest. The track soon swings east then north-east and starts descending steeply. Beauchamp Falls are heard before they are seen and stone steps lead to the base of the falls. A short sidetrack to the right leads to a good view of the falls. Return the same way to the track junction.

2.8km Head north towards Evans Lookout following a fern-filled side gully. As the track climbs higher it ascends some cliffs to enter drier eucalypt forest. At a track junction, ignore the unmarked Horse Track to the right and continue on the left heading northward to Evans Lookout.

3.9km Evans Lookout is fenced and has a stone picnic shelter. It provides excellent views of the deep valley to the north-east. Head west to the car park then turn left onto the signposted walking track to Neates Glen. Follow the track south-west through dry eucalypt forest to pass through picnic grounds to Evans Lookout Road. Turn left and follow the sealed road for 100m then turn left onto a walking track. The walking track parallels the road to the end of the walk at Neates Glen car park.

View from Evans Lookout

21 BLUE GUM FOREST

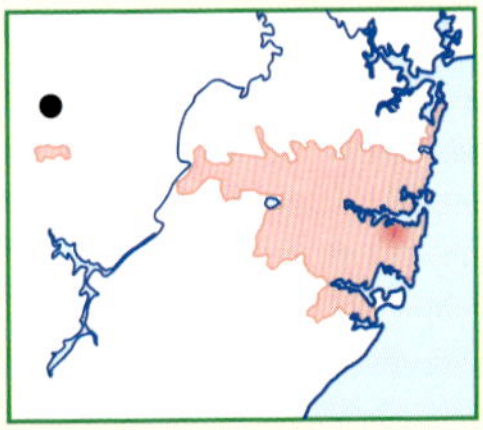

Length: 18.1km, circuit
Time: 8½ hours
Grade: Hard
Total Climbing: 860m
Maximum Height: 980m
From Sydney: 122km
Closest Town: Blackheath 5km
Map: LPI 1:25,000 *Katoomba, Mount Wilson*

Blue Gum Forest is a unique stand of trees comprising mainly of a single eucalypt species. It is located in the Grose Valley in the Blue Mountains near Blackheath. In 1930, the forest was leased for a farm with the intention of felling the trees. Fortunately, the lease was purchased by bushwalkers in 1931 and then donated to the government as a public reserve. This saved the forest and it subsequently became famous. In 1959, the Blue Mountains National Park was declared with the forest being a core feature.

The forest survived many bushfires, but in 2006 a huge fire burnt much of the Grose Valley including Blue Gum Forest. Many trees were killed and today the forest is slowly regenerating from seed. While not as beautiful as it once was, the tall, dead trees are still a feature. This long walk also includes many cascades, waterfalls and scenic views. During the last two decades, landslides occasionally close tracks into the valley – check with park management about track closures before starting.

Access

From Sydney, follow the Great Western Highway west for 118km to Blackheath then turn right onto Govetts Leap Road. Follow the road eastward for 2.8km to the car park at the end of the road at Govetts Leap Lookout.

Public transport – from Sydney Central, trains operate on the 'Blue Mountains Line' to Blackheath Railway Station – refer www.cityrail.info for timetables. Blue Mountains Bus www.bmbc.com.au operate a bus around Blackheath that stops in Govetts Leap Road at the National Parks Visitor Centre. This leaves a 400m walk to the start.

Variations:

1. **Rodriguez Pass Track**, 10.7km, circuit, 6 hours, Medium-Hard. Follow the first 2.9km of the walk. At the track junction, do not cross the creek, instead scramble to the right along the creek to Junction Rock then follow the notes from the 10.3km point to the end of the walk.
2. **Blue Gum Forest & Grand Canyon**, 20.1km, circuit, 10 hours, Hard. Follow the first 14.1km of the walk then turn left and reverse the notes for Walk 20 through Grand Canyon to Evans Lookout then continue from the 15.2km point to the end of the walk.

0.0km Start at the northern end of the car park and follow the track north to a track junction. Ignore the track on the left to Horseshoe Falls and turn right towards Grose Valley Walks. The track descends very steeply south via stone steps towards

Govetts Leap

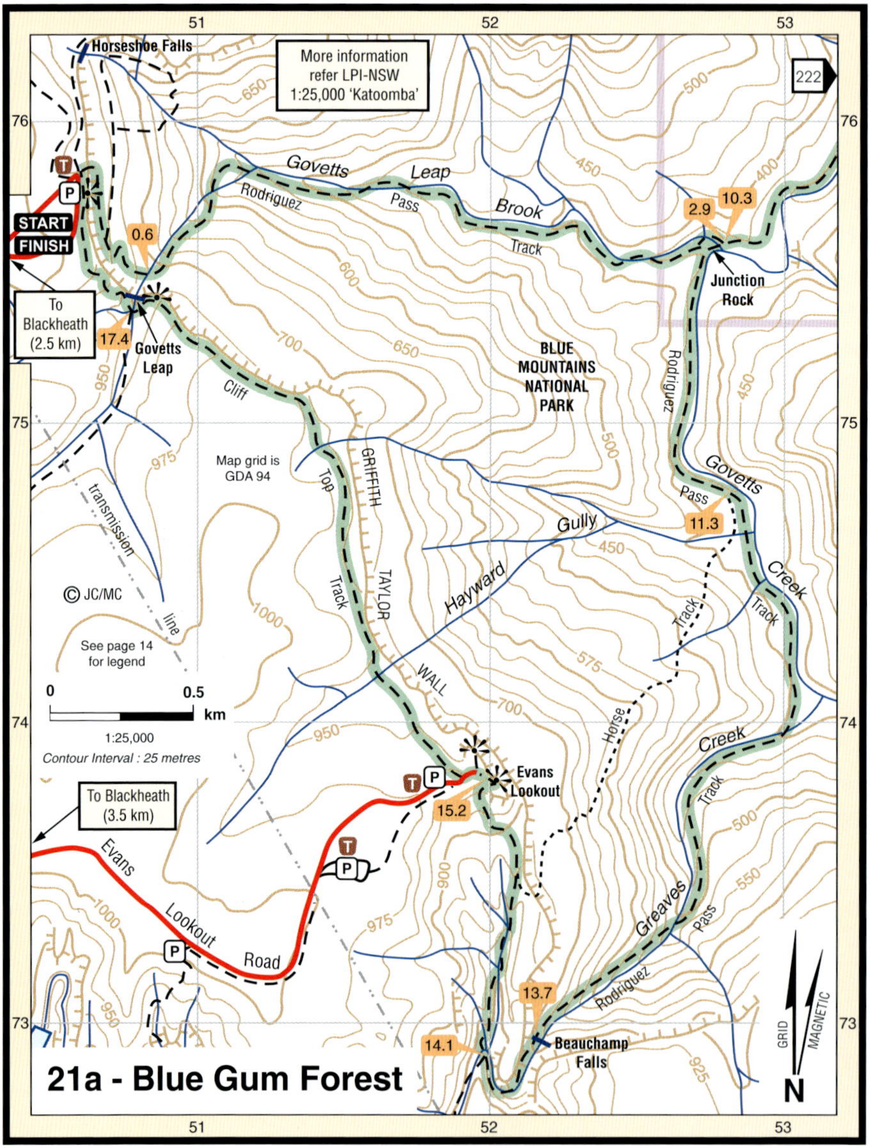

Govetts Leap. There are good views of the tall, wispy waterfall before the track swings north to descend below an arch then down a steel staircase to the base of the cliffs. An easier, but still steep, descent south-east leads to the base of Govetts Leap.

0.6km The falls are an impressive sight tumbling over a sheer cliff. Cross the creek below the falls and follow Rodriguez Pass Track north-east then east alongside Govetts Leap Brook. The track descends and soon enters forest passing several,

Start of the track

small falls and cascades. Continue to a track junction beside a rocky cascade – this is 50m before Junction Rock. Cross the creek via rock slabs to the north bank and continue downstream 50m to another track junction. To the right across the brook is Junction Rock.

2.9km Turn left heading east following Greaves Creek downstream. Continue for 1.0km to cross a side creek then sidle along a narrow ledge 5m above the creek. Cross Fortress Flat then continue on a rough track which rises onto a spur. The track swings right descending east on the spur to cross Orang Utan Gully. Level walking along broad creek flats leads to the camping area at Acacia Flat where there is a toilet. Continue north-east a further 600m to a junction with the track to Perrys Lookdown. This is located on the southern edge of Blue Gum Forest.

6.6km Blue Gum Forest is a stand of eucalypts that was burnt by wildfire in 2006. The forest is regenerating from seed and walkers are requested to stay on the track. Explore the forest then return to the Perrys Lookdown track junction. Return the same way across Acacia Flat to the track junction near Junction Rock.

10.3km Keep to the left and cross Govetts Leap Brook to another track junction beside Junction Rock. Keep left again and follow Rodriguez Pass Track southward following a ledge above Govetts Creek. The track continues through open forest and 1.0km of easy walking following the western side of the creek leads to a signpost. The unnamed track to the right is Horse Track – it does exit the valley, but is not very scenic and is not maintained.

11.3km Keep to the left and continue following Govetts Creek. Pass several cascades and pools and continue for 500m to a wide flat near the junction of two major creeks.

Head south across the flat to cross Greaves Creek. The track swings south-west and starts climbing steeply following Greaves Creek. Pass some small waterfalls and cascades then cross Greaves Creek to its western bank at a series of cascades and terraces. Continue climbing steeply to the base of Beauchamp Falls. A short sidetrack on the left provides a clear view of the falls.

Beauchamp Falls

13.7km From the falls the track climbs steeply zigzagging to meet the creek above the waterfall. Follow Greaves Creek through the pass between two large cliffs. The track and creek soon swing around to the north to a track junction. To the left is Grand Canyon.

14.1km Keep to the right and follow the track north towards Evans Lookout along a fern-filled creek. As the track climbs higher, it passes through the cliffs to enter drier eucalypt forest. At a track junction, ignore the unmarked Horse Track to the right and continue on the left heading northward to Evans Lookout.

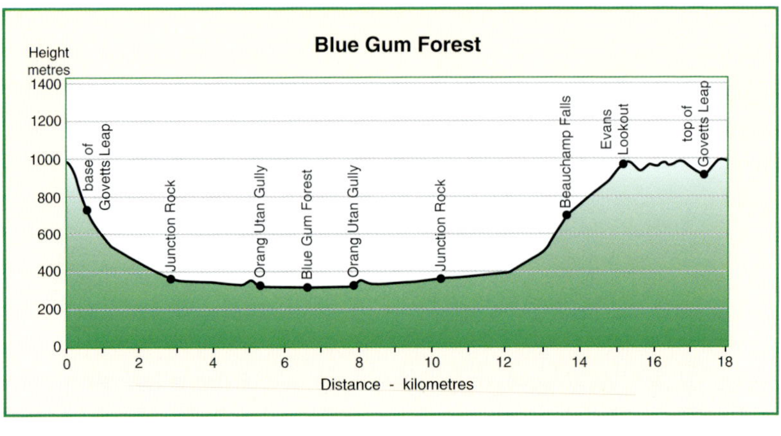

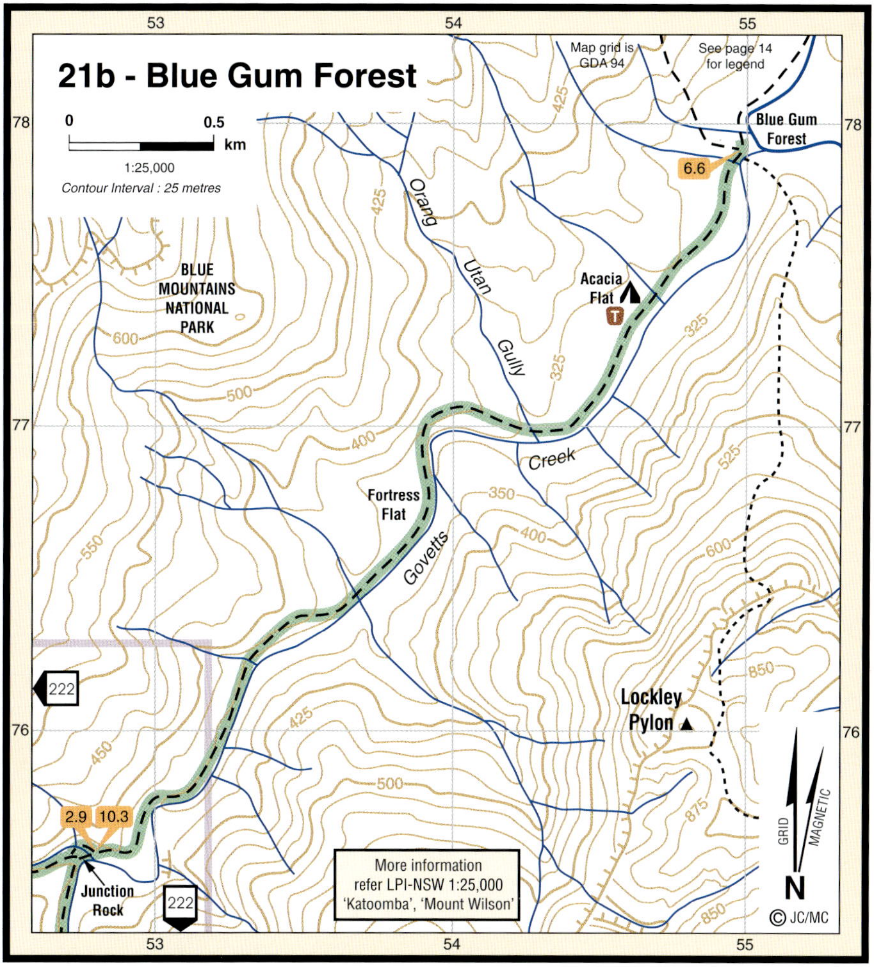

15.2km Evans Lookout is fenced and has a stone picnic shelter. It provides excellent views of the valley of Govetts Creek and Blue Gum Forest to the north-east. Head west to the car park and on its northern side locate Cliff Top Walk. Follow the track north-west. This descends steadily to cross Hayward Gully then rises steadily northward to a broad ridge above Griffith Taylor Wall. The track does not provide many views as it keeps away from the cliff edge. When it swings north-west it begins to descend steadily to a fenced lookout area near Govetts Leap with good views to the north. Cross Govetts Leap Brook on concrete stepping stones just above the waterfall to a track junction. To the left is a minor track leading to Blackheath.

17.4km Keep to the right and a steady climb leads to the end of the walk at the south-east end of Govetts Leap car park.

22 PENNANT HILLS CIRCUIT

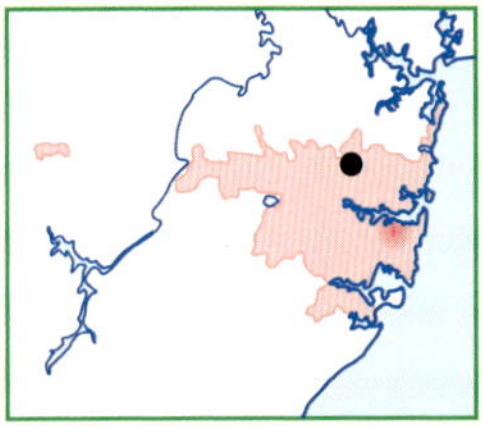

Length: 8.2km, circuit
Time: 3½ hours
Grade: Medium
Total Climbing: 210m
Maximum Height: 145m
From Sydney: 25km
Closest Town: Pennant Hills 1km
Map: UBD 1:19,000 p153, 173 or SYDWAY p214, 234

The western section of Lane Cove National Park is wider than other sections of the park as it includes a number of side creeks that feed into the Lane Cove River together with the intervening ridges. This area was not developed into suburbs as the steep-sided, sandstone valleys were deemed unsuitable. The Great North Walk (GNW), that runs from Sydney to Newcastle, passes through the park and this walk follows part of it. There has been some small development in the park region with one block being leased to the Scouts and, on a flat ridge, there are a series of sporting fields. These have minimal effect on the walk and most of this circuit is in sparse native forest. The park has numerous, minor, unmarked foot pads and these should be ignored when walking the main trails. Track markers are common although they are highly varied ranging from simple arrows to signs to nearby suburbs. On a clear day there is a good view of the city centre from City View Lookout.

Crossing Lane Cove River

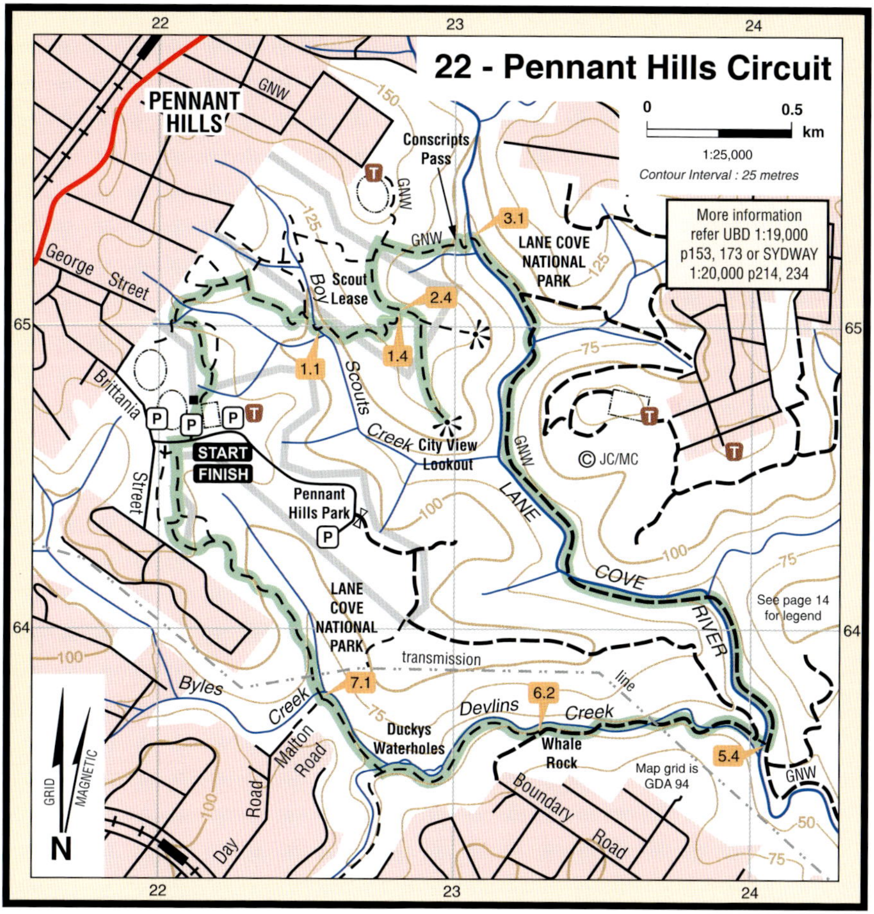

Access

From Sydney follow the Pacific Highway then Epping Road for 19km to Epping. Turn right and follow Beecroft Road for 4km then turn right and follow Pennant Hills Road (also known as Cumberland Highway) for 1km to Pennant Hills. Turn right into The Crescent then left and right into Brittania Street. At the second roundabout, turn left and park near the soccer ground.

Public transport – from Sydney Central, trains operate on the 'Northern Line' to Pennant Hills Railway Station. This leaves a 1km walk along The Crescent and Brittania Street to the start of the walk.

Variations:

1. **Pennant Hills to Cheltenham**, 8.9km, one-way, 4 hours, Medium. Follow the first 7.1km of the walk then turn left and follow Malton Road then Day Road to Cheltenham Railway Station.

0.0km Head north along the west side of the soccer ground to the dressing rooms where a walking track starts on the right. Follow the track northward into forest, ignore two tracks from the right and continue to cross a gully to a track junction. Turn right to cross a northern gully and rise to another track junction. From here, posts with arrows assist at track junctions. Turn right at this and the next two junctions then head south-east along a spur. The track descends through thick scrub to another junction.

1.1km Turn right and cross Boy Scouts Creek ignoring minor foot pads in both directions beside the creek. The track climbs east passing an overhang then zigzags onto the ridge above to a track junction in low woodland. This area is part of a Scout Lease – public access is allowed.

1.4km Turn right for a sidetrip to City View Lookout. Follow the track south-east for 150m then turn right and continue southward to a rock outcrop on the end of the ridge. The harbour bridge and the tall buildings of the city centre can usually be seen from here. Return to the track junction.

2.4km Continue northward, turn right at the next intersection and shortly after meet the Great North Walk (GNW). Turn right and follow the GNW descending for 200m then veer right at a track junction. Continue through Conscripts Pass to a crossing of Lane Cove River. On a rock face in the pass is a faint engraving of the NSW premier during the Great Depression.

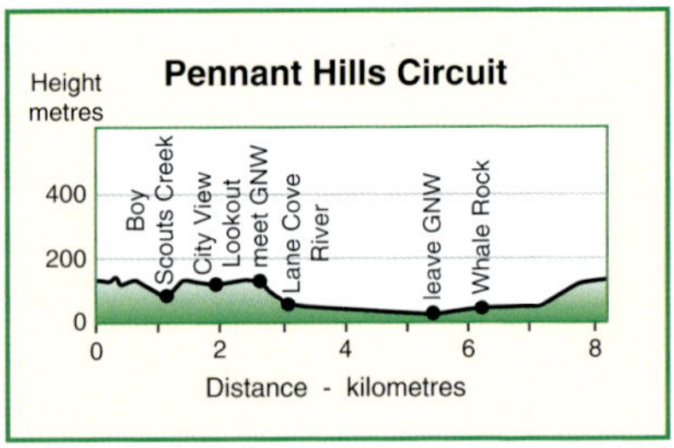

3.1km Follow the eastern bank of the river downstream for 250m to meet a fire trail and continue straight ahead. The fire trail follows the river downstream for 2.1km crossing the river four times. Continue to a junction with a walking track on the right towards Epping.

5.4km Leave the GNW by turning right. Descend steeply, rock hop across Lane Cove River then climb steeply for 30m to meet a fire trail. Turn left and follow the fire trail west along Devlins Creek. The trail crosses the creek three times on concrete fords and leads to a track junction below Whale Rock.

6.2km Veer right onto a walking track and continue following Devlins Creek upstream for 400m to pass along the top of a cliff above Duckys Waterholes. Continue a further 200m then turn right, cross Devlins Creek and follow the scrubby valley of Byles Creek for 300m to the next track junction. Left leads to Malton Road and Cheltenham Railway Station.

7.1km Turn right again to cross Byles Creek, ignore minor side tracks along the transmission line then climb steadily north-west through forest. The track levels out as it nears housing. Continue to a track junction and either may be followed. Turn left and shortly after turn right onto a concrete walking track. Follow this north, ignoring minor side tracks and when the track swings west, follow a rougher track north for 50m to the meet the sealed road near the soccer ground where the walk began.

THORNLEIGH TO HORNSBY 23

Just east of Hornsby is the Berowra Valley Regional Park. The main track through the valley is the Benowie Walking Track which is part of the Great North Walk (GNW) that runs from Sydney to Newcastle. The Benowie Track is 27km long and the southern section is followed on this walk.

The valley and forest of the headwaters of Berowra Creek provide some fine walking. While some sections follow fire trails, much of this walk is along rocky, bush tracks that climb and descend several small cliff lines. After rain, wet feet can be expected as the track fords several creeks. The crossing of Waitara Creek is unusual as the stream bed is a series of deeply eroded circular holes. Two lookouts provide a view over the valley and in most seasons, there is a wide range of wildflowers including boronia, banksia, grevillea, persoonia and flowering eucalypts.

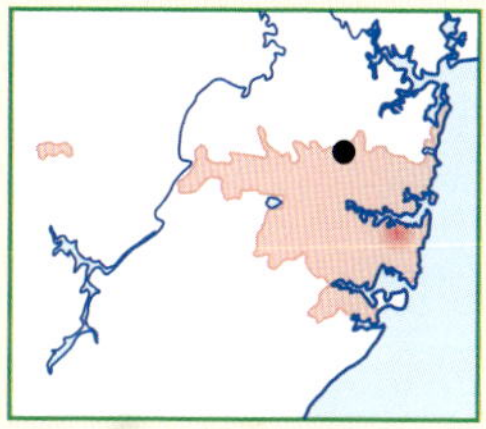

Length: 9.2km, circuit
Time: 4 hours
Grade: Medium-Hard
Total Climbing: 300m
Maximum Height: 185m
From Sydney: 25km
Closest Town: Thornleigh 0km
Map: LPI 1:25,000 *Hornsby*

Access

From Sydney, follow the Pacific Highway north-west for 22km to Wahroonga then turn left onto Pennant Hills Road (also known as Cumberland Highway) and follow it south-west for 3km to Thornleigh. Just past the railway station turn right into Wells Street and park. Alternatively, park near Hornsby Railway Station and catch a train to Thornleigh to begin the walk.

Public transport – from Sydney Central, trains operate on the 'Northern Line' to Thornleigh Railway Station. The return is from Hornsby Railway Station which is on the same line. Refer www.citytrail.info for timetables.

Benowie Track near Zig Zag Creek

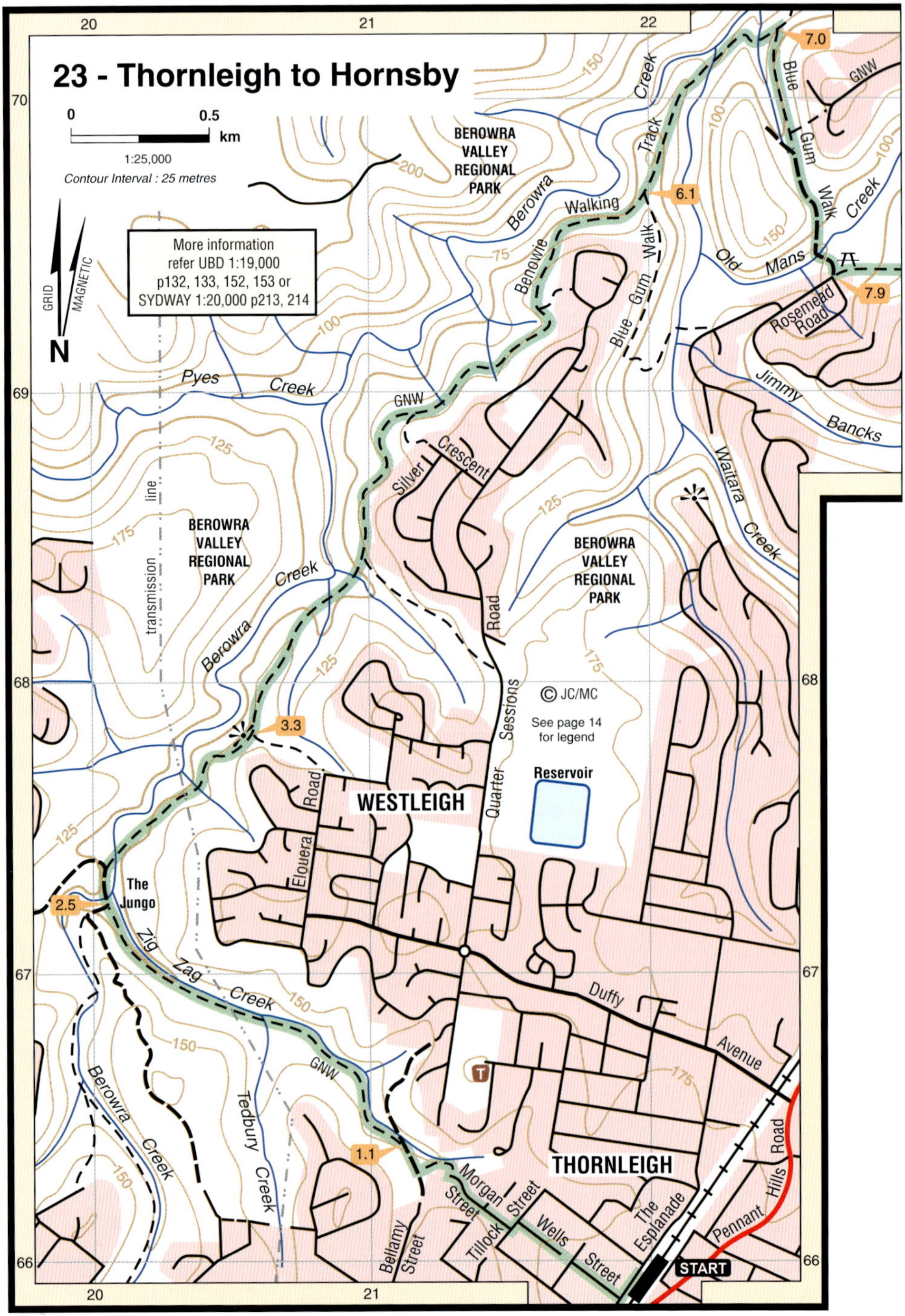
23 - Thornleigh to Hornsby
0 0.5 km
1:25,000
Contour Interval : 25 metres
GRID
MAGNETIC
N
More information refer UBD 1:19,000 p132, 133, 152, 153 or SYDWAY 1:20,000 p213, 214
BEROWRA VALLEY REGIONAL PARK
Berowra Walking Track
Berowie Creek
Blue Gum Walk
Blue Gum Walk Creek
Old Mans Creek
Rosemead Road
Jimmy Bancks
Waitara Creek
Pyes Creek
GNW
Silver Crescent
Sessions Road
Quarter Sessions Road
transmission line
Berowra Creek
© JC/MC
See page 14 for legend
Reservoir
WESTLEIGH
Elouera Road
The Jungo
Zig Zag Creek
Duffy Avenue
Tedbury Creek
THORNLEIGH
Bellamy Street
Morgan Street
Tillock Street
Wells Street
The Esplanade
Pennant Hills Road
START
7.0
6.1
7.9
3.3
2.5
1.1
20
21
22
70
69
68
67
66
200
175
150
125
100
75

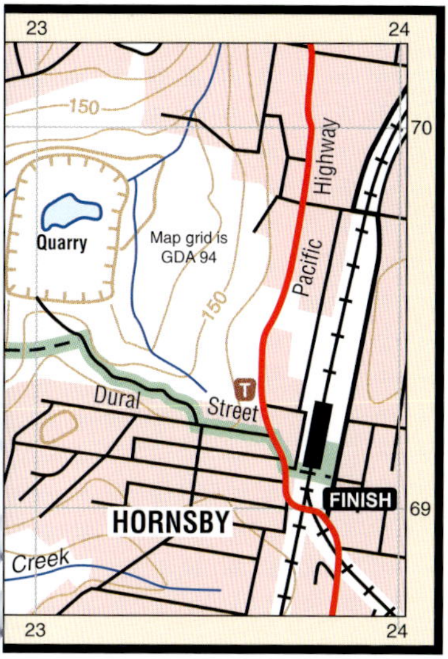

0.0km From Thornleigh Railway Station cross The Esplanade and follow Wells Street north-west until it ends. Turn left into Tillock Street then right into Morgan Street. When it ends in a court the walking track starts on the right. Head north across grass then swing left and follow a rough track across the back of private property to meet a concrete fire access road. Turn right and descend following the road for 200m to a bridge over Zig Zag Creek above a small weir.

1.1km Turn left and follow a walking track north-west along the southern bank of Zig Zag Creek. Descend gently to cross a gully via a bridge. Continue descending steadily to a clearing to meet a vehicle track – this location is known as The Jungo.

2.5km Turn right and follow the vehicle track north across the ford over Berowra Creek. Climb steeply for 100m then turn right onto a walking track. Descend quickly to cross Berowra Creek again. Ignore a minor track to the right and continue north-east following the valley downstream. The track rises gently to pass below a small waterfall then soon climbs steeply to the top of rocky outcrops. Pass a fenced lookout to a second lookout and track junction. Right leads to Elouera Road in Westleigh.

3.3km Continue straight ahead and descend steadily for 700m to cross a large creek. Continue for 100m to cross a second creek. In the next 2.0km keep left at each

Along the fenced lookout

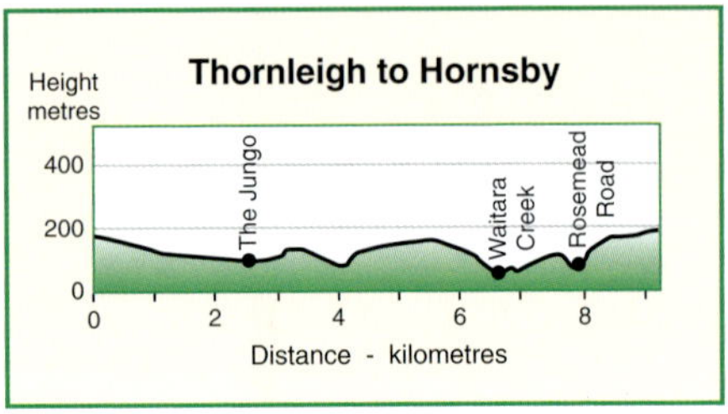

junction and ignore all side tracks on the right. Rise steadily following the base of a cliff line then pass just below private property in Westleigh. Past the houses the track swings east to a major track junction in a saddle on a ridge. To the right is one end of Blue Gum Walk.

6.1km Turn left and continue northward on the Great North Walk (GNW). The track soon swings right and zigzags steeply north-east. It passes through a large overhang and continues descending to cross Waitara Creek. Follow a series of rocky terraces downstream then sidle around the end of a spur. Cross a small side creek and rise to a track junction with the other end of Blue Gum Walk. The GNW continues north through a rifle range.

7.0km Turn right and follow Blue Gum Walk southward. This follows an alternative route for the GNW that avoids the rifle range. Climb steadily following the small creek for 400m to a track junction where the alternative GNW turns left. Continue on the right to meet a fire road. Turn left and follow the road through a wide saddle then descend to cross Old Mans Creek. This is named after the kangaroos that once lived in the valley. Rise south-east to a picnic area at the corner of Rosemead Road.

7.9km From the eastern end of the picnic area, follow a walking track east into the gully. This ascends a cliff via many steps then continues east through light forest to a private, sealed road to a quarry. Turn right and follow the road to Dural Street. Turn left to meet the Pacific Highway. Cross this with care and to the right is the entrance to Hornsby Railway Station. Catch a train back to Thornleigh – be careful to catch the correct train as there are 2 lines from here to Sydney.

Blue Gum Walk

MT KURING-GAI – BEROWRA CIRCUIT 24

The roads that link Sydney to Newcastle follow a high ridge toward the Hawkesbury River. The ridge has small towns on its crest, but the remainder of the ridge is protected native bushland. To the east is the Ku-ring-gai Chase National Park, the second oldest national park in Australia. To the west is the Berowra Valley Regional Park. Both reserves have open forest on the spurs, patches of rainforest in the narrow gullies and mangroves along the creek banks. An historical boat building site is one of the unusual features seen on this walk.

The ridge is bordered by tidal creeks which, during the last ice age were small but as sea levels rose, their valleys were drowned. There are some good views of the peaceful creek waters. Tracks follow both creeks and these can be linked into a long day walk. The walk is readily broken into two shorter walks using a train from the railway station near the half way point to return to the start.

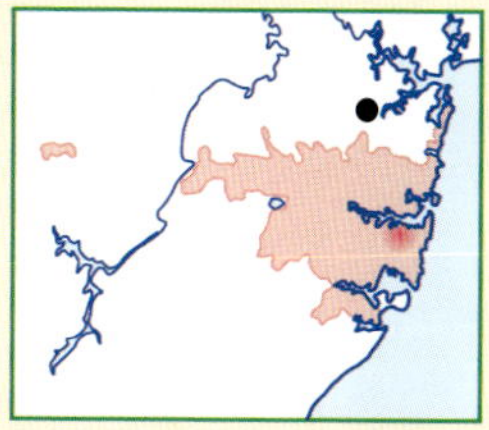

Length: 17.5km, circuit
Time: 8 hours
Grade: Medium-Hard
Total Climbing: 500m
Maximum Height: 220m
From Sydney: 31km
Closest Town: Mt Kuring-gai 0km
Map: LPI 1:25,000 *Cowan, Hornsby*

Waratah Bay

Cowan Creek from Mt Kuring-gai Walking Track

Access

From Sydney, follow the Pacific Highway north-west for 22km to Wahroonga then follow the Sydney - Newcastle Freeway north for 4.6km and exit at Ku-ring-gai Chase Road. Turn left and after 800m turn right onto Pacific Highway and follow it north for 3.2km to Mt Kuring-gai. Park on the left in Glenview Road or near the railway station.

Public transport – from Sydney Central, rains operate on the 'North Shore Line' to Mt Kuring-gai Railway Station. Berowra Railway Station is the next station to the north on the same railway line – it is about half way around the circuit and can be used to complete a circuit for the shorter variations. Refer www.cityrail.info for timetables.

Safety

After heavy rain, do not attempt this walk as there are a large number of creeks that need to be forded.

Variations:

1. **Mt Kuring-gai to Berowra via Cowan Creek**, 9.1km, one-way, 4 hours, Medium. Follow the first 9.1km of the walk to Berowra Railway Station. Use the train to complete a circuit.
2. **Berowra to Mt Kuring-gai via Berowra Creek**, 8.4km, one-way, 4 hours, Medium. Start from the 9.1km point of the walk at Berowra Railway Station and follow the notes to the end of the walk. Use the train to complete a circuit.

0.0km From Glenview Road, follow the Pacific Highway south-west for 100m then turn left and follow the road bridge east over the Sydney-Newcastle Freeway. Almost immediately, turn left and follow a walking track north-east between fences for 300m to meet the end of Harwood Avenue. The pedestrian footbridge on the left leads into the railway station – if arriving by train start the walk by crossing this bridge. Follow Harwood Avenue east for 300m to its end. Enter the Ku-ring-gai Chase National Park by passing through a gate and follow the Mt Kuring-gai Walking Track north-east. Initially, this is a wide fire trail – continue for 600m to a track junction.

1.5km Follow the side track on the right for 100m to a rocky lookout – this has a good view east of Cowan Creek. Return to the track junction and continue north-east along the fire trail for 300m to a set of rocks. Descend these via a series of stone steps passing underneath some overhangs. A gentler descent follows the crest of the ridge eastwards. There are some views then a final zigzagging descent leads to a track junction near Cowan Creek.

3.3km Turn left and follow Berowra Track northwards along the shores of Cowan Creek. Pass a series of aboriginal middens then round a point. A timber walkway crosses a collapsed section of the track and leads into a narrow cove. In rainforest, rock-hop across the creek then continue following Berowra Track climbing high over a point into Winson Bay. Follow the shore around the next point to Lords Bay.

5.7km Cross two creeks then follow a narrow, rock ledge. The track then undulates passing several small overhangs before gradually swinging around to the west as it rounds a wide point into Waratah Bay.

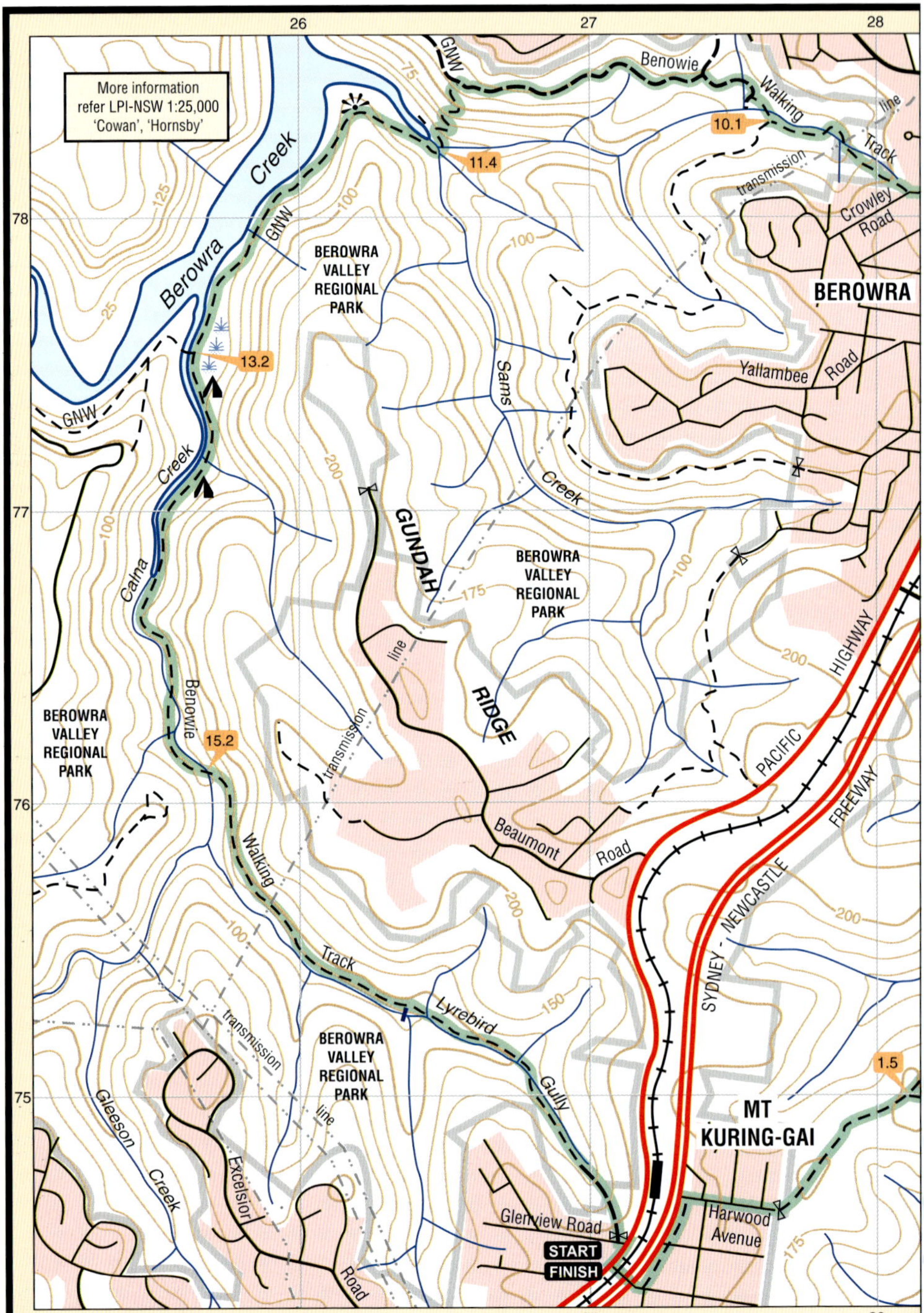
More information refer LPI-NSW 1:25,000 'Cowan', 'Hornsby'
Berowra Creek
Benowie Walking Track
transmission line
Crowley Road
BEROWRA
Yallambee Road
BEROWRA VALLEY REGIONAL PARK
Sams Creek
GUNDAH RIDGE
Calna Creek
GNW
Beaumont Road
PACIFIC HIGHWAY
SYDNEY - NEWCASTLE FREEWAY
Lyrebird Gully
Gleeson Creek
Excelsior Road
Glenview Road
START
FINISH
Harwood Avenue
MT KURING-GAI
10.1
11.4
13.2
15.2
1.5
26
27
28
78
77
76
75

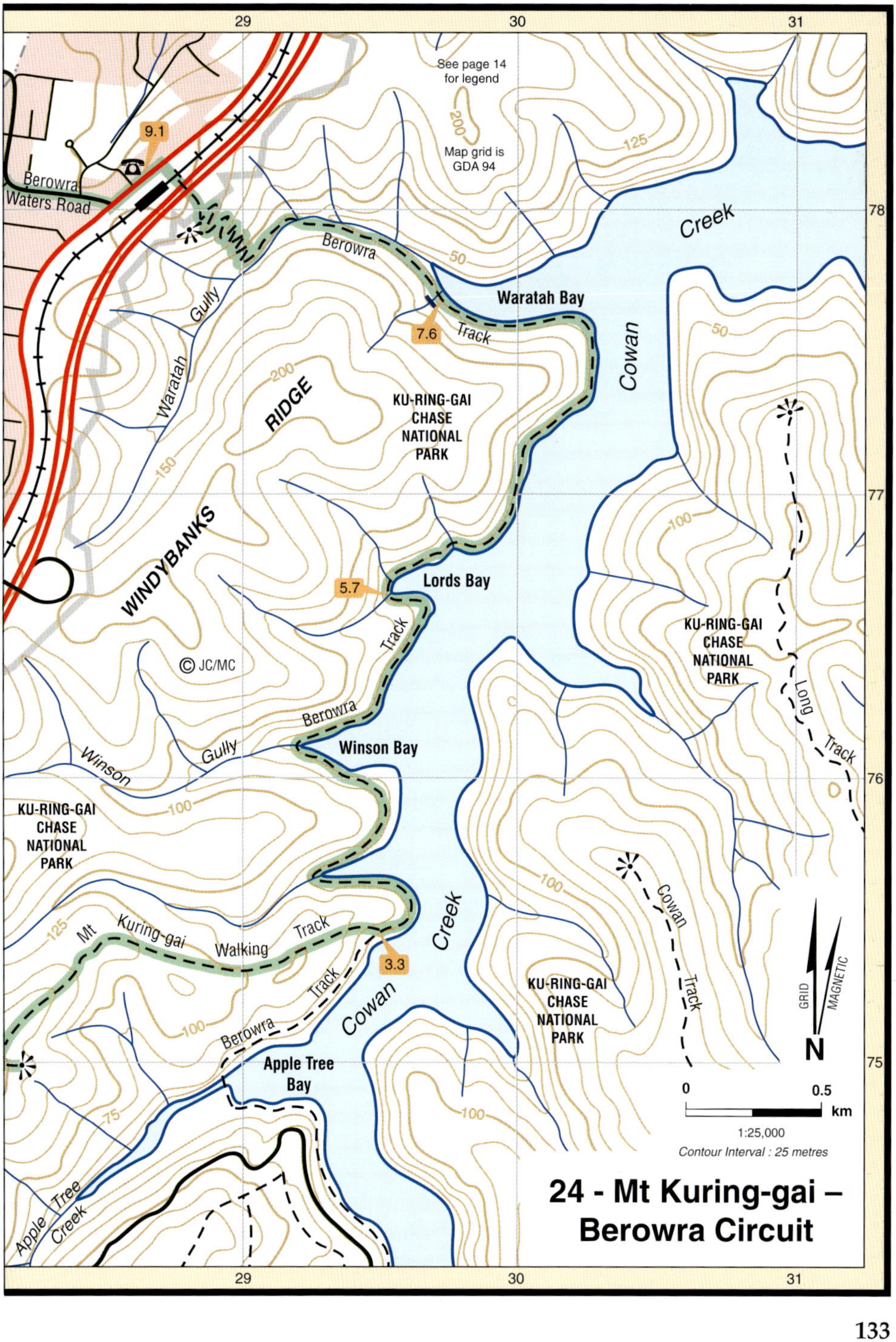

24 - Mt Kuring-gai – Berowra Circuit

Rusting boat frame, Waratah Bay

7.6km Pass the foundations of an old jetty then a rusting boat frame – the bay was settled by a boat builder in 1890. Pass below a waterfall then head north-west climbing gently into Waratah Gully. The track crosses the creek at a slippery rock slab next to the foundations of a long-vanished bridge. A steep climb north-west up a zigzagging track leads to Berowra. Cross the bridge over the freeway then turn left to the Berowra Railway Station.

9.1km From the railway station, cross Pacific Highway at the traffic lights then follow the highway south-west passing the shops. Turn right into Berowra Waters Road and follow it west for 400m to a roundabout. Continue straight ahead on Crowley Road for 50m then turn right and follow the Benowie Walking Track towards Crosslands. The track descends north-west on a steel stairway through a cliffline. It soon crosses to the northern bank of the creek, crosses a side gully then returns to the main creek crossing back to the southern bank. Continue to a track junction.

10.1km Turn right, cross the creek and rise to meet a vehicle track. Turn right again to cross a gully then, at the next junction, veer left and follow the vehicle track sidling the hillside. Follow the vehicle track west for 900m to a track junction to meet the Great North Walk (GNW).

11.4km Turn left onto the GNW and follow the walking track which descends steeply south. The zigzagging track has many steps and some handrails as it passes down a cliff to the banks of Sams Creek. Cross multiple creek channels then follow the track north-west keeping above the mangroves and rise onto a spur. A short scramble onto rocks on the right of the track provides excellent views of Berowra Creek. Continue following the undulating track south-west for 800m to

Crossing the salt marsh, Berowra Creek

the north end of a salt marsh. A boardwalk crosses the swampy plain to a track junction beside Berowra Creek.

13.2km The GNW turns right and crosses the bridge. Leave it by keeping to the left and follow Benowie Walking Track south. At the end of the salt marsh, pass a campsite then follow the east bank of bank of Calna Creek upstream passing another campsite. Pass the end of the tidal zone and soon after cross Calna Creek at a slippery rock crossing. Follow the western bank of Calna Creek crossing a normally dry side creek then re-cross Calna Creek to its eastern bank.

15.2km Climb high above the valley then sidle south-east along the base of a long cliffline. Pass through several overhangs then descend a little to meet the creek in Lyrebird Gully above a waterfall. Follow the creek bed upstream for 200m then follow the north side of the gully upstream. Cross the creek and climb steadily to merge with a road leading into a clearing. Veer right and follow a closed, sealed road climbing steeply to a gate in Glenview Road and the end of the walk. Mt Kuring-gai Railway Station is just around the corner to the left.

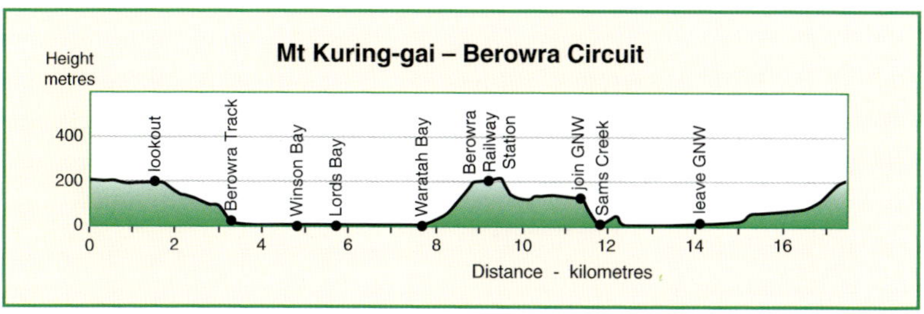

25 SMUGGLERS RIDGE

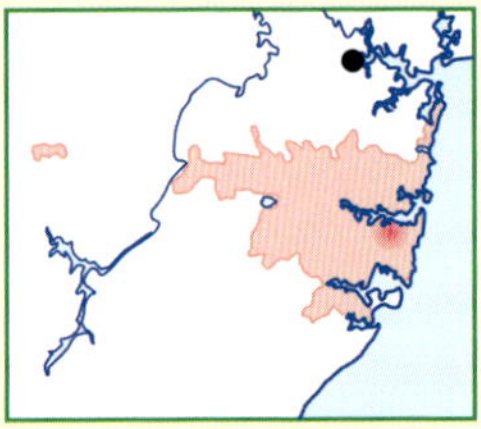

Length: 12.6km, circuit
Time: 5 hours
Grade: Medium
Total Climbing: 340m
Maximum Height: 220m
From Sydney: 51km
Closest Town: Galston 14km
Map: LPI 1:25,000 *Cowan*

Marramarra National Park is one of the lesser known national parks near Sydney. It is located south of the Hawkesbury River and protects a large section of natural landscape that includes a sandstone plateau and associated ridges and creeks. The park was created in 1979 and is believed to contain some significant aboriginal heritage.

The area is a good example of the original vegetation as it was never heavily settled by Europeans. Most development was minor and restricted to farming of the rich river flats in the valleys – some old orchards will be seen on this walk. The walk follows a fire trail to Marramarra Creek then returns via an unmarked walking track that ascends Smugglers Ridge. This ridge is named as it was rumoured to have been used for smuggling in the early days of settlement near Sydney. This an enjoyable walk through natural bushland.

Access

From Sydney follow the Pacific Highway then Epping Road for 19km to Epping. Turn right and follow Beecroft Road for 5km then turn right then left onto Boundary Road. Follow this then New Line Road for 7.5km to meet Old Northern Road in Dural. Dural can also be accessed from Parramatta and Castle Hill. Follow Old Northern Road north for 2km then turn right and follow Galston Road for 4km to Galston. Turn left into Arcadia Road and continue for 4km then turn left into Cobaw Road. Continue north for 3.4km to where the name changes to Bloodwood Road. Follow the gravel road northward a further 4.9km to a Y-junction. Turn left onto Marramarra Ridge Track and 1.3km leads to a signposted junction of Smuggler and Marramarra Ridges. Park near the junction. There is no public transport to the start.

0.0km Follow Marramarra Ridge Trail north-east. The vehicle road follows the electricity transmission line and minor access tracks to the pylons should be ignored. Follow the road for 1.8km to the start of an open paddock left of the track. Follow

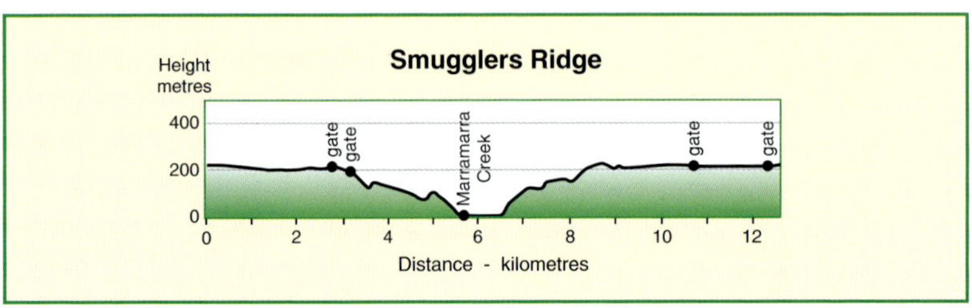

Marramarra Creek from Smugglers Ridge

the road north-east a further 1.0km to a locked gate. Descend east for 400m to another gate and swing north-east descending steeply to the junction with Kulpas Trail.

Smugglers Ridge

3.5km Turn left to cross the headwaters of a creek and continue descending northwards to a creek crossing. Rise over a spur ignoring the service track to the transmission tower. Instead, swing right and descend steeply to a track junction beside a backwater channel of Marramarra Creek. The track to the right is a dead-end.

5.6km Turn left and follow the grassy track, which passes through light forest, to a clearing with the remains of an abandoned orchard. Continue westward along the flats beside Marramarra Creek. Pass another clearing and more orchard then cross a side creek and 100m further on meet a track junction. The track to the north-west leads into a campsite, known as The Orchard, which has a pit toilet.

6.5km Turn left and follow the faint track through grass and ferns to the base of Smugglers Ridge. Initially, Smugglers Ridge Track does not follow the ridge crest. Instead it climbs up steeply on the east side of the ridge for 100m before veering west back to the crest. Follow the top of the ridge towards some rocky outcrops and bypass these by veering left and crossing an old stone wall. Continue climbing up the east side of the ridge for a further 200m to a large, rocky outcrop on the ridge crest. From here the faint track follows the ridge crest – there are some good views of Marramarra Creek from rocky outcrops. Continue following the crest, bypassing one rocky outcrop on its left side, and rise steadily to a large, open rock slab.

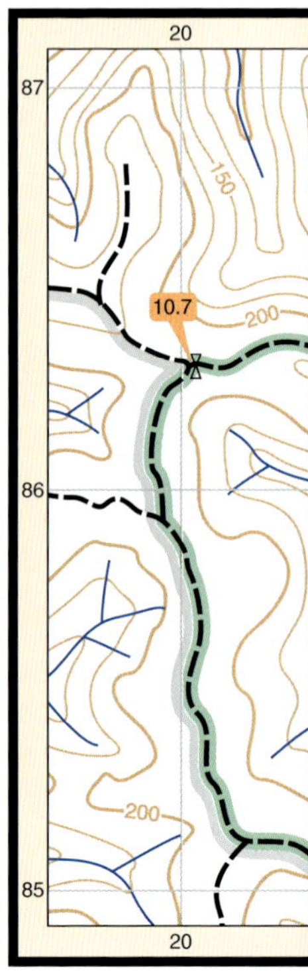

8.4km Just past the slab the track widens into an old road formation on top of the very broad crest of Smugglers Ridge. Follow this south-west for 2.3km, ignoring an old track to the right, to an old gate and track junction.

10.7km Veer left and follow the old vehicle track south for 400m then veer left again. A further 900m leads to a T-intersection. Turn left and head east, passing through a gate to a quarry, and soon after meet Marramarra Ridge Trail at the end of the walk.

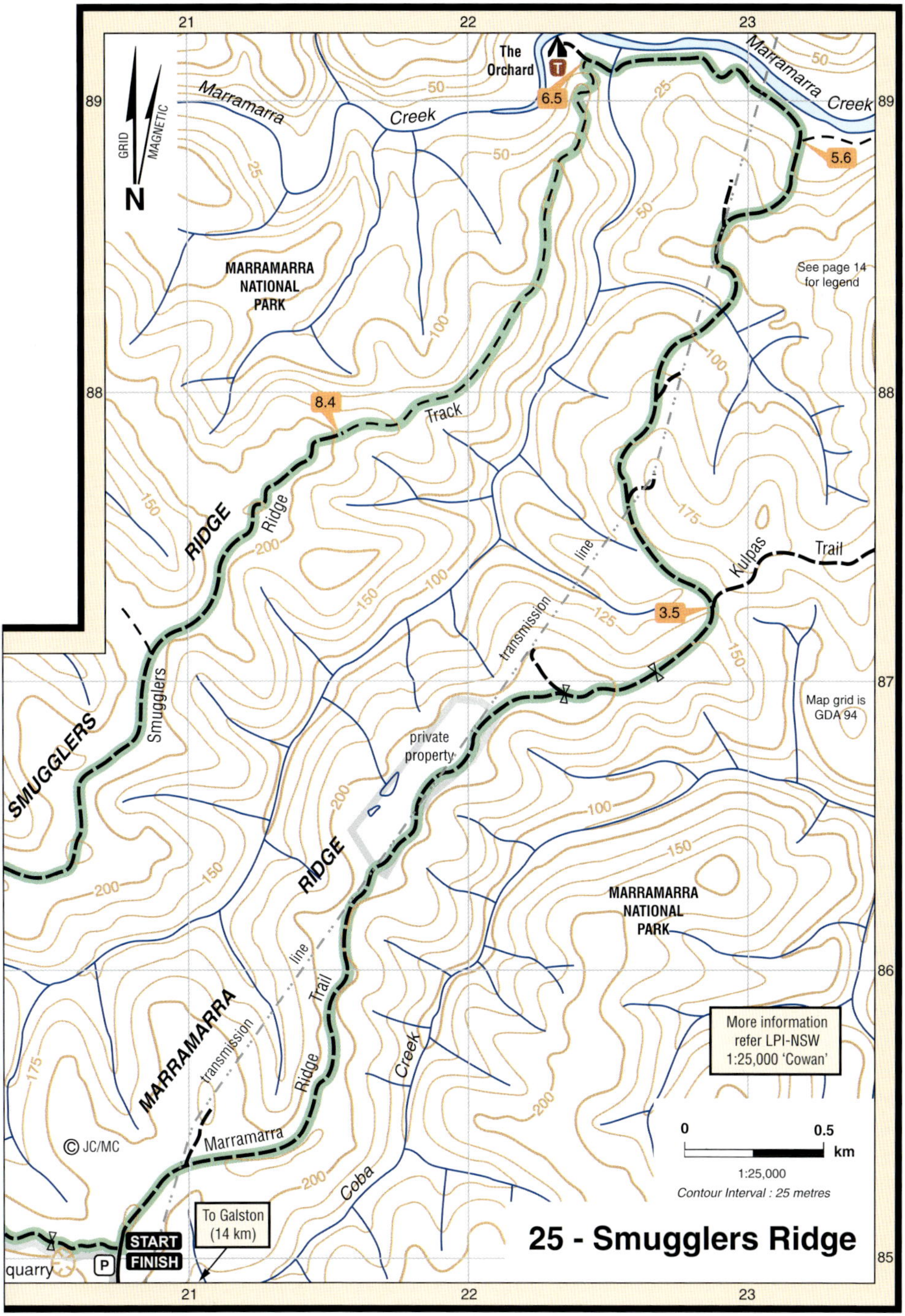
25 - Smugglers Ridge
GRID
MAGNETIC
N
The Orchard
Marramarra Creek
MARRAMARRA NATIONAL PARK
See page 14 for legend
Track
SMUGGLERS RIDGE
Smugglers Ridge
Kulpas Trail
transmission line
Map grid is GDA 94
private property
MARRAMARRA RIDGE
Marramarra Ridge Trail
Coba Creek
More information refer LPI-NSW 1:25,000 'Cowan'
© JC/MC
To Galston (14 km)
START
FINISH
quarry
0
0.5
km
1:25,000
Contour Interval : 25 metres
6.5
5.6
8.4
3.5

26 COWAN TO BROOKLYN

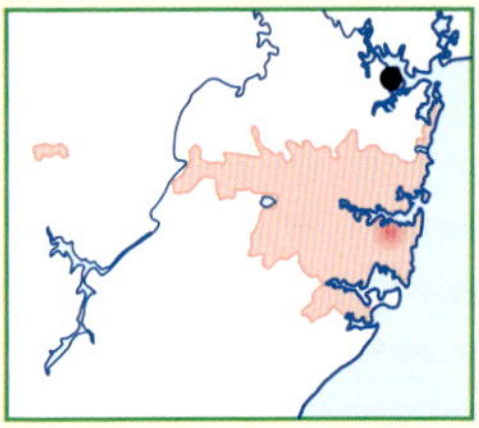

Length: 10.9km, one-way
Time: 5 hours
Grade: Medium
Total Climbing: 400m
Maximum Height: 200m
From Sydney: 39km
Closest Town: Berowra 6km
Map: LPI 1:25,000 *Cowan*

The north-west section of Ku-ring-gai Chase National Park is a less frequented area due to the restricted number of access points into this part of the park. The rugged, sandstone landscape is bounded on the west by the deep cuttings of the Sydney - Newcastle Freeway and on the other sides by the Hawkesbury River. One of the few tracks in this section of the park is the Great North Walk (GNW). This track links the small railway stations of Cowan and Brooklyn making an ideal one-way day walk. The track has some rough sections as it was never constructed as a road. Walkers marked the route and over time it has consolidated into a well-defined track. There are some steep descents and ascents and the track passes through a wide variety of vegetation. It also provides some good views of the Hawkesbury River.

Access

From Sydney, follow the Pacific Highway north-west for 22km to Wahroonga then follow the Sydney - Newcastle Freeway north for 10.5km and take the Berowra exit. Continue north following the Pacific Highway for 6km to Cowan Railway Station.

Heading towards Jerusalem Bay

Jerusalem Bay

Public transport – from Sydney Central, trains operate on the 'Northern Line' to Cowan Railway Station. The return is from Hawkesbury River Railway Station in Brooklyn which is the next station on the same line. Refer www.cityrail.info for timetables.

Variations:

1. **Jerusalem Bay**, 4.6km, return, 2½ hours, Medium. Follow the first 2.3km to the point in Jerusalem Bay. After enjoying the view return the same way to the start.
2. **Campbells Crater**, 11.5km, one-way, 5½ hours, Medium. Follow the described walk and include the sidetrip to Campbells Crater.

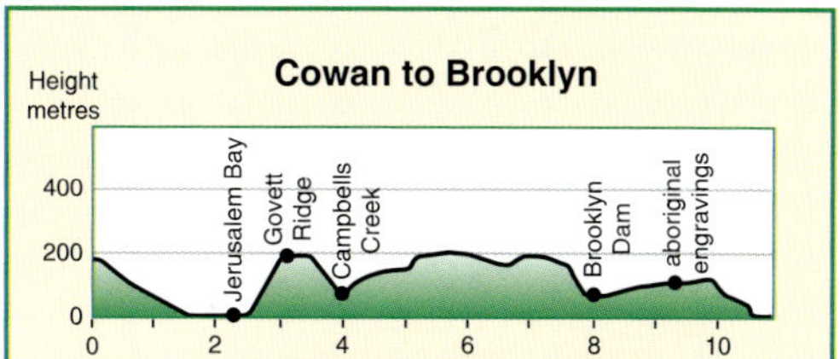

0.0km From the east side of the railway station, follow a vehicle track beside the railway north for 100m. Turn right onto the signposted Great North Walk (GNW) and cross the Sydney - Newcastle Freeway on a foot bridge. The track descends steadily into a creek bed which is then followed. Pass through a patch of rainforest, cross the creek on rock slabs just above a small waterfall then follow the north side of the valley. Continue above the creek through a narrow part of the valley then descend to reach the tidal shore of Yatala Creek. The track heads through forest just above the shore to an open area on a point in Jerusalem Bay.

2.3km At the back of the clear area on the point, climb some steps then continue northwards into a small bay. A rough section of track leads into a rainforest-filled gully. Cross the gully and pass along the base of a cliff. Cross a second gully and climb north-east up a spur onto Govett Ridge. Pass a signpost to 'Brooklyn' and continue to a second signpost to 'Brooklyn'.

Sidetrip: Campbells Crater 600m, 20 minutes return

At the second signpost to 'Brooklyn', an unmarked track on the left leads to Campbells Crater. Follow the track north-east for 300m into a saddle. The depression on the right is an eroded, volcanic crater filled with bracken and palms that are different to the surrounding forest – it is not easy to gauge the size of the feature as there are no viewpoints. After exploring the depression, return the same way to the main track.

3.3km Continue on the more major track towards Brooklyn. The forest soon opens up providing some views. Descend northwards to cross Campbells Creek and rise to an unmarked track junction. Keep to the left and climb northward to pass below a cave then ascend a rock band with metal steps and 50m on meet a management road.

5.2km The road is high above the deep cuttings on the Sydney - Newcsatle Freeway. Turn right and follow the vehicle track north-east along the ridge top. This track is used to service a powerline and minor sidetracks to each power pole should be ignored. There are good views along the way of the Hawkesbury River and its inlets. Continue following the ridge for 2.4km to where a rough, rocky track on

Brooklyn Dam

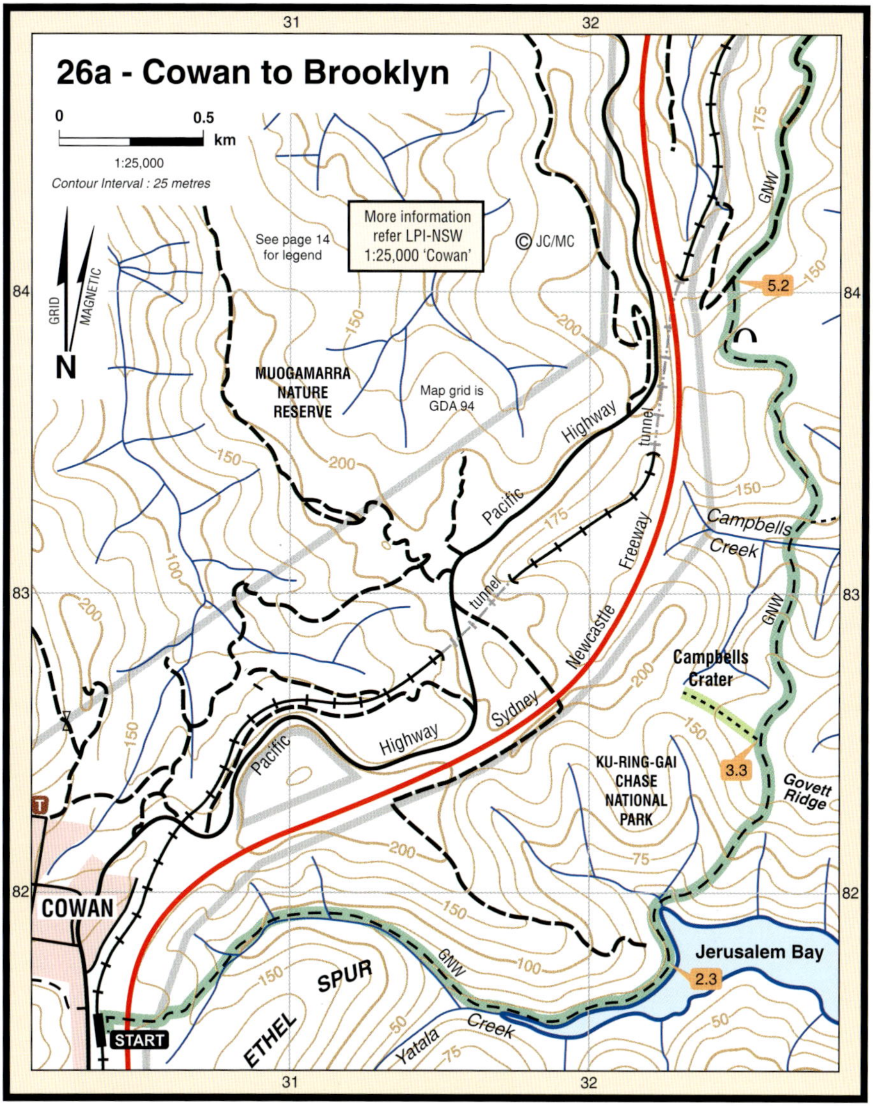

the right descends steeply east towards Brooklyn Dam. Head down this track until close to the dam.

8.2km Turn left onto a vehicle track and 50m on turn right to enter a camping area beside Brooklyn Dam. Follow a walking track east descending to cross the outlet creek from the dam then rise into a wide, open area to meet another vehicle track.

8.4km Turn left, follow the vehicle track 400m, then turn right and 50m further on, turn right again. The track follows a powerline for 300m then turns sharp right to pass under the powerline before swinging back left.

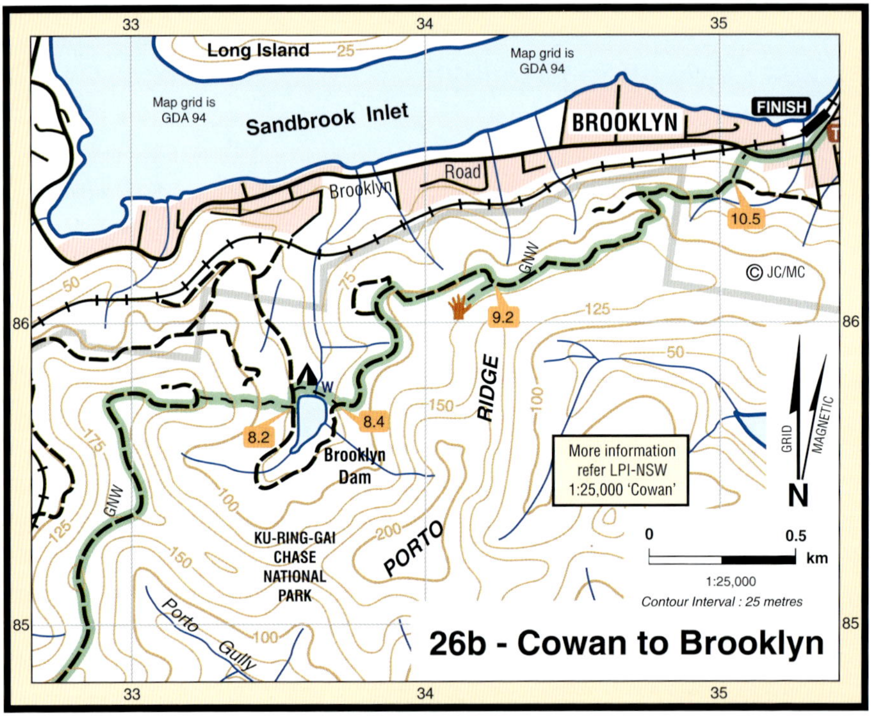

9.2km A minor walking track on the right heads south-west for 200m to a series of rock slabs. Aboriginal engravings include fish, a whale, some human figures and several markings that could be works in progress. Return to the main track and continue north-east following the vehicle track. Ignore minor side tracks to power poles. After 500m the track swings north and comes to a track junction. Turn right and continue a further 400m to where the powerline turns sharp left and descends into Brooklyn.

Engraving

10.5km Turn left and a walking track follows the powerline descending steeply to meet Brooklyn Road. Turn right and follow the foot path east for 200m to the railway station. Catch a train back to Cowan – trains run about once each hour.

PILES CREEK 27

On the north side of the Hawkesbury River is the Brisbane Water National Park. While many see the park from the Sydney-Newcastle Freeway, only a few stop to explore this large area. One of the best bases for a visit is the picnic area at Girrakool where a network of tracks was constructed in the 1960s. The tracks lead to aboriginal engravings and a waterfall and pass many cliffs, caves and overhangs. The described walk starts on the sandstone plateau and descends into the steep-sided valley of Piles Creek where there is a forest of coachwood and water gums. It continues to a major creek junction where mangroves dominate the shoreline then returns to the picnic area. The many lookouts along the way are all fenced, but often don't provide distant views. More than 650 plant species exist in the park, so wildflowers can be found here at most times of the year.

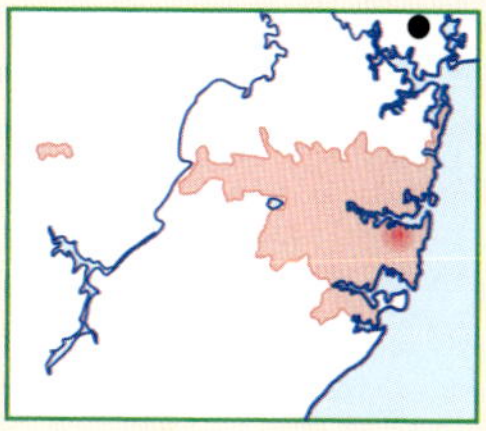

Length: 8.1km, circuit
Time: 4 hours
Grade: Easy-Medium
Total Climbing: 190m
Maximum Height: 130m
From Sydney: 73km
Closest Town: Gosford 11km
Map: LPI 1:25,000 *Gosford*

Access

From Sydney, follow the Pacific Highway north-west for 22km to Wahroonga then follow the Sydney-Newcastle Freeway north for 48km and exit the freeway towards Gosford and Woy Woy. At the first intersection, turn left, follow Pacific Highway

Bundilla Lookout

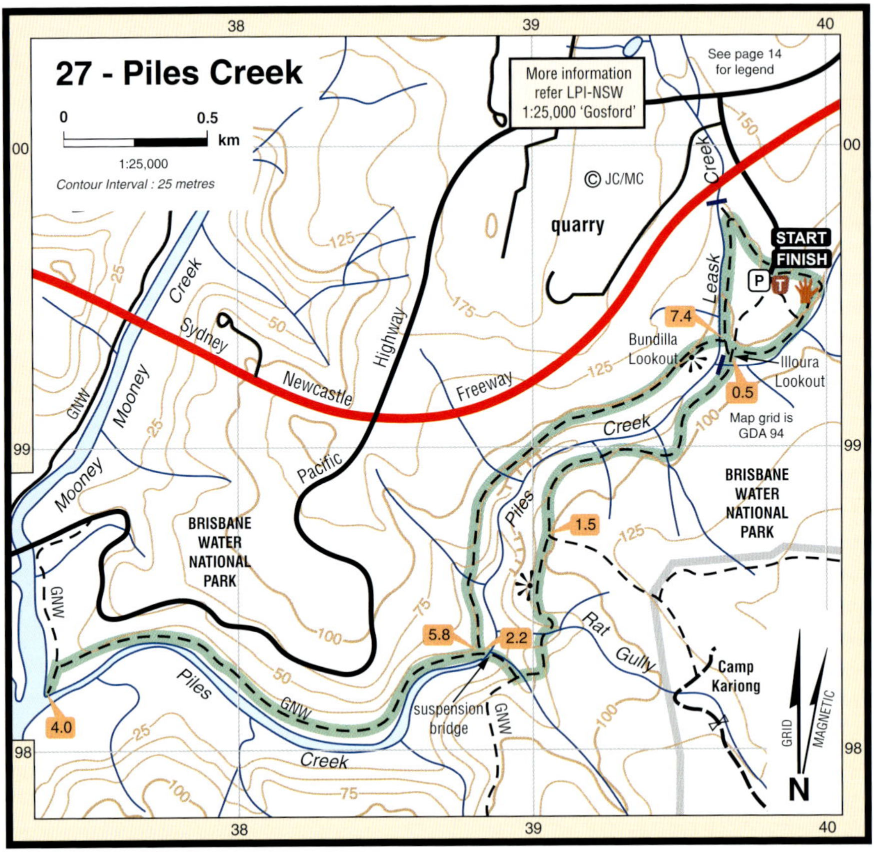

north for 800m, turn left at the roundabout and continue to follow the Pacific Highway south-west for 1.5km. Turn left and head southward for 600m to the Girrakool Picnic Area in Brisbane Water National Park. Park entry fees apply. There is no public transport to this walk.

Variations:

1. **Girrakool Loop**, 1.3km, circuit, 30 minutes, Easy. Follow the first 0.5km of the walk to Illoura Lookout. Turn right and continue 100m to a track junction then follow the described walk from the 7.4km point to the end.
2. **Piles Creek Circuit**, 4.5km, circuit, 2½ hours, Easy-Medium. Follow the main walk without including the sidetrip to Mooney Mooney Creek. Follow the first 2.2km of the walk to the suspension bridge, turn right and follow the notes from the 5.8km point to the end of the walk.

0.0km Four tracks meet at the car park. Head east to follow Girrakool Loop Track. Descend gently though open forest to a sandstone outcrop where there are some aboriginal carvings of a fish and a man. The track then circles around to the south to a fenced lookout above a forested gully. Continue south-west 30m to a track junction – right leads back to the car park. Continue on the left to the next track junction, turn left to a track junction beside Illoura Lookout.

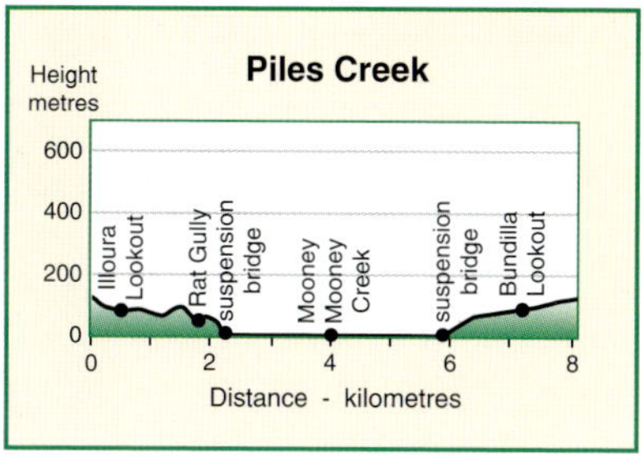

0.5km Leave Girrakool Loop by turning left towards Piles Creek. Cross the creek via a set of concrete stepping stones then continue south-west sidling a heath-covered ridge. The track crosses some small gullies then rises slightly to follow the base of a cliff. Pass below some overhangs then continue through more heathland to a track junction. Left leads to a Scout facility called Camp Kariong.

1.5km Continue on the right for 200m to timber steps. At the base of the steps, to the right, an unmarked, 20m long sidetrack leads to a fenced lookout with a view of the deep gully of Piles Creek. Return to the track and zigzag down into Rat Gully. Cross the creek via steps in large boulders then climb steeply over a spur into another deep gully. Cross the creek to a track junction to meet the Great North Walk. Turn right and descend in open forest to a suspension bridge over Piles Creek. This is the tidal limit for Piles Creek – left of the bridge are reeds and mud banks while to the right is rainforest. Cross the bridge to a track junction on the western bank. The unmarked track to the right will be used for the return.

Bridge over Piles Creek

2.2km Turn left for a return sidetrip to Mooney Mooney Creek. Initially the track is not clear as it crosses a camping flat. It soon becomes better defined and follows the northern bank of Piles Creek downstream keeping just above the swampy floodplain. Continue for 1.5km to a long boardwalk across the floodplain and soon after there is a track junction. Turn left and follow the wide track south along the bank of Mooney Mooney Creek for 100m to a campsite at the junction of Piles and Mooney Mooney Creeks.

High above Piles Creek

4.0km The stream junction provides good views across the wide waters of both creeks where mangroves line the banks. Return the same way for 1.8km to the track junction beside the suspension bridge.

5.8km Turn left and climb steeply to the base of ridge top cliffs. The track rises and falls as it follows the cliff base north – handrails are provided on narrow ledges. When the cliff ends, the track remains high above Piles Creek as the valley swings north-east. Easier walking leads to a track junction. Just off the track on the right is Bundilla Lookout where there is a good view of a small waterfall. Continue on the main track descending to cross Leask Creek via a concrete bridge then rise to a track junction. To the right is Illoura Lookout which was visited earlier.

7.4km Turn left onto Girrakool Loop and head north for 400m to a junction on a sharp bend. Directly ahead is a lookout and nearby waterfall – the view is obscured by trees, but an easy descent leads to the pool at the base of the falls. Return to the main track and climb south-east to another lookout. Continue south-east through light forest to the picnic area 50m north of the car park.

Native Rose

PUTTY BEACH TO BOUDDI SPUR 28

The entrance to the Hawkesbury River is a wide expanse of water known as Broken Bay. On the north side of the bay, the coastline consists of a series of rocky, forested headlands and secluded, sandy beaches. The beauty of this section of coastline was recognised by Marie Byles. She first visited the coast in 1922 and with the help of the Confederation of Walking Clubs, she developed walking tracks and camping areas and urged protection for the area. This happened in 1935 when much of the coast became a Natural Park and in 1974, it was changed to a National Park.

The main track through the park is a one-way track along the coast. This walk includes a long section of the coastal track then leaves it to climb to the natural viewpoint on Bouddi Lookout. The return to the start is along a closed fire trail, then on a short section of sealed road and concludes on a well-used, but unmarked track back to Putty Beach.

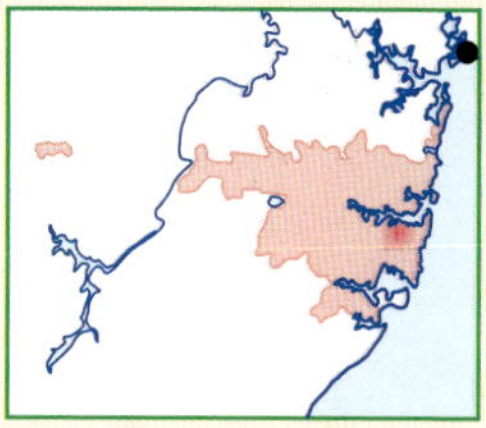

Length: 12.0km, circuit
Time: 4½ hours
Grade: Medium
Total Climbing: 360m
Maximum Height: 150m
From Sydney: 96km
Closest Town: Woy Woy 12km
Map: LPI 1:25,000 *Broken Bay*

Heading towards Gerrin Point

Leaving Putty Beach

Access

From Sydney follow the Pacific Highway north-west for 22km to Wahroonga then follow the Sydney - Newcastle Freeway north for 48km and exit the freeway towards Gosford and Woy Woy. Follow Pacific Highway eastward for 5km to West Gosford then turn right and head south for 9km to Woy Woy. Turn left and follow Blackwell Road south-east for 3km then turn left and follow Maitland Bay Drive eastward for 1.5km to cross the Rip Bridge. From the bridge continue a further 4km then turn right onto Wards Hill Road. Head south for 2km, turn right into Scenic Road and after 1km turn left into Beach Road and park at the end near the Killcare Surf Club.

Variations:

1. **Putty Beach to Maitland Bay**, 7.9km, circuit, 2.5 hours, Easy-Medium. Follow the first 4.0km of the walk to Maitland Bay. After exploring the beach return up the path for 200m to the track junction then turn right and follow Maitland Bay Track north-west for 600m to the carpark. Turn left and follow the notes from the 8.9km point to the end of the walk.
2. **Maitland Bay & Bouddi Spur**, 5.7km, circuit, 2 hours, Easy-Medium. To access the start, turn left into Scenic Road and follow it eastward for 1.7km to the carpark at the start of Maitland Bay Track. Follow Maitland Bay Track south-east for 600m then follow the notes from the 3.8km point to the 8.9km point.

0.0km From the surf club head south-east onto the sandy beach. Turn left and follow the waterline north-east for 1.5km to the end of the beach. Climb steps onto the headland above. Pass through heathland descending gently to follow the top of the cliffs eastward. From the track there are excellent views of interesting rock patterns and of the coast towards Gerrin Point. Continue to a track junction.

2.3km The short sidetrack on the right descends steps to Bullimah Beach. Continue on the left through scrubby heathland to a lookout above Gerrin Point which provides views of Maitland Bay. Follow the track north-east passing through coastal forest just above the cliffs. Cross several gullies and soon after meet a track junction.

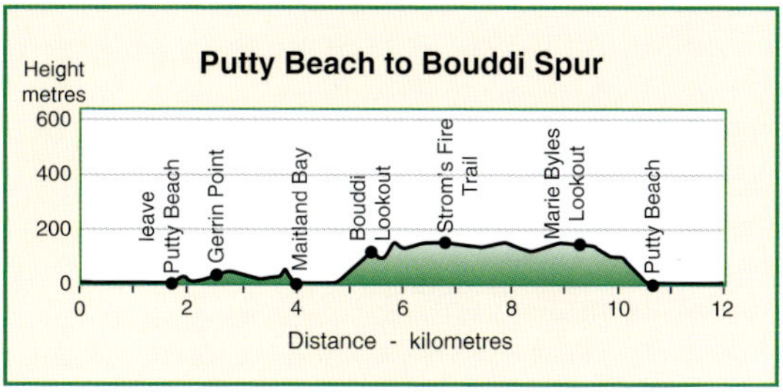

3.8km Left leads to Maitland Bay carpark. Turn right and follow the paved track to Maitland Bay. Follow the sand eastwards as it curves around to the start of the rocks. At low tide, a sidetrip along the rock platform leads to the remains of the paddle-steamer SS Maitland.

4.7km Leave Maitland Bay by climbing steeply south-east to a saddle behind Bouddi Point. After enjoying the views, continue eastward climbing gently up a spur to a track junction. A short 20m sidetrip to the right leads to another viewpoint then return to the junction.

5.1km An eroded track heads northward climbing steadily to Bouddi Lookout. Views are available on the outcropping rocks on the east of the track. Continue north-

Maitland Bay

Bouddi Spur

ward through coastal forest along the crest of Bouddi Spur. The initially level track soon climbs again, passing more rock outcrops, to the top of a timbered knoll. Continue northward through a saddle then rise to Dingledei Picnic Area.

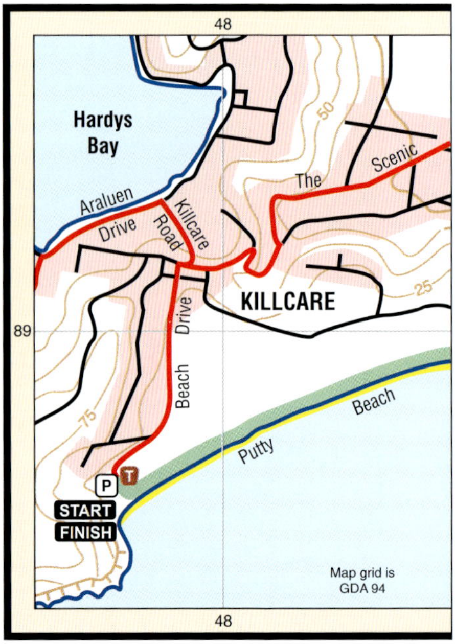

6.4km The picnic area has a shelter, tables and a toilet. Cross the carpark and follow the sealed road northward for 400m. Just before The Scenic Road, turn left to pass through a gate onto Stroms Fire Trail.

6.8km Follow this wide, shady fire trail west then south-west through tall forest. Continue for 2.1km to pass through another gate to Maitland Bay carpark.

8.9km Follow the sealed road south for 200m then follow a walking track beside the road to Marie Byles Lookout. This provides a good view of Putty Beach and the coast. From the lookout continue west for 300m then turn left onto an unmarked foot track. Follow this south for 50m then descend between a series of boulders to a wide, grassy opening. Follow the clearing south then south-west to the end of Jacqueline Avenue.

9.9km Follow the sealed street south-west for 200m to a street corner. Turn left onto another unmarked walking track and follow this south for 80m to a track junction. The 20m long sidetrack on the left leads to a lookout on a rocky outcrop. Back at the junction head west passing below a house then follow the rocky track south-west descending steeply through open forest into a gully. Enter the campground behind site 7.

10.6km Cross the road, pass a toilet block and walk out onto Putty Beach. Turn right and follow the beach south-west to the surf club and the carpark behind from where the walk started.

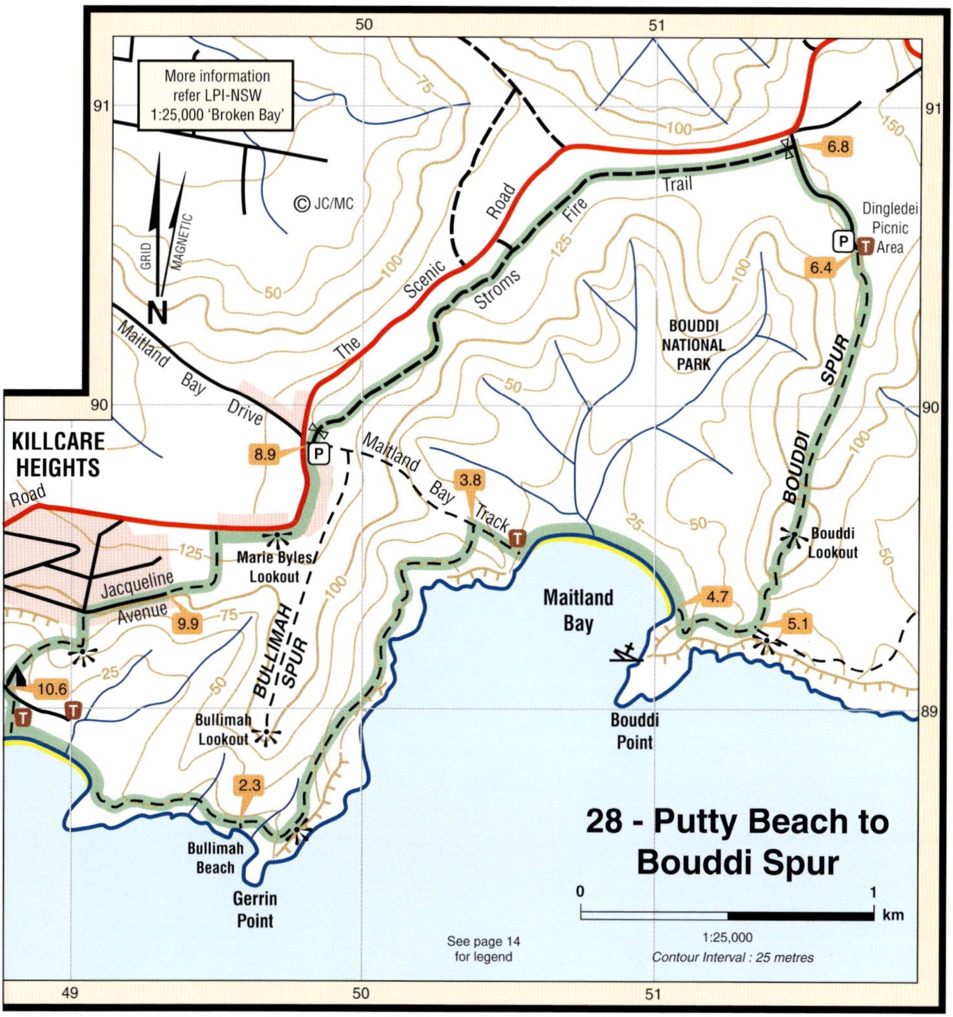

29 ELVINA BAY

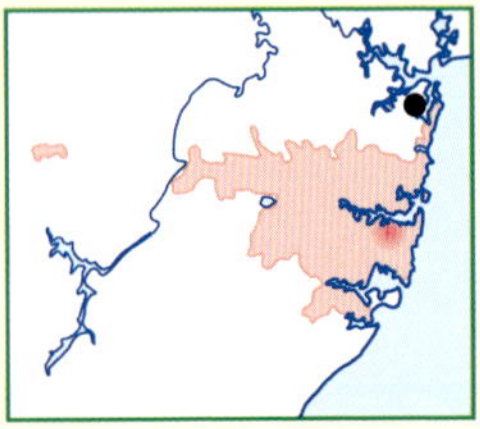

Length: 5.1km, circuit
Time: 2 hours
Grade: Easy-Medium
Total Climbing: 170m
Maximum Height: 160m
From Sydney: 33km
Closest Town: Terrey Hills 8km
Map: LPI 1:25,000 *Mona Vale*

The north-east corner of Ku-ring-gai Chase National Park is a wide peninsula that overlooks the Hawkesbury River. A single road follows the spine of the peninsula to West Head and there are a number of service tracks on both sides of the road that are also used by walkers. The first track on the peninsula is to the small settlement at Elvina Bay which is the destination for this walk.

While short, this walk has great variety. Initially a major aboriginal engraving site is visited then an old road is followed to pools and a waterfall in a rainforest-filled gully. The top of the waterfall has a popular swimming hole and also provides one of the best views in the park. The walk continues by descending to the small settlement at Elvina Bay which is serviced by a ferry from Church Point. The ferry provides an optional starting point for the walk. The rest of the walk climbs through open forest to the plateau then passes through heathland.

Tessellated pavement

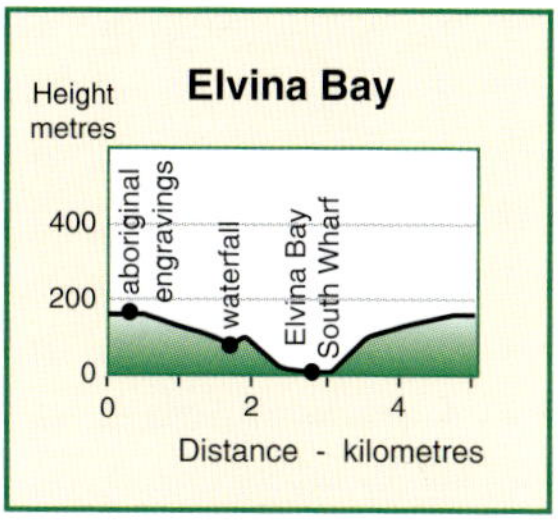

Access

From Sydney follow the Pacific Highway north-west for 17km to Pymble then turn right onto Mona Vale Road and follow this north-east for 9km to Terrey Hills. Turn left onto McCarrs Creek Road and follow it north then east for 5km then turn left onto West Head Road. After paying the park entry fee at the toll gate, continue northwards along West Head Road for 2.5km to a car parking area on the right at the start of the service road to Elvina Bay.

Public transport – the only public transport is to Elvina Bay. From Circular Quay, take a ferry to Manly. From the terminal, walk west 50m to Stand B in West Esplanade and take a 155 or 156 bus to Church Point. From there a ferry operates once each hour to Elvina Bay. Alight at South Wharf and join the circuit at the 2.8km point.

0.0km Pass through the locked gate and follow the service road, Elvina Track, east for 200m to a track junction. Turn right and follow a walking track south for 100m rising onto a large, rock slab where there are many aboriginal engravings. The engravings are not marked by signs and can be hard to see – there are fish, shields, birds, an emu and a human figure. The edge of the rock slab is a tesselated pavement which is common in sandstone – it weathers into long lines or square-patterned shapes. Return to Elvina Track, turn right and 50m further meet another track junction.

0.5km Turn left onto the minor track – this is not marked, but is fairly well defined. It is an old road that has overgrown into a narrow walking track. Follow the lightly

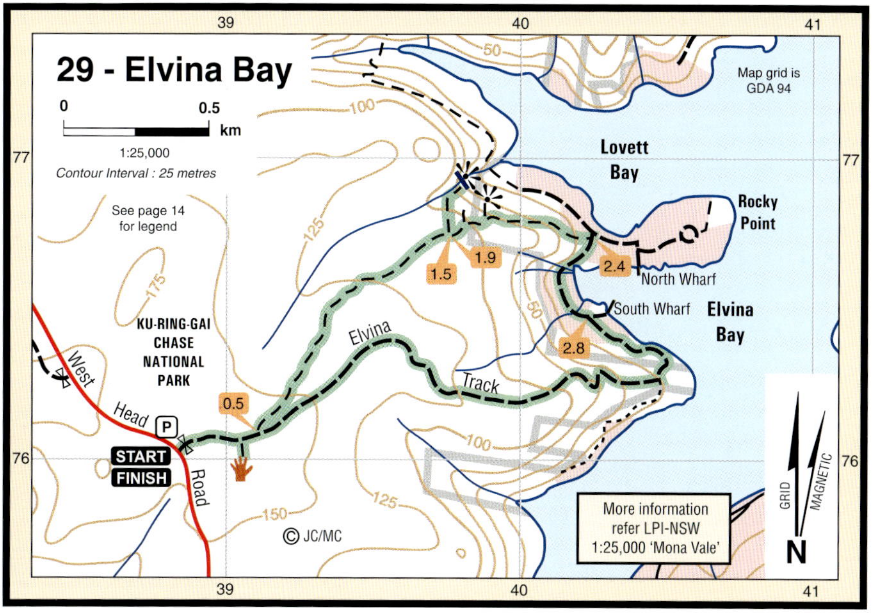

scrubby, eroded track north-east through heathland. Continue for 1.0km to another unmarked track junction.

1.5km Turn left for a return sidetrip. The track descends gently to meet a creek at a series of waterholes. Turn right and follow a rough track along the southern bank of the creek for 50m. While short, some scrambling is needed to get to the top of a tall waterfall. The large pool is a popular swimming spot and there are good views of Lovett Bay. Return to the main track.

Lovett Bay from the waterfall

1.9km Head east ignoring two minor tracks to the left – they lead to viewpoints that are not as good as the waterfall. The track soon descends through dense forest passing a grave site. Continue eastward to meet a service road behind the large, white, swiss-style house in the saddle.

2.4km Turn right and follow the service road through the settlement of Elvina Bay. Continue for 400m to a sidetrack on the left that leads down to a grass-covered park close to South Wharf at Elvina Bay.

2.8km Continue following the service road south-east for 300m to the last house in the settlement. The track turns right and the gravel road begins climbing steeply zigzagging onto the plateau above. Continue westward passing the two track junctions near the start of the walk to return to the car park beside West Head Road.

Christmas Bell

SPHINX TO BOBBIN HEAD 30

This circuit is one of the more popular walks in Ku-ring-gai Chase National Park and is located in the south-western corner of the park. Initially it visits the unexpected feature of the sphinx – this is a carved sandstone outcrop that is a miniature version of an Egyptian sphinx. From there the track enters bushland and descends a damp gully then follows the shores of Cowan Creek. The tidal stream banks are dominated by mangroves and above the shore is tall, mixed forest with blackbutt, turpentine and grey ironbark trees. There are also numerous smaller flowering plants. The track is easy to walk apart from one slippery creek crossing. Just over halfway around the circuit, a short sidetrip leads to the very popular picnic area at Bobbin Head. Complete with visitor centre, kiosk and picnic shelters this makes a good lunch stop. The walk returns by following an old road formation along a heathland-covered ridge passing some aboriginal engravings.

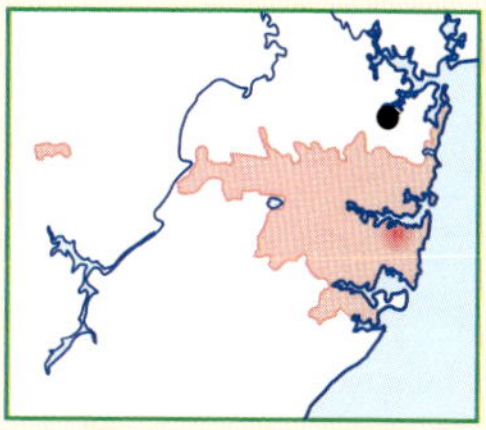

Length: 10.2km, circuit
Time: 4 hours
Grade: Easy-Medium
Total Climbing: 210m
Maximum Height: 180m
From Sydney: 25km
Closest Town: North Turramurra 1km
Map: LPI 1:25,000 *Hornsby*

Access

From Sydney follow the Pacific Highway north-west for 19km to Pymble. Turn right onto Bobbin Head Road and follow it north for 6km to the gated entrance to Ku-ring-gai Chase National Park. Park before the gate as entry fees apply for cars.

Public transport – from Sydney Central, trains operate on the 'North Shore Line' to Turramurra Railway Station. Take bus 577 to the Bobbin Head Road park entrance.

Cowan Creek

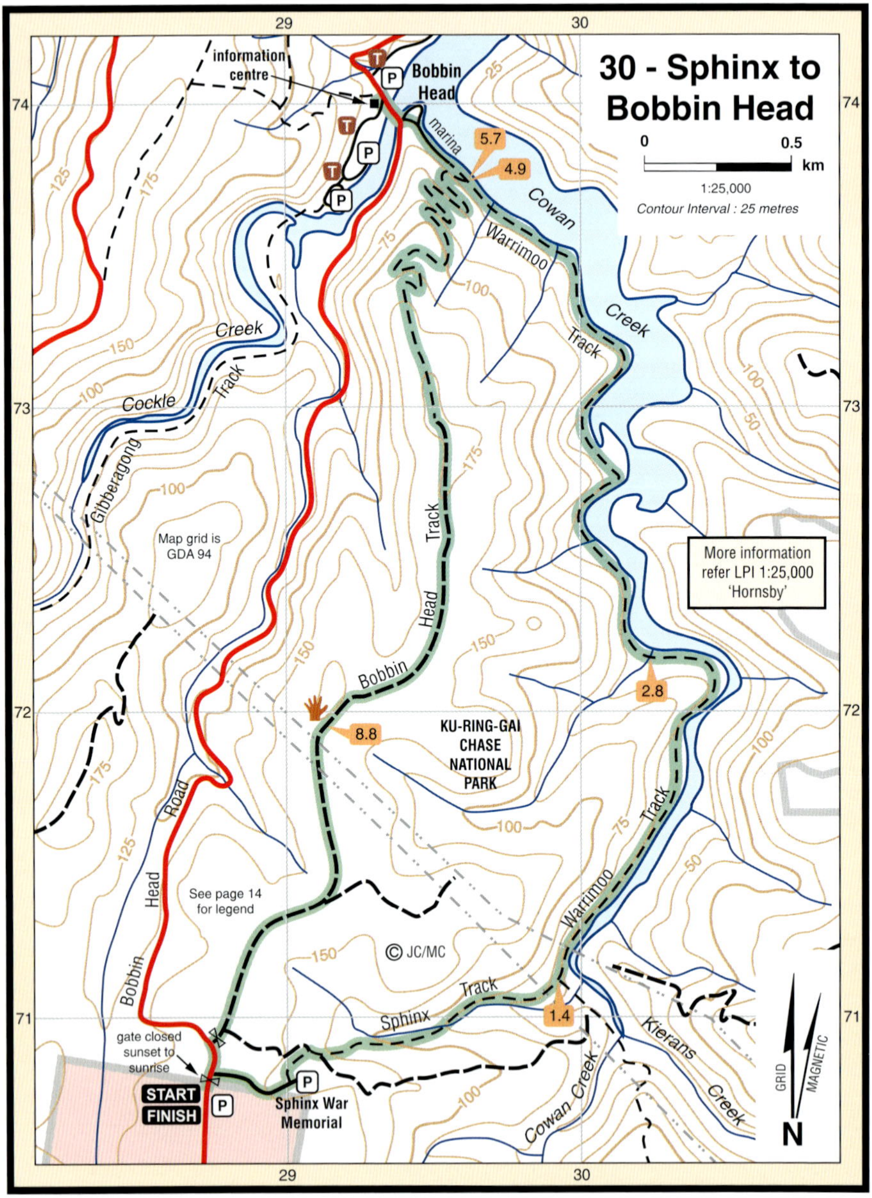

0.0km Head north past the entrance gate and straight after turn right and follow a sealed road east for 400m to the car park near the Sphinx War Memorial. This replica of an Egyptian sphinx was carved after the first world war by a returned soldier. From the sphinx, follow a sealed track north for 50m to a track junction. Turn right and after 20m turn left to follow a walking track east. The track gradually descends into a gully, crosses the creek and continues along the north side of the gully to a track junction.

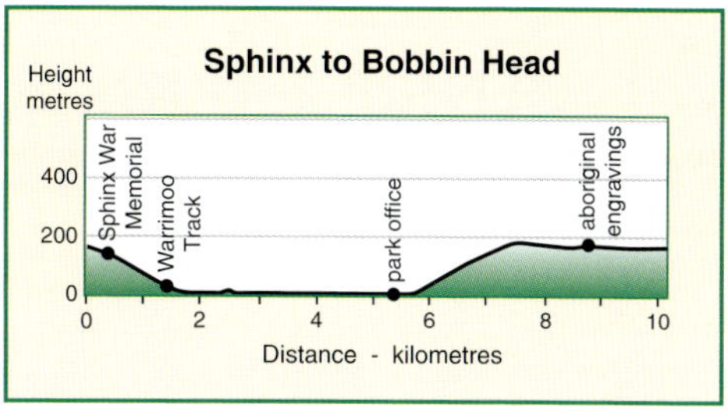

1.4km Turn left onto Warrimoo Track. This track heads north-east along the banks of Cowan Creek where mangroves line the tidal shore. Continue for 1.0km to a clearing then a short climb over a spur leads around a bend to a creek crossing.

2.8km Wade or rockhop across the slippery creek bed and continue to follow Cowan Creek north to an overhang at the base of some cliffs. The track continues northward following the meandering waters of Cowan Creek. It passes below more cliffs and shortly after crossing a rainforest–filled gully there is a track junction. To the left is Bobbin Head Track which will be used for the return.

4.9km Continue straight ahead and walk north-west across the back of a marina to meet a road. Follow the road across the bridge to picnic areas, a kiosk and the park information centre. Return the same way to the Bobbin Head Track junction.

5.7km Turn right and start climbing steeply up steps passing through several small cliffs to meet the original road to Bobbin Head. Turn left onto the old road formation and continue climbing. Old stone work can be seen beside the road. The wide, zigzagging track leads onto the ridge top. Continue southward along the level ridge top for 1.5km until 50m before a powerline where there is an unmarked sidetrack on the right.

8.8km On the side track, 10m off the track, is a set of aboriginal engravings. These are not easily seen and include a goanna and a male figure. Do not walk on these engravings. Return to the track and continue southward along the ridge for 1.3km to meet Bobbin Head Road. Turn left and 100m away is the park gate and the end of the walk.

Sphinx War Memorial

31 CENTRE & DUCK HOLE TRACKS

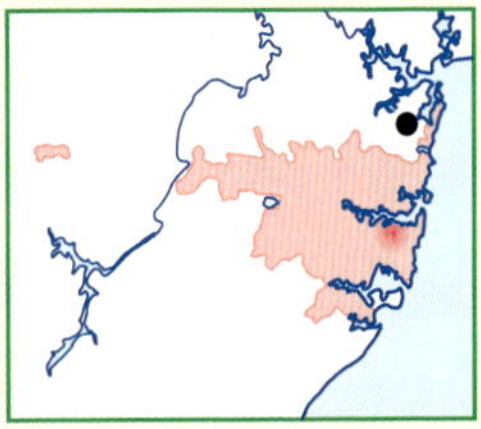

Length: 11.2km, circuit
Time: 3½ hours
Grade: Easy-Medium
Total Climbing: 210m
Maximum Height: 185m
From Sydney: 28km
Closest Town: Terrey Hills 2km
Map: LPI 1:25,000 *Hornsby, Mona Vale*

The southern end of Ku-ring-Gai Chase National Park is an old sandstone plateau that has been dissected by numerous valleys. This walk initially follows a management road along one of these high ridges. There are plenty of views from the track and also from rocky outcrops beside the track and the observant walker will also discover aboriginal engravings. The walk continues along a sealed road into a valley then follows walking tracks past a picnic area and pools. It deviates for a sidetrip to a waterfall then ends by following another management track through bushland around the headwaters of McCarrs Creek. Many flowering plants including banksia, grevillea, tea-tree and heath can be found along the way.

The walk avoids the entry fee to Ku-ring-Gai Chase National Park by starting just before the toll gate. Walkers on foot can enter the park without paying fees.

Terrey Hills Track

McGarrs Creek from Centre Track

Access

From Sydney follow the Pacific Highway north-west for 17km to Pymble then turn right onto Mona Vale Road and follow this north-east for 9km to Terrey Hills. Turn left onto McCarrs Creek Road and follow it north for 2km then turn left onto General San Martin Drive and park on the left before the toll gate. There is no public transport to this walk.

0.0km Follow the sealed road north-west and just past the toll gate turn right to pass through a gate onto Centre Track. Follow the wide track north-east along a high ridge. There are plenty of views of surrounding ridge lines. Continue north-east for 1.1km to pass right of a rocky hill. Follow the undulating track eastward then north-east a further 1.4km to a sharp bend to the right. Rock slabs to the left provide good views. Follow the road around to the right then back to the left.

2.9km An open, rock slab left of the track provides good views to the south-east. Faint engravings of a whale, fish and some people made by aborigines are located here. Return to the track and continue eastwards over several rises before a short, steep descent leads to a gate and the sealed General San Martin Drive.

3.4km Turn right and follow the road for 350m to a road junction. Take care to avoid traffic – it's usually safest to step off the road when vehicles are around. Turn right and follow the sealed road downhill for

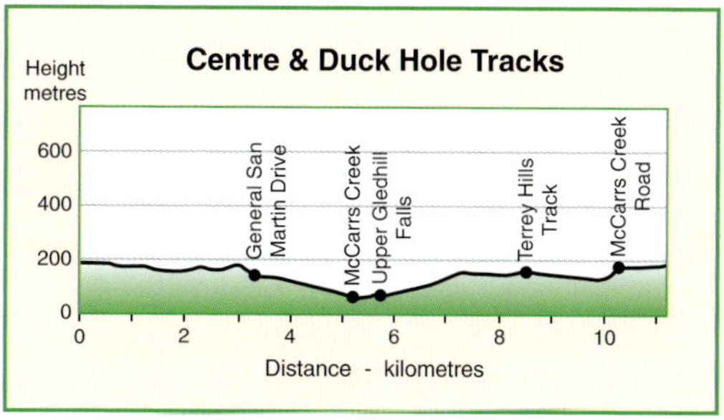

1.2km to the toll gate. Follow the sealed road a further 200m then turn left into a car park and picnic area beside McCarrs Creek. The attractive pools in the creek are known as The Duckhole.

5.2km Cross McCarrs Creek below the road bridge and climb to a road junction. Cross McCarrs Creek Road to an unmarked foot track. Follow this south-west into bush and turn right at a track junction. Follow the foot track westward – it stays about 10 to 20m above the road and after 400m meet the gravel-surfaced Duck Hole Track. The walk will follow this trail after a short sidetrip to the nearby Upper Gledhill Falls.

Upper Gledhill Falls

5.6km Cross the sealed road and follow an unmarked foot pad downstream for 100m. A steep descent and short scramble leads to the plunge pool at the base of Upper Gledhill Falls. Return to the same way to Duck Hole Track.

5.8km Follow Duck Hole Track west then south. It passes through heathlands and patches of light forest and climbs steadily for 2.6km to a gate. Pass the gate and 100m further on meet the signposted Terrey Hills Track. Left leads to the suburb of Terrey Hills.

8.5km Turn right onto Terrey Hills Track which soon swings around to the north passing through dense forest. It undulates a little crossing the heads of several small gullies then follows private property boundaries. After 400m the track swings sharp left and climbs to a gate beside the Coal and Candle Rural Fire Brigade. Follow the sealed road west climbing to meet McGarrs Creek Road.

10.3km Turn right and follow McGarrs Creek Road northwards for 800m to a road junction. Turn left to the end of the walk at the car parking area before the toll gate.

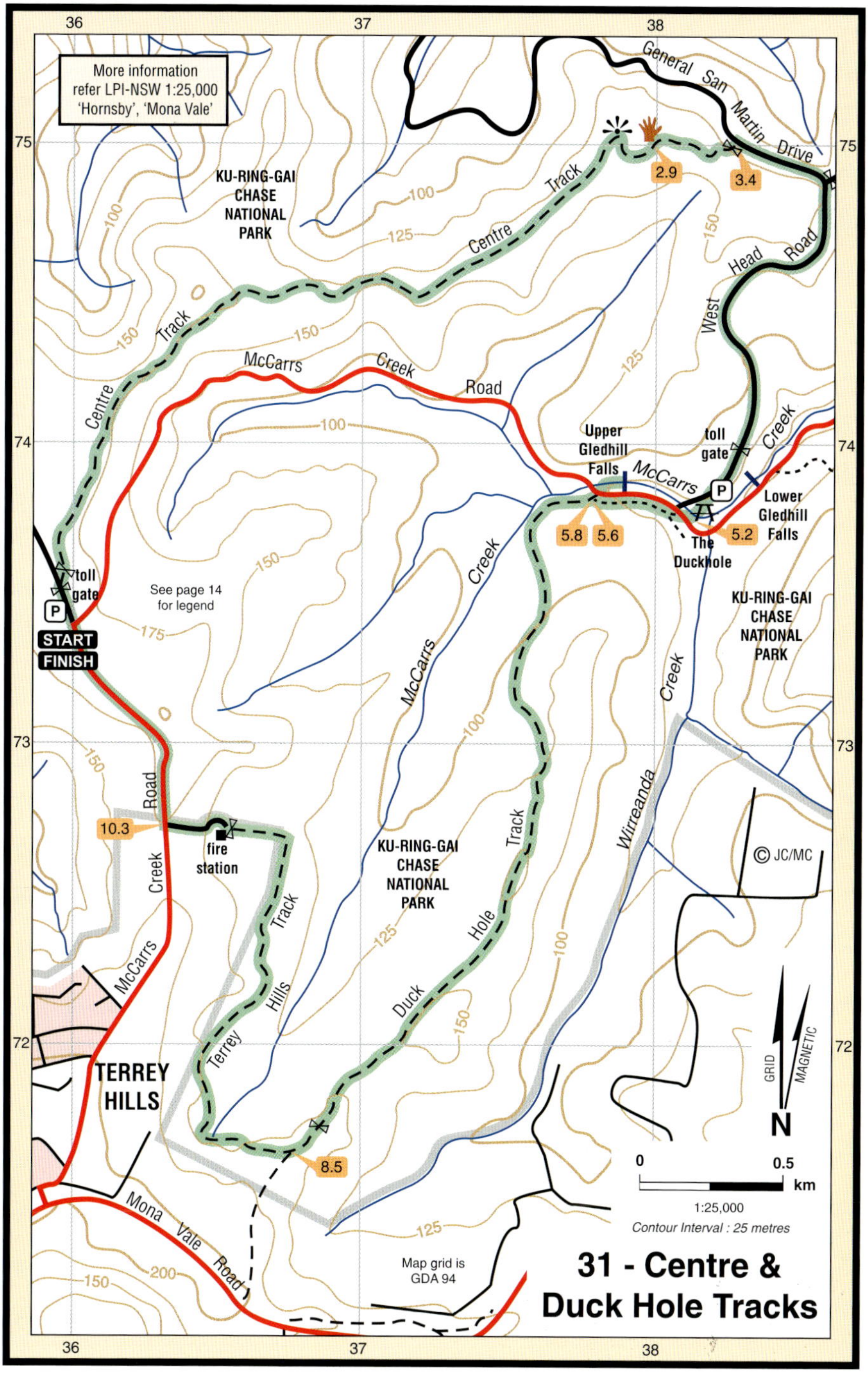
More information
refer LPI-NSW 1:25,000
'Hornsby', 'Mona Vale'
KU-RING-GAI
CHASE
NATIONAL
PARK
General San Martin Drive
Centre Track
West Head Road
McCarrs Creek Road
Upper
Gledhill
Falls
toll
gate
Lower
Gledhill
Falls
The
Duckhole
START
FINISH
See page 14
for legend
fire
station
Terrey Hills Track
Duck Hole Track
Wirreanda Creek
McCarrs Creek
TERREY
HILLS
Mona Vale Road
© JC/MC
GRID
MAGNETIC
N
0
0.5
km
1:25,000
Contour Interval : 25 metres
Map grid is
GDA 94
31 - Centre &
Duck Hole Tracks

32 BELROSE CIRCUIT

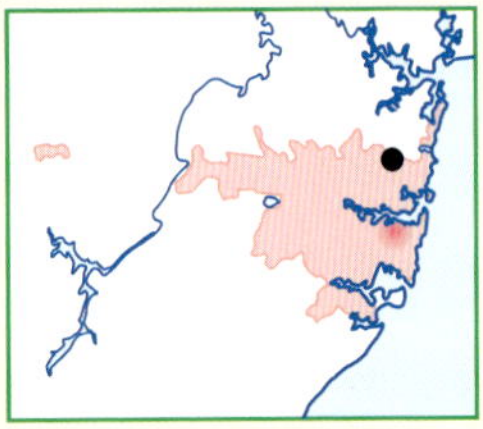

Length: 8.5km, circuit
Time: 3½ hours
Grade: Medium
Total Climbing: 190m
Maximum Height: 170m
From Sydney: 19km
Closest Town: Belrose 0km
Map: UBD 1:19,000 p155, 156 or SYDWAY 1:20,000 p217

Middle Harbour Creek is one of the major streams that drains into the northern section of Sydney Harbour. The upper reaches of this creek along with two of its side creeks are explored on this walk which first heads through the streets of Belrose, before entering Garigal National Park.

The walk has considerable diversity. It visits several natural lookouts and passes numerous cascades, waterfalls and rockpools. The vegetation is also varied as the walk passes through heathland, light forest and damp gullies. Such diverse habitats support a huge range of native plants with many having colourful flowers. Wildflowers that can be found here most of the year include banksia, grevillea, epacris and westringia.

Do not attempt the walk after heavy rain as there are several crossings at fords and some of these can become impassable.

Access

From Sydney, follow the Warringah Freeway north across the Harbour Bridge then turn right onto Miller Street and continue north along Strathallen Avenue then East-

Bare Creek Track

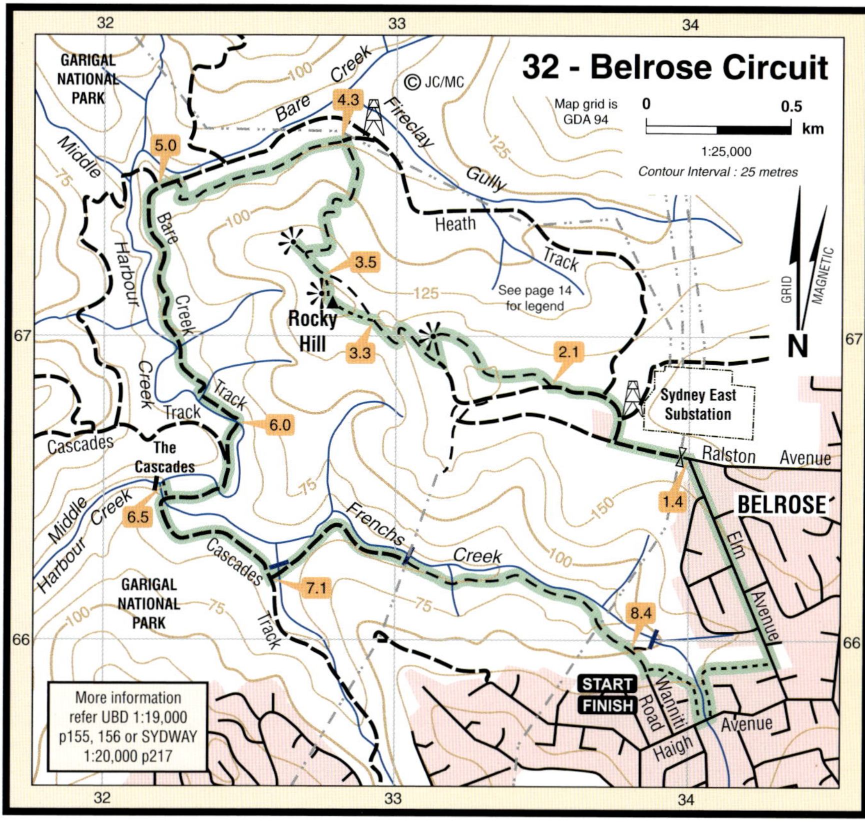

ern Valley Way to merge with Babbage Road in the suburb of Roseville Chase. Follow Babbage Road, which becomes Warringah Road, for 5km then turn left into Forest Way and continue north for 1.5km. Turn left into Glen Street, right into Pringle Street, left into Haigh Street then right again to park in Wanniti Road.

Public transport – from Sydney take the 270 bus to Haigh Avenue in Belrose. Follow Wanniti Road north-west for 250m to join the walk at the end of the street. Alternatively, from Chatswood Railway Station take bus 282 or 283 to Haigh Avenue in Belrose.

0.0km Turn right and follow the grassed reserve south-east behind the houses to a creek then follow this to meet Haigh Avenue. Cross the creek then turn left and follow the grassy reserve on the other side of the creek north then west to Elm Avenue. Turn left and follow Elm Avenue north-west to its end to meet Ralston Avenue.

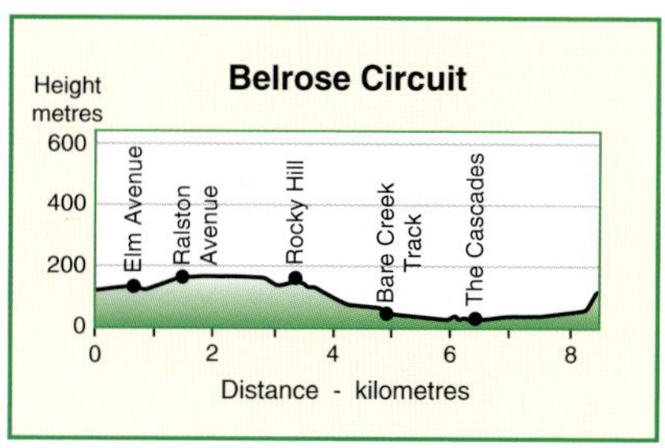

1.4km Turn left and head west on the continuation of Ralston Avenue. Pass through a locked gate via a walker entrance on the right. Follow the road west for 250m then turn right and follow a gravel track north between a house and a tower. Keep to the left at the next two intersections as the track swings around towards the west. When the track divides, veer right onto a walking track.

2.1km Head west then north-west through heathland – flowers are common for much of the year. The track circles around the edge of a plateau swinging around to the south to a natural lookout on a rock slab. Continue south another 100m then turn right and descend gently north-west. The rocky track soon leaves the ridge to descend south then swings back north-west and rises gently to a track junction in a saddle. The track on the right bypasses Rocky Hill.

3.3km Turn left and follow the track to the summit of Rocky Hill then head north-west to a viewpoint on top of a cliff. Follow the cliff-top north 20m then descend to meet the alternative track that bypassed the hill.

3.5km Turn left and continue north-west for 100m to a short sidetrack on the left to another lookout rock. Continue to the right descending steadily to the top of a long, rock slab. Continue directly ahead descending steeply then swing right below the slab to meet an alternative route down the eastern side of the rock. Continue north through light forest to a T-junction. Just 30m to the right is an electricity transmission tower and management tracks.

4.3km Turn left and follow the walking track south-west through banksia forest then swing north and descend steeply to meet Bare Creek Track. Turn left and follow the management track 100m to a junction.

5.0km Keep to the left as the track undulates and follows the valley downstream. Pass below some cliffs and a rock shelter, cross two side gullies to a ford across Middle Harbour Creek. Cross on rocks above the ford – take care when wet.

Middle Harbour Creek

Frenchs Creek

6.0km Climb south-west for 150m then veer left onto Cascades Track. Descend to another ford across Middle Harbour Creek – cross on rocks just below the ford. Rise west over a low spur to meet Frenchs Creek. Leave the track and follow a foot pad along the northern creek bank downstream for 100m to The Cascades.

6.5km The Cascades is a popular site for an extended stop. It is a large, open slab of rock at the junction of the Frenchs and Middle Harbour Creeks. Just downstream of the junction are the concrete and stone remains of a dam wall. Return to Cascades Track, cross Frenchs Creek and follow the track south-eastwards for 500m to another track junction.

7.1km Turn left and immediately cross a side creek on rocky slabs above a waterfall. Continue following the track north-east for 500m to meet Frenchs Creek at a sewer overflow pipe. The track conitnues south-east and soon narrows to a rough walking track as it heads upstream. Initially it climbs away from the creek then follows the top edge of a rocky, sandstone cliff eastward. It soon returns to the creek and then follows it closely to pass a small waterfall. Pass more cascades then swing south-east climbing away from the creek to a vent pipe then a track junction. To the left is a sidetrack to a poor view of another small waterfall.

8.4km Turn right and climb steps south-east to the end of the walk at Wanniti Road.

Heath Banksia

33 TWO CREEKS TRACK

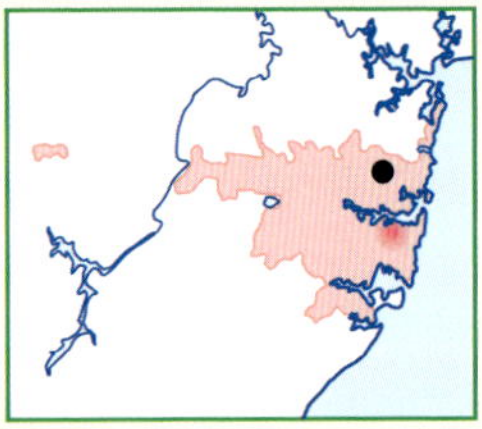

Length: 10.9km, circuit
Time: 4 hours
Grade: Medium
Total Climbing: 180m
Maximum Height: 100m
From Sydney: 14km
Closest Town: Lindfield 1km
Map: UBD 1:19,000 p175, 176 or SYDWAY 1:20,000 236, 237

The narrow gullies of the creeks near Lindfield are lined with numerous, low clifflines. There are several, small falls and cascades in the creeks and the low cliffs are popular training areas for rockclimbers. The steep gullies were not easy to develop so they were left as housing spread in this area. Eventually these undeveloped strips became reserves and now form part of Garigal National Park. A network of walking tracks provide access to many of the area's features. This walk follows the narrow valley of Gordon Creek to the wide waters of Middle Harbour Creek, which is tidal and lined with mangroves. These live in salt water and have roots with vertical breather tubes. The walk continues along the creek passing under Roseville Bridge to picnic grounds at Echo Point. This is an ideal lunch site or some might prefer the nearby kiosk. The return is along Little Digger Track passing two, small waterfalls then it's a short walk through the streets of East Lindfield back to the start.

Access

From Sydney, follow the Pacific Highway northward for 11km then in Roseville turn right onto Boundary Road. Follow this north-east for 1.2km then turn left into Archbold Road. Continue north-west for 1.8km then turn right into Tryon Road and park on the left near Lindfield Oval.

Public transport – from Sydney Central, trains operate on the 'North Shore Line' to Lindfield. This leaves a 1.2km walk north-east along Tryon Road to the start of the walk. Alternatively, from Wynyard Railway Station in central Sydney take bus 207 or 208 to East Lindfield to the corner of Tryon and Sydney Roads.

Variation:

1. **Gordon & Moores Creeks**, 6.9km, circuit, 2½ hours, Easy-Medium. Follow the first 4.6km of the walk then turn left and follow the notes from the 8.6km point to the end of the walk.

0.0km Starting on the eastern side of Lindfield Oval, head north-east then north across grass slopes to a timber bridge at the start of Two Creeks Track. Follow the track north-west into bush and sidle westward around a broad ridge to a track junction. Turn right and descend to a bridge over a small gully. This area has many rocky outcrops and is popular with rockclimbers. Ignore all minor side tracks and zigzag down to meet a wide track in the valley. An alternative start to the walk is from the left.

Long overhang above Gordon Creek

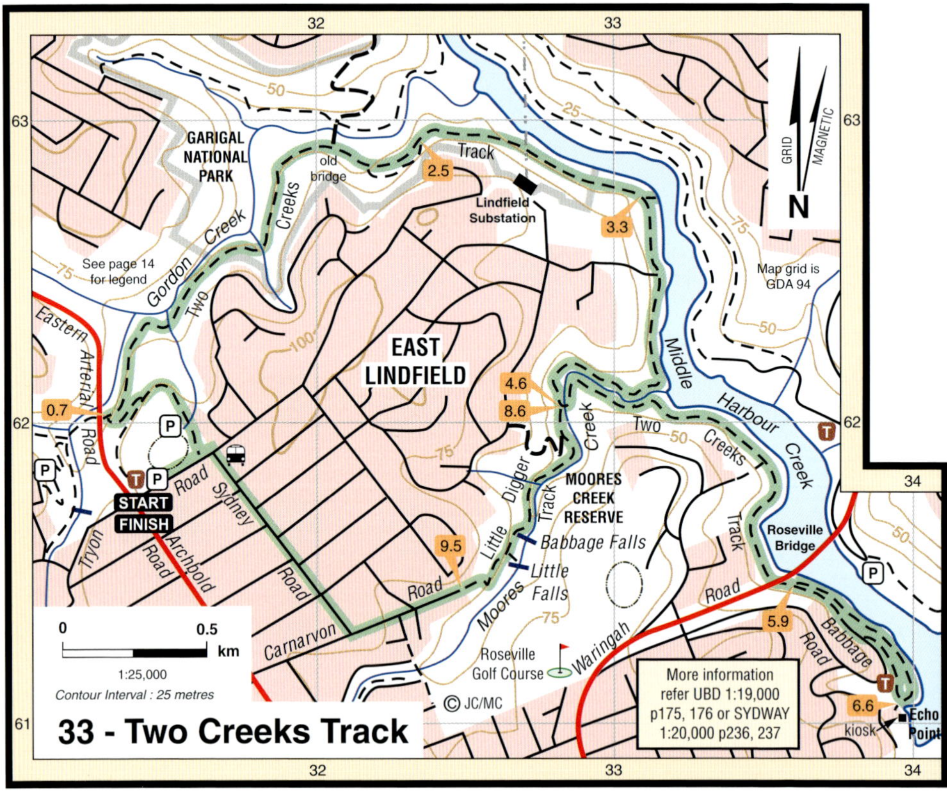

0.7km Turn right and follow the wide Two Creeks Track along the valley of Gordon Creek for 1.4km to a track junction. The left track leads to a closed bridge. Continue on the right and the track soon narrows rising to the next track junction. The sidetrack on the right climbs steps to a rock shelter then rejoins the main track 200m further on. Continue on the left following the main track passing under a long overhang then meet the sidetrack again.

2.5km Two Creeks Track now descends gently to some view points over Middle Harbour Creek. Ignore several minor, sidetracks on the left leading to the shoreline. Continue south-east following the valley of Middle Harbour Creek. Pass below the Lindfield Substation and 400m further on round a bend to an unmarked track junction.

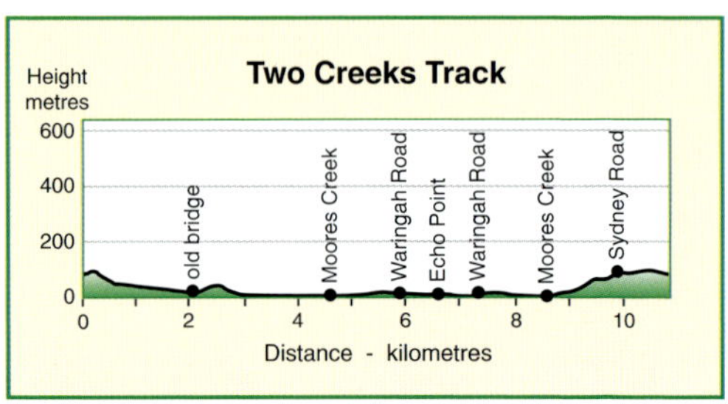

3.3km Turn left and a short, steep sidetrack leads to a sandy bank beside Middle Harbour Creek – this is a good place to see the mangroves and their aerial roots. Return to the main track and continue south – ignore three, minor sidetracks on the right leading to streets above. Continue for 900m to the junction of Moores and Middle Harbour Creeks. The track swings west and follows Moores Creek for 300m then crosses a side creek at a series of cascades. It then heads south for 100m to a track junction. The walk will later continue on Little Digger Track on the right.

4.6km Turn left and stay on Two Creeks Track. Cross Moores Creek on a timber bridge then follow the southern bank of the creek for 300m to more views over Middle Harbour Creek. On the opposite side of the creek the picnic areas of Davidson Park can be seen. Continue along the level track as it heads south passing behind a mangrove forest to Roseville Bridge.

5.9km Just past the bridge, the track divides and the return will be from the left. Veer right and climb gently to a gate then descend a short access road onto Babbage Road. Follow the road 50m then turn left to pass through the gap in the fence. Keep right following the level track, passing play equipment, to a picnic area above Echo Point. From the picnic shelter descend steps south-east to the shoreline below Echo Point.

Davidson Park

6.6km The nearby kiosk/cafe is usually open from Wednesday to Sunday. To return to Moores Creek, turn left and follow a track along the shore. Ignore all tracks to the left and continue close to the shore for 300m to a grassy flat which was the site of the old Roseville Baths. Keep to the right following the narrow fenced track over and around rocks then rise to the track junction just before Roseville Bridge. Keep to the right and reverse 1.3kms of the outward track back to the track junction beside Moores Creek.

8.6km Turn left and follow the track south for 200m to the junction with Little Digger Track. Turn left onto Little Digger Track and follow Moores Creek upstream. Pass under two, rock overhangs to the top of Babbage Falls. Continue upstream for a further 150m to a sidetrack on the left to Little Falls – these are a cascade falling into a shady glen. Continue climbing and a zigzag leads to the end of Carnarvon Road.

9.5km Follow Canarvon Road south-west for 300m climbing steeply to Sydney Road. Turn right and follow Sydney Road north-west for 800m to Tryon Road. Turn left and walk along Tryon Road to Lindfield Oval at the end of the walk.

34 FORESTVILLE CIRCUIT

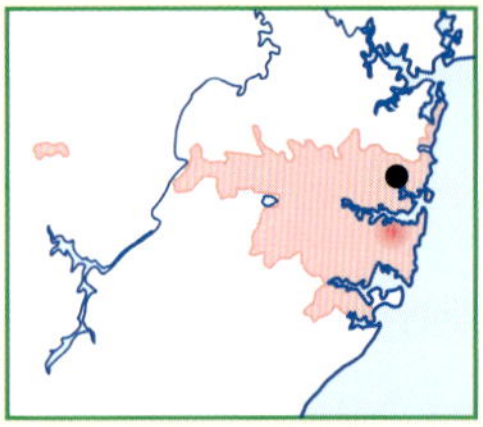

Length: 13.4km, circuit
Time: 5 hours
Grade: Medium
Total Climbing: 200m
Maximum Height: 125m
From Sydney: 15km
Closest Suburb: Forestville 0km
Map: UBD 1:19,000 p175, 176, 196 or SYDWAY 1:20,000 p237

Garigal National Park contains the largest area of natural forest beside Sydney Harbour. The park protects the shores of Middle Harbour and Bantry Bay in the northern arm of the harbour. The reserve began in 1923 when Davidson Park was created as a grassed picnic ground for recreation. In 1992, Davidson Park was integrated with the newly declared Garigal National Park which also incorporated large sections of undeveloped native forest. These are mainly steep creek valleys and the park is a long corridor of creeks filled with native forest surrounded by housing.

This walk is a circuit at the southern end of the park and passes a wide variety of native plants and wildflowers. Common trees are bloodwoods, coachwoods and peppermints with mangroves along the tidal creeks. On the heathlands and forest floor fuschias, hakeas and banksias provide splashes of colour. The walk also passes several, small waterfalls, cascades, rock platforms and fern-filled gullies.

Access

From Sydney, follow the Warringah Freeway north across the Harbour Bridge then turn right onto Miller Street and continue north along Strathallen Avenue then Eastern Valley Way to merge with Babbage Road in the suburb of Roseville Chase. Follow Babbage Road which becomes Warringah Road. Cross Roseville Bridge and continue for 2.3km then turn left into Ferguson Street. Park anywhere after the first street intersection.

Public transport – from Sydney Central, trains operate on the 'North Shore Line' to Chatswood. Take any 278 to 284 bus to the shopping centre near Ferguson Street in Forestville.

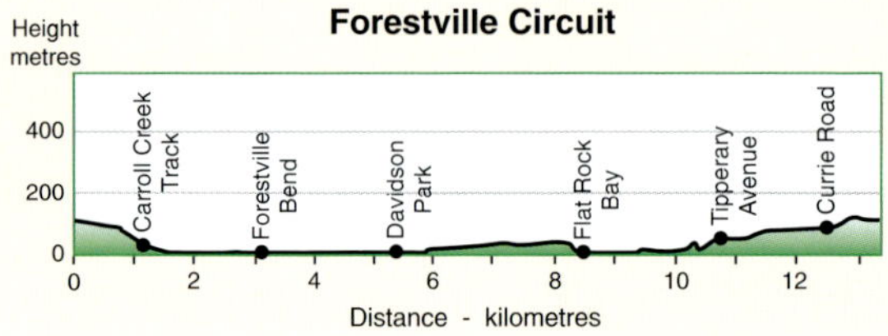

0.0km Follow Fergusson Street north-west to its end. Enter Garigal National Park through a gate and pass the park office and buildings. Follow the management

Roseville Bridge from Davidson Park

Waterfall on Carroll Creek

road north-west 100m then turn right following an old road. This descends steeply east then north-west to the start of two walking tracks.

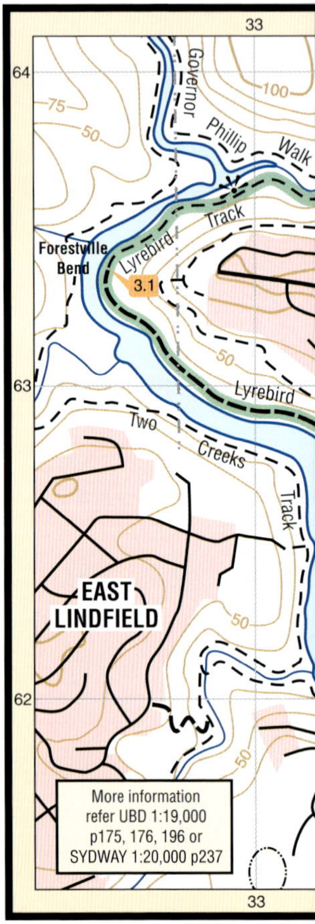

1.2km Turn right onto Carroll Creek Track, descend a series of concrete steps then turn left – don't cross the bridge over the creek. Follow the southern bank of Carroll Creek downstream passing through a dense forest of coachwood. The rough track runs along the base of a long overhang then follows rocky slabs in the creek for 50m to a waterfall. Continue on the south side of the creek through open forest and ferns following the creek to a track junction at a wide, rock slab. The Governor Phillip Walk crosses the creek to the right via stepping stones – don't attempt that track during floods or at high tides.

2.0km Keep to the left and follow Lyrebird Track which continues downstream – the creek is now tidal. Rise onto the top of a small cliff where there are good views of the junction of Carroll and Middle Harbour Creeks. A short, steep descent follows then the track continues close to the creek bank to reach a clearing at Forestville Bend.

3.1km The track widens into a management road and this is followed south-east along the creek bank to a carpark. Leave the road and cross the open grass of Davidson Park. This provides good views of the creek and Roseville Bridge. Follow the creek bank through the park using footbridges to cross three, small creeks. Pass underneath Roseville Bridge and then below a pipeline bridge. When the access road turns sharp left, head north-east to the start of Flat Rock Track.

5.8km Flat Rock Track climbs steeply to a wide, sandstone terrace then swings south-east to sidle the forested slopes above Middle Harbour. Continue for 700m to the end of a road on the left. Continue straight ahead for 600m to a minor track to the right that descends to the rowing club on Killarney Point. Ignore it and continue for 200m to a second track to the rowing club. Continue following Flat Rock Track eastwards for 800m to another track junction.

Grey Spider-flower

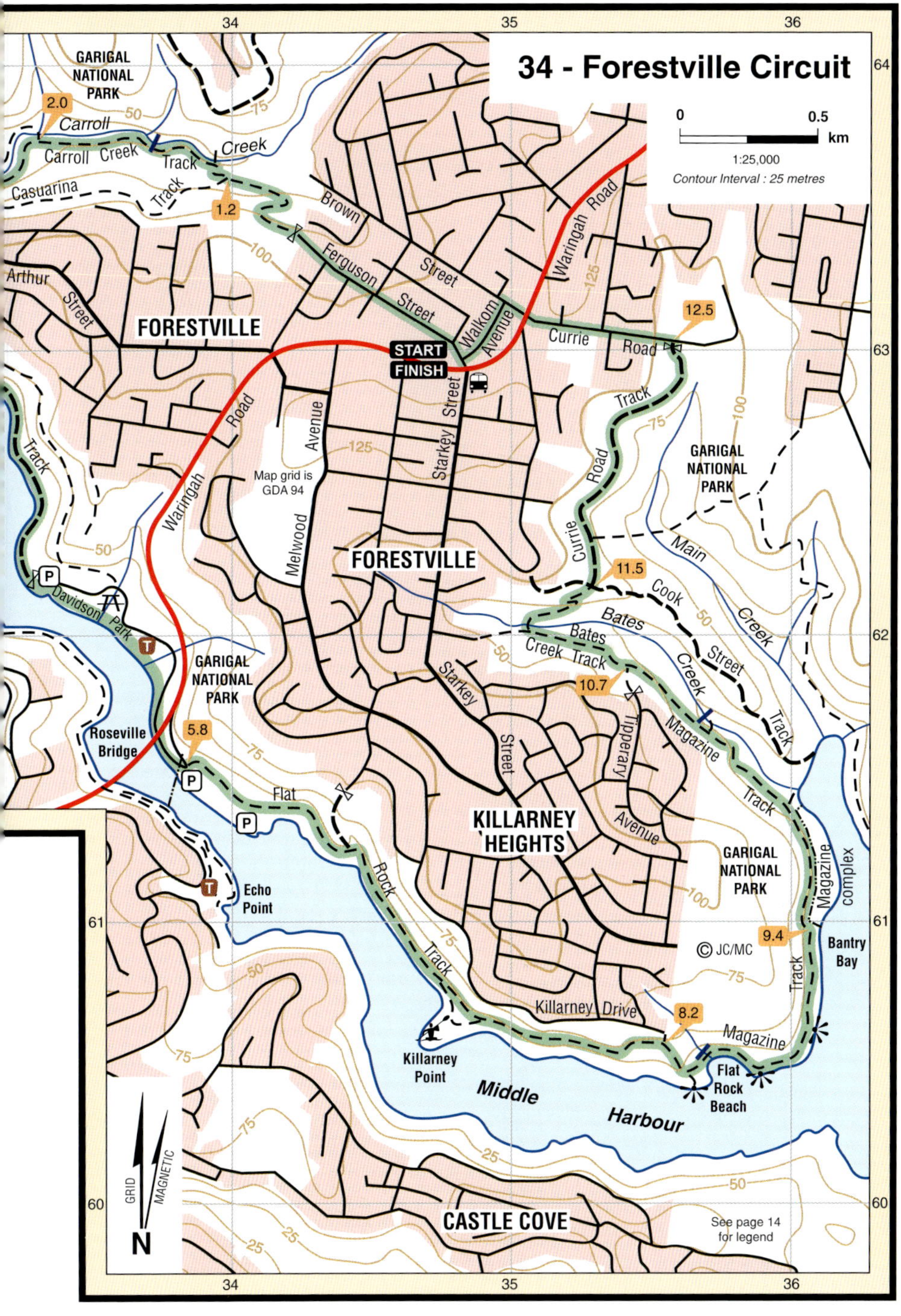
34 - Forestville Circuit
0
0.5
km
1:25,000
Contour Interval : 25 metres
34
35
36
64
63
62
61
60
GARIGAL NATIONAL PARK
Carroll Creek
Carroll Creek Track
Casuarina Track
Brown Street
Ferguson Street
Walkom Avenue
Waringah Road
Currie Road
Currie Road Track
Arthur Street
FORESTVILLE
START
FINISH
Starkey Street
Melwood Avenue
Map grid is GDA 94
Main Creek
Cook Street Track
Bates Creek
Bates Creek Track
Magazine Track
Tipperary Avenue
Starkey Street
KILLARNEY HEIGHTS
Davidson Park
Track
Roseville Bridge
Flat Rock Track
Echo Point
Killarney Point
Killarney Drive
Magazine complex
Magazine Track
Bantry Bay
Flat Rock Beach
Middle Harbour
CASTLE COVE
© JC/MC
See page 14 for legend
GRID
MAGNETIC
N
2.0
1.2
12.5
11.5
10.7
9.4
8.2
5.8

Middle Harbour

8.2km Turn right onto Magazine Track and descend steeply south for 200m to yet another track junction – right leads to a lookout. Turn left and continue eastward towards Flat Rock Beach. Keep left at each track junction to pass underneath a waterfall then scramble across large boulders. Continue past Flat Rock Beach to enter sheoak forest above the short, coastal cliff. There are numerous viewpoints as the track heads east then north along the shore of Bantry Bay to meet a fence. The fence encloses the Magazine Complex where explosives were once stored.

9.4km The track follows the fence initially climbing steeply west then heading north for 400m. When the fence ends, ignore minor tracks on the right and continue north-west through forest. Cross a side creek then climb to a track junction – right leads down to some waterfalls on Bates Creek. Keep to the left and climb steadily to a track junction where Magazine Track veers left to Tipperary Avenue.

10.7km Continue on the right on Bates Creek Track for 500m to the next track junction. Turn right onto a walking track to cross Bates Creek via a small concrete weir – be careful if water is flowing strongly. Follow the foot track north-east through forest to a zigzag climb through a rocky outcrop. Continue north-east to meet a road – Cook Street Track.

11.5km Continue straight across the road and follow the vehicular Currie Road Track northward. After 200m ignore a walking track on the right to Natural Bridge. Continue northward a further 900m to Currie Road.

12.5km Turn left and follow the sealed street west for 500m to meet Warringah Road. Cross at the traffic lights and follow Brown Street north-west for 100m then turn left into Walkom Avenue. Follow it south-west then turn right into Fergusson Street to end the walk.

MONA VALE TO MANLY 35

The coastline of the northern suburbs of Sydney provides some excellent walking. There are long, sandy beaches, rocky headlands and narrow coastal reserves. An almost continuous track follows the coast – signs indicate this as the Bicentennial Coastal Walk, but track markers are poorly maintained and a wide variety of other track markers are also used. The track is often squeezed into a narrow corridor between housing and the ocean and a large number of side tracks are passed. Generally, these should be ignored as many of them lead into private property.

Swimming is a popular activity along this coast. Either swim between the flags at one of the patrolled beaches or have a dip in one the five sea baths. These are swimming pools that have been built beside the ocean and are designed so that the water is replaced at each high tide. While suburban development is ever present, the magnificent scenery from the headlands and the wild ocean beaches make this a memorable walk.

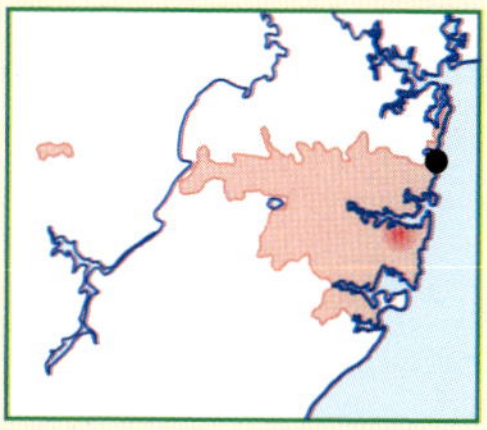

Length: 18.8km, one-way
Time: 5 hours
Grade: Medium
Total Climbing: 270m
Maximum Height: 40m
From Sydney: 31km
Closest Town: Mona Vale 0km
Map: UBD p138, 158, 178, 198 or SYDWAY p199, 219, 239, 259

Curl Curl Beach

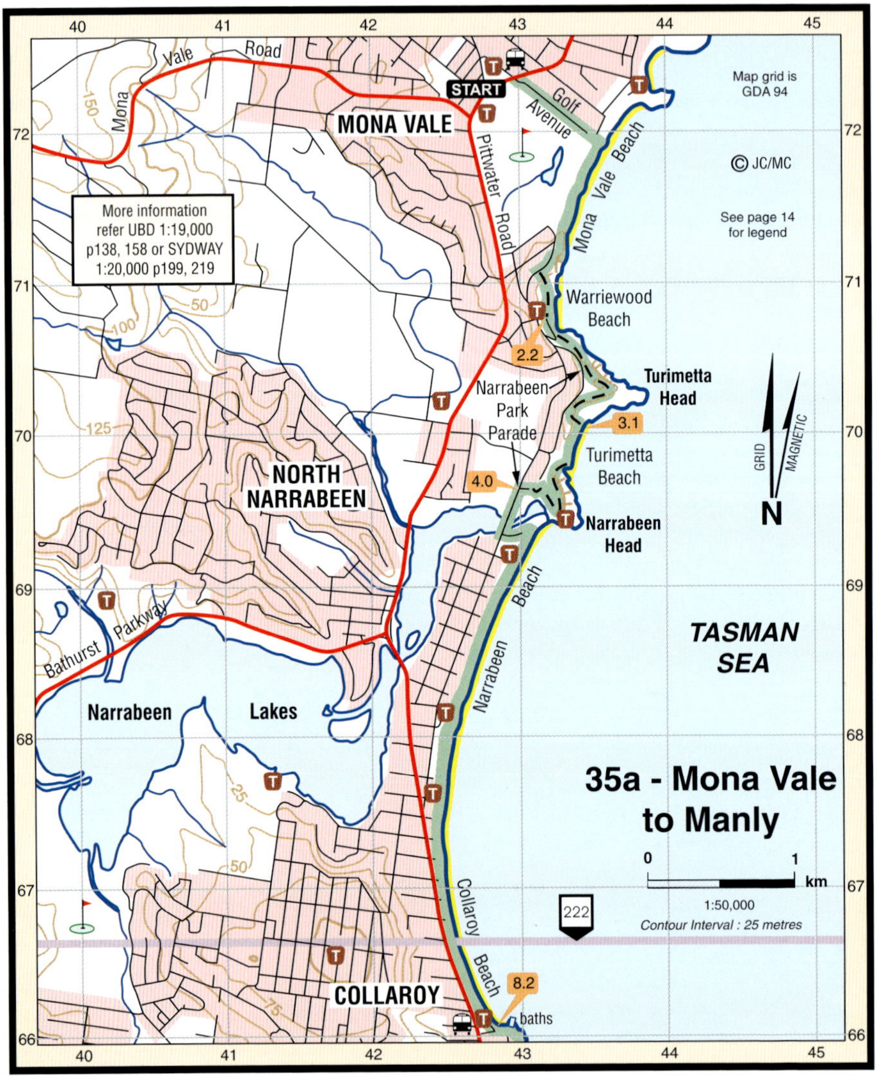

Access

From Sydney follow Waringah Highway north across Sydney Harbour Bridge. Exit to follow Military Road east then Spit Road north crossing Spit Bridge to Seaforth. Continue northward on Burnt Bridge Creek Deviation into Condamine Street. Follow this north for 4km then merge with Pittwater Road and continue northwards for 12km to Mona Vale. Turn right onto Barrenjoey Road and after 500m turn right and park in Golf Avenue. The walk is not a circuit and parking at the other end in Manly is not free. To return to the start catch bus 151 from the bus stands near Manly Wharf.

Public transport – from Circular Quay, take a ferry to Manly Wharf then take bus 151 to Mona Vale. Alternatively, from Sydney bus L90 runs to Mona Vale then return to the city on the Manly Ferry.

Variations:

1. **Mona Vale to Collaroy**, 8.4km, one-way, 2½ hours, Easy-Medium. Follow the first 8.2km of the walk to the south end of Collaroy Beach. Leave the coast and head west 200m to Pittwater Road and catch a 151 or L90 bus north to Mona Vale or south to Manly.
2. **Collaroy to Manly**, 10.8km, one-way, 3 hours, Medium. Start from the corner of Pittwater Road and Birdwood Avenue in Collaroy and head east for 200m then descend steps to the baths and join the walk at the 8.2km point. Continue southward to the end of the walk in Manly. To return to Collaroy catch the 151 bus.

0.0km Follow Golf Avenue south-east for 700m to its end then follow a walking track onto the beach. Turn right and follow the sand of Mona Vale Beach south-west for 800m. At the end of the beach turn right and climb steps to the top of the cliff. Turn left to follow Narrabeen Park Parade southward then turn left at the next set of steps. Descend, ignoring all turns to the right, to the sand on Warriewood Beach. Turn right and cross the sand to a car park and toilets.

2.2km Continue 100m south to the Surf Life Saving Club and climb the steps on its left – this is the start of a walking track to Turimetta Head. The track leads through coastal scrub just above the cliffs and passes a lookout. Soon after it crosses a clearing with trig marker on top of the headland. At a track junction, veer left and descend south-east to where there are good views to the south. The track then sidles to a track junction beside a road, turn left then, after 20m, left again and descend steps to Turimetta Beach.

Track to Turimetta Head

Outlet of Narrabeen Lakes

3.1km Follow the sand south for 200m. At low tide the coast can be followed around the base of Narrabeen Head to the baths then north-west along the outlet of Narrabeen Lakes to a car park beside Narrabeen Park Parade. At high tide, leave the coast and follow a signposted walking track south-west climbing to a lookout. Continue climbing to the open top of Narrabeen Head then walk south through scrub to a fenced lookout just left of the track. Follow the track west and descend a long set of steps to a car park beside Narrabeen Park Parade.

4.0km Turn left and cross the road bridge over the outlet of Narrabeen Lakes. Turn left again to cross a car park and follow a walking track east onto Narrabeen Beach. Turn right and follow the beach southward. The sand is at times soft and can be tedious to walk. The beach is backed by a low sand dune with housing behind. Halfway along the beach it changes name to Collaroy Beach and multi-storey apartments become more common. Continue to the end of the sand. The walk can easily be shortened here as Pittwater Road is just 200m to the west.

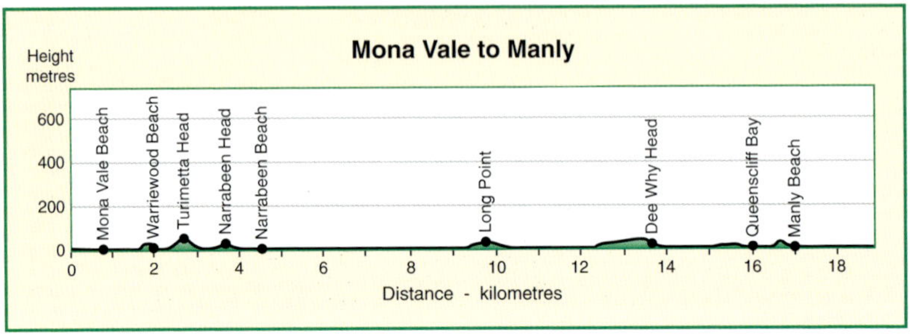

8.2km Continue following the coastline around a small point passing a rock sea bath to the next sandy beach. Follow sand around the shores of The Basin to the end of the beach then climb south passing the Surf Rescue shed and the Long Beach Fisherman's Shed. Continue up the grassy embankment to the road above. Either follow a pad on the left through scrub or follow the road 100m to a car park. Pass through a locked gate and follow a wide, walking track south-east rising steadily to Long Reef Point. The lookout on the top of the point has the best all round view on the walk.

9.8km From Long Reef Point follow the walking track south-west along the southern edge of the golf course. Cross a bridge over a gully and shortly after the track divides. Turn left and descend to Long Reef Beach. Follow the sandy shore south-west to cross the outlet of Dee Why Lagoon – sometimes this is a shallow wade. Continue south-west to the end of Long Reef Beach then follow a path to the sea baths on the rocky point.

12.2km From the baths, climb steps to the cliff top, turn left and follow the street briefly to an old quarry on the corner. Veer left across the quarry to the start of a walking track. The narrow track is rough at times following a thin strip of land between the cliff edge and the houses. There are several track junctions to nearby streets – keep to the left at each one. There are some reasonable views of the cliffs below and a lookout close to Dee Why Head provides views to the north.

13.7km Dee Why Head has a trig point, but it is covered in scrub. Stay left at track junctions and descend west to an open slab that provides good views to the south. At the next track junction turn right and descend a long set of steps to the Surf Life Saving Club. Just past the club, turn left and follow the edge of Curl Curl Lagoon

Baths below Dee Why Head

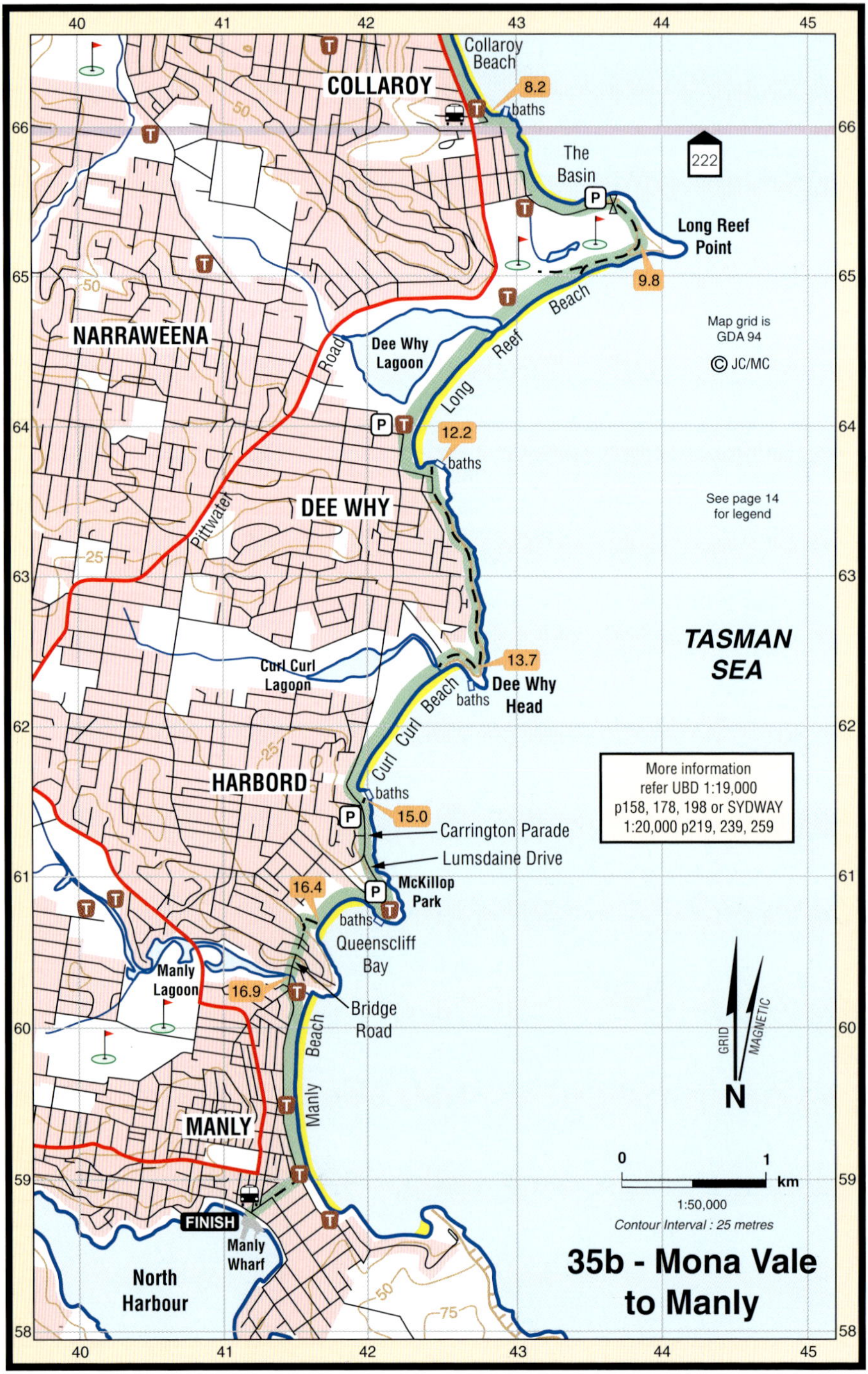
COLLAROY
Collaroy Beach
8.2
baths
The Basin
222
Long Reef Point
9.8
NARRAWEENA
Dee Why Lagoon
Long Reef Beach
Road
Pittwater
Map grid is GDA 94
© JC/MC
12.2
baths
DEE WHY
See page 14 for legend
TASMAN SEA
Curl Curl Lagoon
13.7
Dee Why Head
baths
Curl Curl Beach
HARBORD
baths
15.0
Carrington Parade
Lumsdaine Drive
McKillop Park
16.4
baths
Queenscliff Bay
More information refer UBD 1:19,000 p158, 178, 198 or SYDWAY 1:20,000 p219, 239, 259
Manly Lagoon
16.9
Bridge Road
Manly Beach
GRID
MAGNETIC
N
MANLY
0
1
km
1:50,000
Contour Interval : 25 metres
FINISH
Manly Wharf
North Harbour
35b - Mona Vale to Manly

to the beach. Turn right and follow Curl Curl Beach south-west to the sea baths at the end of the sand.

15.0km Climb steps behind the baths to the car park above and turn left following a rough track along a terrace in the cliff for 300m then turn right and ascend a set of steps to Carrington Parade. Turn left and follow this street south then turn left into Lumsdaine Drive. Follow this road south-east through McKillop Park to a car park. Head south to the toilet block and descend steps towards the sea baths. Just before the baths, turn right and follow a concrete path west. This is close to the rocky shoreline and leads to the beach in Queenscliff Bay. Follow the short beach south-west to its end.

Manly from Queenscliff Bay

16.4km At end of the beach, turn right and climb a concrete ramp to meet Undercliffe Road – do not follow the obvious steps at the end of the beach as they lead to private houses. Turn left and follow Undercliffe Road briefly then veer right up a ramp and steps to the end of Bridge Road. Follow Bridge Road south-west over the ridge then follow two sets of steps to a road bridge crossing the outlet of Manly Lagoon.

16.9km Cross the bridge then turn left onto the promenade above Manly Beach. Follow either the beach or promenade south for 1.4km. About 300m before the end of the beach, turn right and follow The Corso south-west. This street is a mall with a large number of shops. Follow it for 500m to Manly Wharf.

36 MANLY DAM CIRCUIT

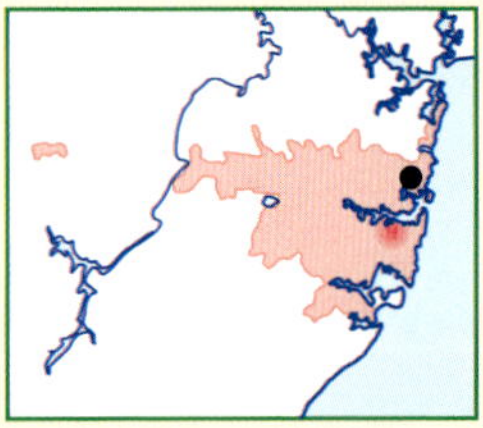

Length: 7.9km, circuit
Time: 3 hours
Grade: Easy-Medium
Total Climbing: 130m
Maximum Height: 100m
From Sydney: 15km
Closest Town: Brookvale 3km
Map: Sydway 1:20,000 p238

Since 1892, fresh water for Manly has been supplied from a dam in the nearby hills. To maintain water quality, most of the catchment area was retained as a reserve of native bushland. Much of the surrounding area has been developed into suburbs making the reserve a valuable remnant of original vegetation. Plant life is varied with around 300 different species in the reserve and bird watching is also a popular pastime as both waterbirds and forest species live here.

The most popular walk in a network of walking tracks and management roads is a circuit of the dam. One section of the circuit follows a popular mountain bike route and walkers should allow bicycles to pass. There are also a number of minor, unmarked, walking pads branching off the main track and these are best ignored. The reserve has four parking and picnic areas and is popular on weekends and holidays.

Access

From Sydney follow Warringah Highway north across Sydney Harbour Bridge. Exit to follow Military Road east then Spit Road north crossing Spit Bridge to Seaforth.

Manly Dam

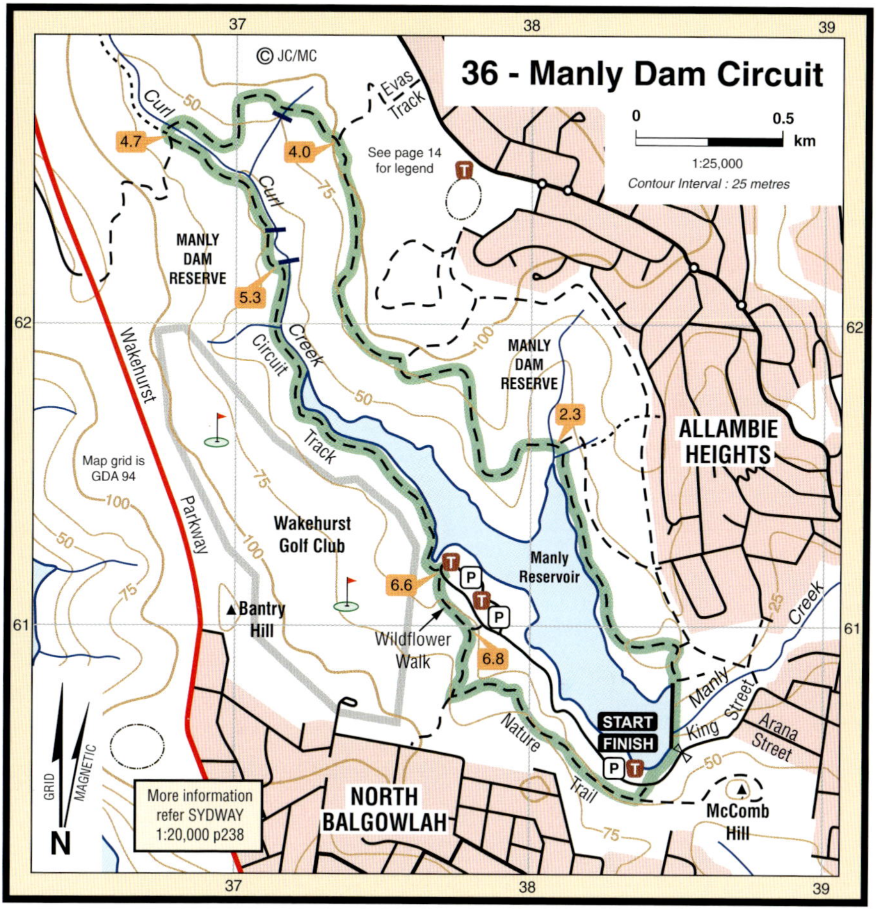

Continue northward on Burnt Bridge Creek Deviation into Condamine Street. Follow this north for 800m then turn left into King Street and follow it to its end to enter Manly Dam Reserve and park in the first of the four parking areas. From the north, King Street is 1.7km south of Warringah Mall shopping centre. The entry gate is locked at 7pm and on some days an entry fee applies.

Public Transport – from Sydney Central, trains operate on the 'North Shore line' to Chatswood Railway Station. Take bus 143 or 144 to Seaforth then change to a 145 bus to the corner of King and Arcana Streets in Manly Vale. This is 300m from the park entrance.

0.0km From the first picnic area head east along the shore to the dam wall. Turn left and cross the bridge above the dam wall to a track junction on the northern bank. Turn left and ascend steps onto a low, rocky ridge where there are views of the ocean. At the next track junction turn left and descend gently to the dam shore. Pass signs marking the limit of the power boat region and continue following the shore northwards along an inlet to the next junction.

2.3km Turn left and a 50m long boardwalk crosses the swamp behind the inlet. Continue west rising onto a sandstone ridge – the track winds around as it climbs. Head northwards crossing the edge of heathland where there are views of surrounding ridges and the ocean. The track swings west again, then continues north to meet a wide, rough road that is also used by mountain bike riders. Turn left and follow the wide track northwards.

Track crossing a wet area

4.0km At the junction with Evas Track keep to the left and descend to cross a rock slab above a small waterfall. The winding track climbs over a low spur before descending to cross Curl Curl Creek. A short climb leads to a four-way track junction.

4.7km Turn left and head southward following a walking track towards the picnic areas. The track passes through light forest to a small waterfall. Continue 100m to a larger waterfall and descend to the pool at its base.

5.3km The track continues southwards and soon enters tall heathland with views over the dam. Ignore minor foot tracks on the left to the dam shore and follow the main track. When the track divides, either may be followed as they soon rejoin and shortly after cross a small gully and climb to a car parking area near a picnic ground.

6.6km About 20m to the right is the start of Wildflower Walk. Head south-west along this track following markers for 200m to a track junction. Left leads back onto the sealed road through car parks.

6.8km Turn right onto Nature Trail and follow the track as it climbs gently to a track junction. Turn left and sidle a ridge. Keep left at all track junctions ignoring tracks to North Balgowlah and McComb Hill to eventually descend to meet the sealed, entrance road close to the first car parking area.

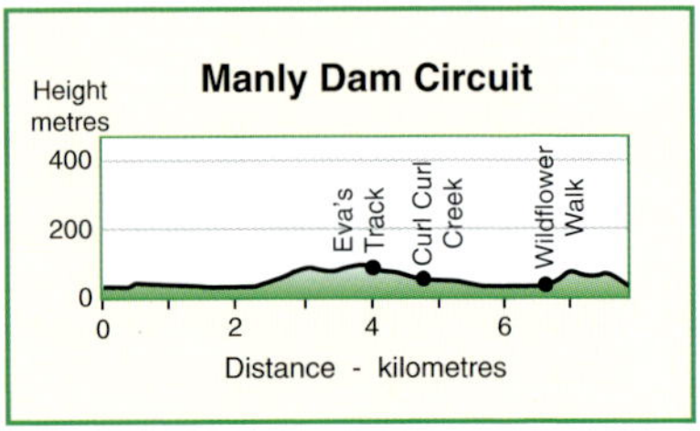

SPIT BRIDGE TO MANLY 37

Sydney Harbour is renowned for the natural beauty of its waterways and headlands. The harbour is extensive and has been divided into several smaller harbours. This walk follows the northern shore from Middle Harbour through to North Harbour beginning at the Spit Bridge. The bridge is unusual as it can be opened to allow large boats to pass. The track follows a series of paths through a number of reserves along the foreshore with the largest being Sydney Harbour National Park. This large patch of remnant bush has changed little since European settlement and provides many fine views of the surrounding harbour. Wildflowers can be found most of the year and the walk passes some aboriginal sites.

This walk was formally opened as a track in 1988 and has a variety of names including Spit to Manly and Manly Scenic Walkway. While its title is not consistent, it is well marked and easy to follow.

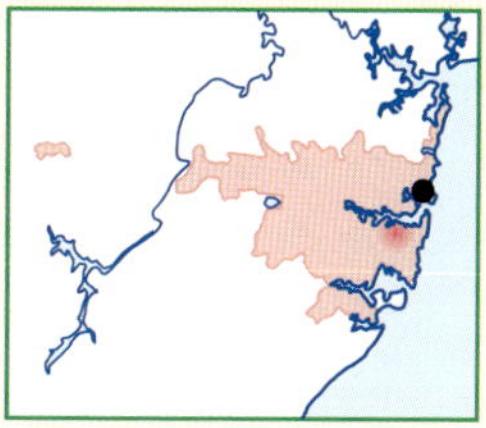

Length: 9.7km, one-way
Time: 4 hours
Grade: Easy-Medium
Total Climbing: 220m
Maximum Height: 90m
From Sydney: 10km
Closest Town: Seaforth 1km
Map: UBD 1:19,000 p197 or SYDWAY 1:20,000 p258, 259

Sydney Harbour entrance from near Cutler Road

Track near Fisher Bay

Access

From Sydney follow Warringah Highway north across Sydney Harbour Bridge. Exit to follow Military Road east then Spit Road north. Cross Spit Bridge and turn left at the first junction to parking areas beside the bridge. Fees apply for parking and a free alternative is to park in one of the streets higher up the hill in Seaforth. The walk is not a circuit and a wide range of buses can be used to return from Manly to the Spit Bridge – check that the bus is not an express service and that it will stop near the bridge.

Public transport – from Circular Quay, take a ferry to Manly. Head north-east 100m to Stand D in Belgrave Street and take a bus to the Spit Bridge. Do not take an express service – a wide range of services are available such as routes 143, 144, 151 and 168.

Variations:

1. **Manly Scenic Walkway**, 8.9km, one-way, 3½ hours, Easy-Medium. Follow the described walk, but leave out the return sidetrips to Grotto Point and Arabanoo Lookout.

0.0km From Spit Bridge, descend to the shore and follow a level track eastwards to Fisher Bay. Climb some steps and cross the creek behind Fisher Bay then more steps lead south to a rock shelter. Round a sharp point where a seat provides an incentive to stop for the view then descend to the sand in Sandy Bay. Cross the beach, cross a road and follow a stepped path over a small spur and down to cross the road again. Follow the footpath south for 100m to Clontarf Reserve. Cross the grass to the kiosk and toilet.

1.7km Continue south to the beach and follow the narrow, sandy shoreline south-east passing below a row of houses. At the end of the sand the track climbs steps then passes underneath a long, high overhang. A steep, zigzagging climb follows after which the track continues and meets an access track. Turn right and descend steps to another junction. The track on the right leads onto Castle Rock Beach.

2.8km Turn left and enter the Sydney Harbour National Park. Initially the track is close to the rocky shore, but soon climbs steps to a signposted track junction.

3.2km Turn right for a return sidetrip to the lighthouse on Grotto Point. The track heads south along the crest of a ridge descending gradually to the lighthouse. Surrounded by a picket fence, the small lighthouse has commanding views of Middle Harbour. Return the same way to the track junction.

3.9km. Continue eastwards towards Manly through heathlands for 200m to a large timber log on the right. This is the entrance to a set of aboriginal engravings. These are scratched outlines on sandstone slabs and a timber barrier surrounds each one. Signs describe the engravings which include a kangaroo, fish and boomerangs. Return to the track and continue north-east. Pass just below Cutler Road where there are several lookouts on rocks on the right. Continue north-east to a good view of Crater Cove and 100m further on is a track junction just below a carpark beside Tania Park. Turn right descending steps to a fenced lookout then continue along a timber ramp into heathland to another track junction.

4.5km Turn left for a sidetrip to Arabanoo Lookout. The track rises for 200m to a car park then turns right to the lookout which provides the first view of Manly. The lookout seat is bordered by an interesting set of tiles depicting animals, plants and birds of the park. Return the same way to the main track.

Castle Rock track junction

North Harbour Reserve

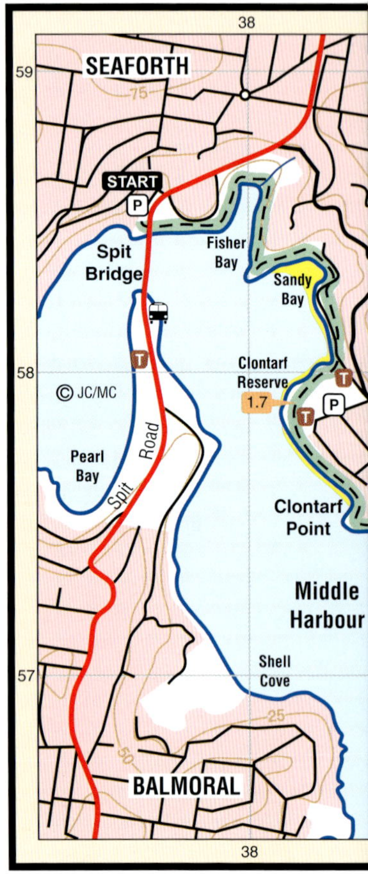

4.9km Descend south-east towards Dobroyd Head passing some fine natural lookouts from outcropping rocks along the way. At the next junction keep to the right and continue for 150m to a short sidetrack on the right to a fenced lookout above Dobroyd Head. This provides good views of Sydney Heads and the Manly ferries crossing the harbour. Return to the track and head northward descending gently through heathland to the sand at Reef Beach.

5.7km Follow the wide boardwalk just above the beach where there is a long seat with more decorative tiles. Rise over a small spur then descend to the rocky shore and follow it north-west for 50m to Forty Baskets Beach. Leave the beach and follow a sealed path above the shore for 400m to meet Gourlay Avenue at a sharp bend.

6.6km Turn left and follow the narrow, sealed road for 250m then turn right and follow a walking track between houses. Cross a gully via a high bridge then turn right into North Harbour Street and follow it north for 100m. At the next corner turn right and descend steps to the foreshore. Follow the concrete path northwards along the edge of North Harbour Reserve then climb steps to Kings Avenue.

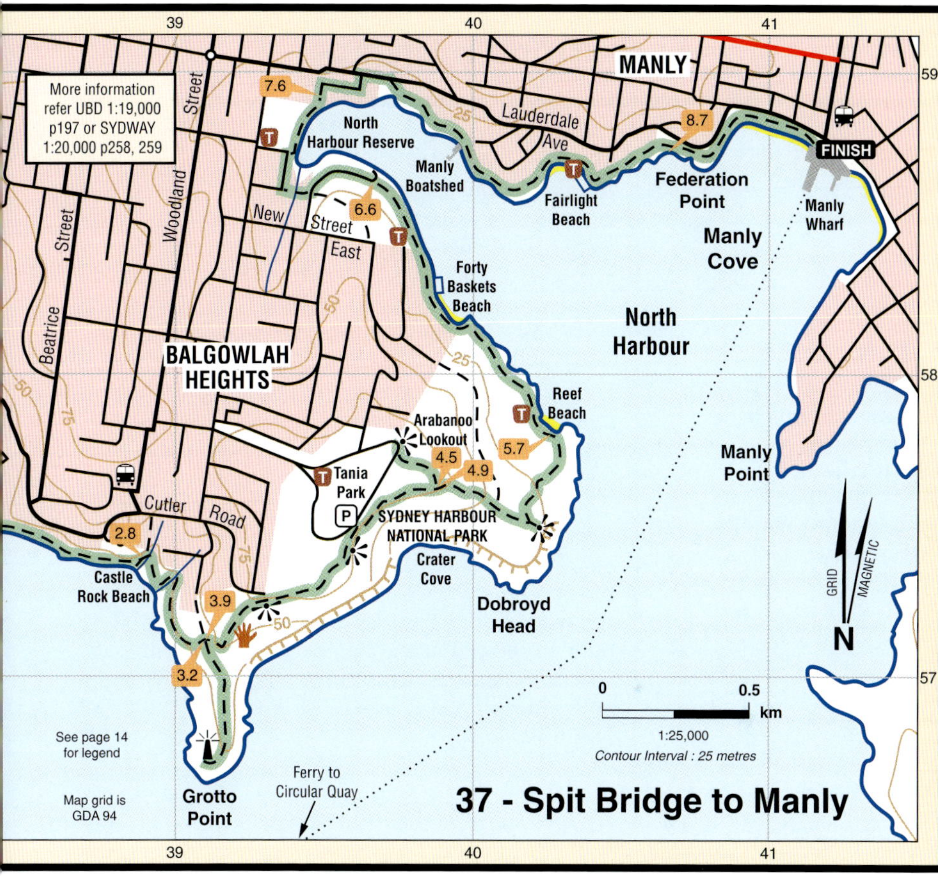

7.6km Follow Kings Avenue east then north then turn right into Lauderdale Avenue. After 70m turn right onto a concrete walking track. This track continues through to Manly and follows the steep slope between the houses and the seaside cliffs. Continue around one point to a walled swimming pool at Fairlight Beach – the water is replaced at each high tide.

8.7km Continue along the path to Federation Point where a plaque describes the life of Australia's first Prime minister – William Barton. When the path ends, turn right to descend steps to a wharf. Follow the wharf north-east to pass behind Ocean World then follow the wide path south-east along The Esplanade to Manly Wharf. Buses to the Spit Bridge leave from Stand D in Belgrave Street, 100m north of Manly Wharf.

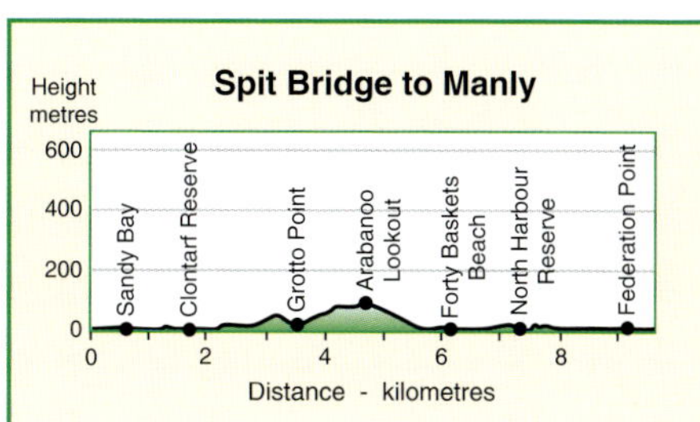

38 LANE COVE THREE BRIDGES

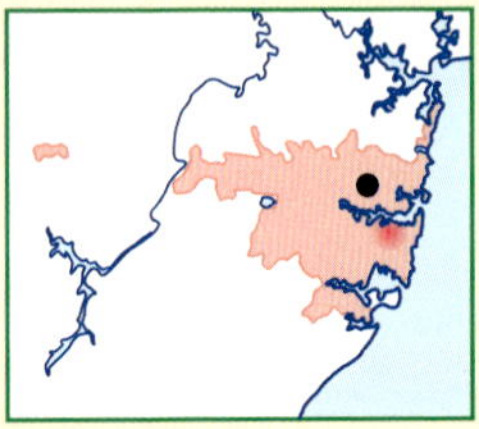

Length: 15.5km, circuit
Time: 5 hours
Grade: Medium
Total Climbing: 270m
Maximum Height: 50m
From Sydney: 13km
Closest Town: Chatswood 2km
Map: UBD 1:19,000 p194 or SYDWAY 1:20,000 p235, 236, 256

The Lane Cove River flows through a steep-sided, forested valley and is one of the larger streams that enters Sydney Harbour. The forests along its banks were of particular interest to the first fleet settlers as a source of timber. In the early 1800s they established several wharfs and sawpits in the valley and cut timber for many years. When logging ceased, other settlers arrived planting orchards and market gardens. In 1910, one of the market gardens was modified to create picnic grounds and became known as Fairyland Tea Gardens. This was very popular and most visitors arrived by boat.

As Sydney grew, the plateau surrounding the river was developed into suburbs. In 1938, the narrow strip of undeveloped land along the river was reserved as Lane Cove National Park. At that time, the weir, walking tracks and stone buildings were built for recreation and they form the core of the current track system. This walk follows tracks along both sides of the river utilising part of the Great North Walk.

Access

From Sydney, follow the Pacific Highway north-west for 10.5km to Chatswood. Turn left into Fullers Road and follow it, then Millwood Road, westward for 2.2km to Fullers Bridge. Turn right just before the bridge then after 200m turn left to enter the Lane Cove National Park. An entry fee applies. Alternatively the walk can be started from any of the picnic areas along Riverside Drive or from the Chatswood Athletic Field near Epping Road.

Public transport – from Sydney Central, trains operate on the 'North Shore Line' to Chatswood. Take bus 545 or 555 to Fullers Bridge. Alternatively, from Chatswood take a train on the 'Epping-Chatswood Link Line' to North Ryde Railway Station – this is 1km from the walk at Ironbark Corner.

Variations:

1. **Fullers & De Burgh Bridges**, 10.4km, circuit, 3½ hours, Easy-Medium. Follow the first 10.1km of the walk to Fullers Bridge, cross the bridge and head north for 200m to the park entrance.
2. **Fullers & Epping Bridges**, 5.7km, circuit, 2 hours, Easy-Medium. From the park entrance, walk south for 200m, cross Fullers Bridge to the west bank of the river and follow the notes from the 10.1km point to the end of the walk.

Rock shelter

0.0km On the west side of Little Blue Gum Creek is a signpost for the Great North Walk (GNW). Head north along the edge of a grassy flat beside the creek in the direction indicated by the signpost – initially there is no track. After 200m turn left at some track markers and rise to meet a sealed road. Follow the road westward for 50m then turn right onto a walking track. This climbs to meet a rough, management road. Continue climbing gently until close to several houses where a walking track veers left and sidles across the hillside to meet a sealed, park road.

0.7km Turn left and 50m down the road turn right onto another walking track. This heads south-west rising gently onto a broad spur with open forest. To protect the nearby housing areas, management fires are regular events that contribute to the open nature of the forest. Ignore minor tracks on the right that lead to the houses. The main walking track swings north-west and a short descent leads to an old road. Turn right and follow the wide track north. This soon narrows and sidles slopes above the Lane Cove River leading to a spur with a good view. Descend the spur west passing a rock slab with a Scout engraving and soon after meet a track junction. Right leads to the grassy opening at Fiddens Wharf Oval.

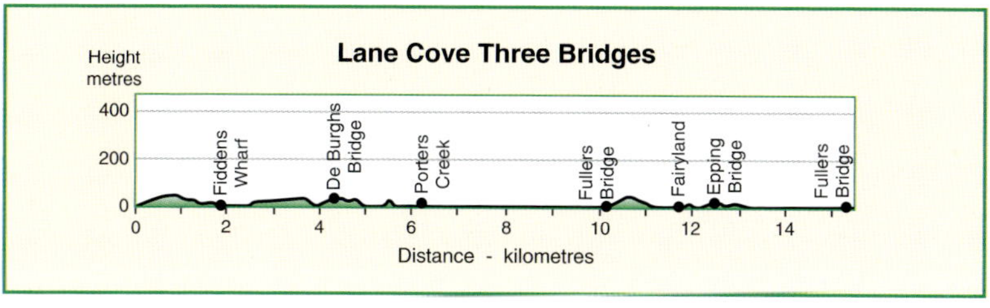

1.9km Keep to the left and descend to an open rock slab beside the river. Soon after pass below a large rock shelter and continue northward through scrubby forest for 200m to a bridge over a small creek. Follow the river upstream another 1.0km to meet a cliff. Follow the fern-covered cliff base north for 100m then a zigzag climb leads to the top.

3.2km Continue northward passing a good view of the river then follow the base of a series of larger cliffs. Ferns hang down the cliffs and there are several overhangs. Continue to rise to a track junction – the wide track to the right leads to Allen Park where there are some aboriginal rock engravings. Turn left and descend, keeping left at minor track junctions, to a ford over De Burgh Creek. Contour around the end of a spur to another track junction – the sidetrack on the left leads down to a sandy beach at Blue Hole. Continue on the right for 100m then leave the GNW by turning right and climbing to Lane Cove Road. Turn left and cross De Burghs Bridge, high above Lane Cove River.

4.3km At the south end of the bridge turn left and a series of wide steps descends to the bicycle track below. Turn right and follow it 200m to a car park near a park gatehouse. Turn left and descend north on a set of stone steps towards Lane Cove River – the river is hidden behind a wall of weeds that choke the rivers edge. Follow the undulating walking track downstream keeping left at track junctions. Continue for 1.4km to where the track swings south-west away from the river to follow Porters Creek. Rise for 200m to meet the sealed road.

6.2km Turn left and cross the road bridge. This was built by workers in the Depression between 1932 and 1938. Across the bridge turn left and return to the walking track. This soon reaches the river and continues downstream for 1.0km to the first of many picnic areas at Fern Valley. Ignore tracks to the right and continue for 1.5km crossing several picnic grounds to Iron Bark Corner.

Lane Cove River near Porters Creek

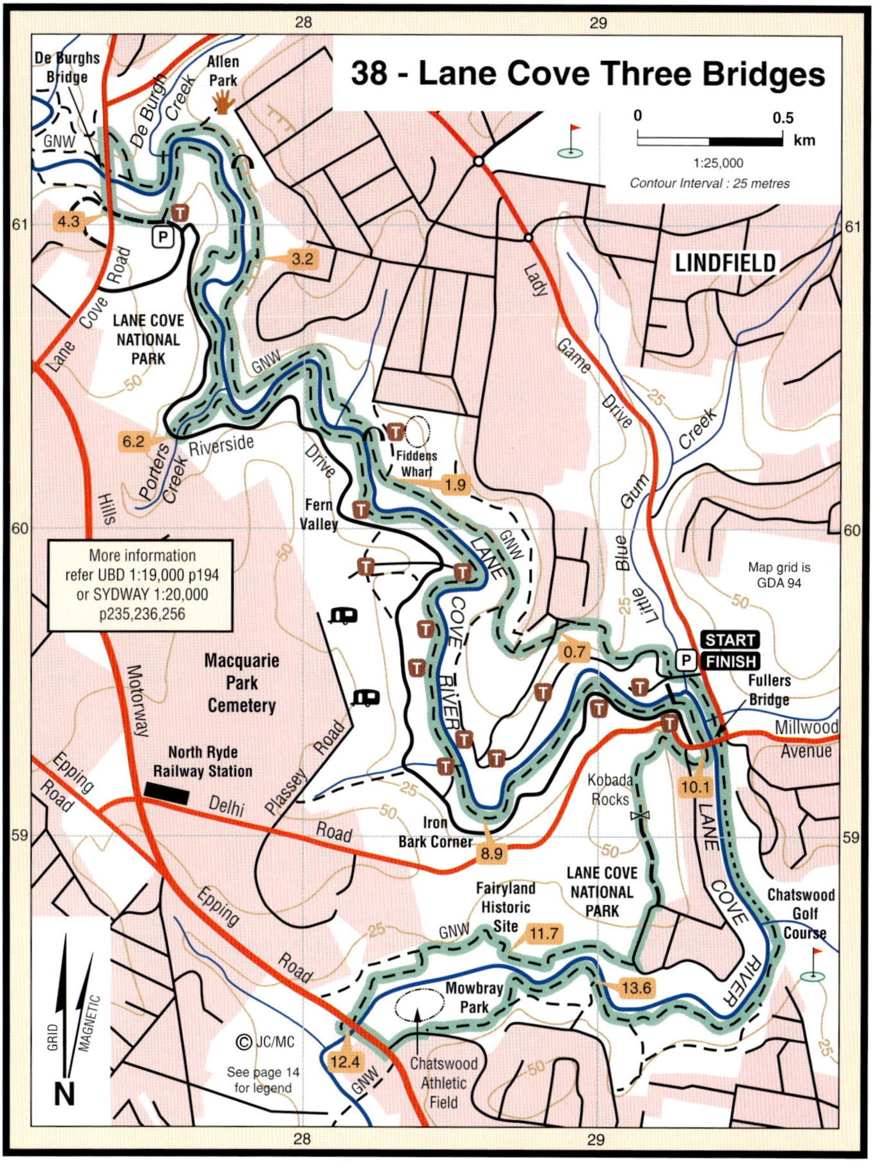

8.9km Cross a small creek then scramble along the base of a low cliff. The track soon improves and leads through more picnic areas. It passes between a boatshed and the river then around one more bend to reach the weir. This was built to create a calm region for boating. At low water levels the weir can be crossed to the car park at the start of the walk. The main walking track continues downstream for 150m to Fullers Bridge.

Kobada Rocks

10.1km Pass underneath Fullers Bridge then turn right to follow a short, sealed street to meet a road. Cross the road and follow the signposted GNW climbing steeply westward to Kobada Rocks on top of the ridge. These are a series of rock slabs and shallow pools. Continue to a gate at the end of a quiet, sealed road. Follow the road downhill and at the street intersection turn right and follow the suburban street south-west for 250m. Turn right at the bend in the street and the walking track continues westward through light forest above the river. Cross a swampy creek via a boardwalk into the Fairyland Historic Site.

11.7km From 1910 to 1960, Fairyland was a popular picnic site complete with swings, a ferris wheel, picnic shelters, playgrounds and a cricket pitch – a wharf attracted many boat-based visitors. There is not much left on the river flat apart from introduced plants and signboards. Continue westward and the undulating track passes below office buildings and several rock shelters to Epping Bridge.

12.4km Pass underneath the bridge then turn right and climb onto the bridge. Cross the bridge to the south-eastern bank, turn right to descend steps and pass underneath Epping Road. Continue eastward following the footpath on the north side of Mowbray Road for 100m to the entrance to Chatswood Athletic Field. From the entrance follow a bicycle track east for 100m then, when the track swings right, leave it and continue straight ahead following a grassy terrace. Cross a concrete access track to the athletics oval and continue north-east 100m to the entrance to Mowbray Park. Cross a short timber bridge to a junction. Turn right then left at the next junction and descend steeply on stone steps to the river passing a rock shelter on the way. Turn right and continue eastward beside the river.

13.6km Ignore all tracks to the right and follow the river eastward to the entrance to Chatswood Golf Course. Walkers are allowed to enter – a sign outlines entry conditions. Keep close to the river and beware of golfers and golf balls. Follow the trees on the left edge of the fairway for 400m then pass through a locked gate and continue on a walking track. This heads north beside the river and rises to meet Millwood Avenue. Turn left to pass underneath Fullers Bridge and continue northward crossing a side creek and soon after is the end of the walk at the entrance to Lane Cove National Park.

IRON COVE 39

Sydney Harbour contains many inlets and bays the foreshores of which are an Intertidal Protected Area. This protection applies to the animals and vegetation around the waters edge. Although the shoreline is a major feature of this capital city, only a few inlets can be walked close to the water's edge. This is because privately owned land extends to much of the shoreline. Iron Cove is one of the inlets with a continuous strip of public land around its shore.

A well made and easy to follow walking track, that also doubles as the annual Bay Run track, leads around the shoreline. While some of this parallels some busy public roads there are also some long sections of quiet walking track. The urban views are interspersed with small parks and pockets of mangroves and native vegetation. The cove is very popular with walkers, joggers and bicycle riders so expect to share the track with many others, particularly on weekends and public holidays.

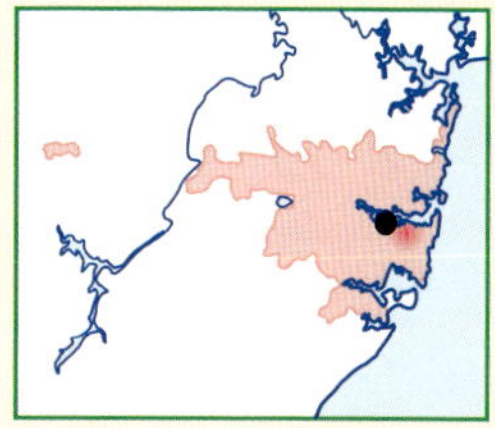

Length: 7.1km, circuit
Time: 2 hours
Grade: Easy
Total Climbing: 20m
Maximum Height: 20m
From Sydney: 4km
Closest Town: Rozelle 1km
Map: UBD 1:19,000 p234, 235 or SYDWAY 1:10,000 p53, 54

Iron Cove Bridge

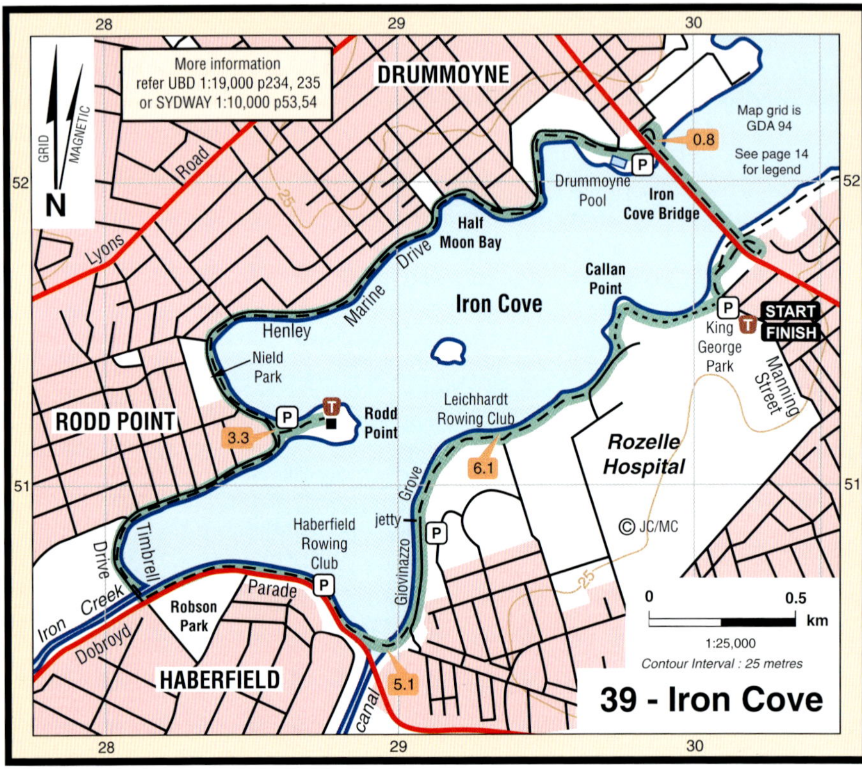

Access

From Sydney, follow Western Distributor west for 3km then turn right into Victoria Road. Follow this north-west for 1km then turn left into Toelle Street. At the end turn right to car parking areas on the left side of Manning Street. Alternatively, continue along Victoria Street, cross Iron Cove Bridge and turn left at the first street then left again to car parking areas beside Henley Marine Drive.

Public transport – from Circular Quay in central Sydney, take any of the Victoria Street buses (routes 500 to 520) to the first stop after Balmain Road.

0.0km From King George Park car park head north-west to the fitness and exercise equipment area beside Iron Cove. Turn right and almost immediately the track around the cove shore divides. Keep to the right and rise towards Iron Cove Bridge. Pass underneath the bridge then turn right onto the bridge. Follow the pedestrian pathway north-west across the bridge – there is no pedestrian path on the other side. At the other end of the bridge keep to the right and follow the sharply curving road to the shore of the cove.

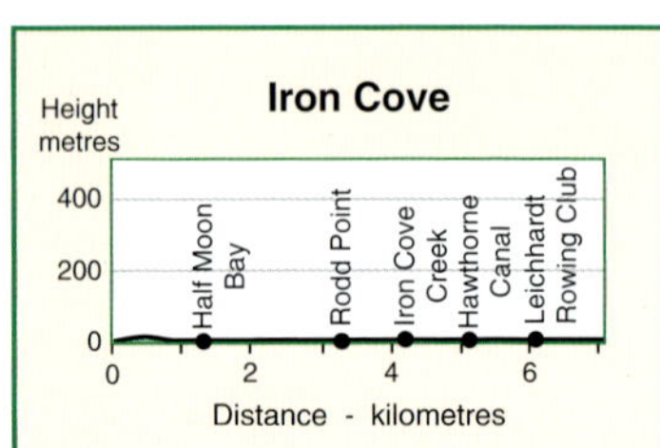

0.8km When safe to do so, cross to the southern side of Henley Marine Drive and follow the footpath west. Pass above the Drummoyne Pool and then the Rowing Club. Informative signs, about the local flora and sea-life, are found beside the path. Although at low tide it looks possible to follow the foreshore, it is suggested this not be attempted as the foreshore comprises tidal mudflats. Continue following the path as it winds westward beside the road and passes below some interesting houses, both old and new. The footpath soon divides into a bicycle path on the right and a walking track on the left. Continue along the walking track to where the road swings south opposite Nield Park. At the end of the park the track crosses a car park. Rodd Point is a short sidetrip to the east and the picnic area has a good view across the cove.

Footpath beside Iron Cove

3.3km From Rodd Point continue following Henley Marine Drive westwards then turn south along Timbrell Drive around the end of the bay to cross Iron Creek. Turn left and the walking track runs parallel to the very busy Dobroyd Parade. Continue eastwards to pass Haberfield Rowing Club then further on pass a mural wall about the club. Climb up steps and cross the old road bridge over a canal. On the other side turn left descending steps.

5.1km Leave the busy roads behind and follow the walking track north along the foreshore to enter Giovinazzo Grove. The line of trees is named after an Italian immigrant who founded an Italian community in the area. The immigrants built a club and created a fishing fleet based at the cove – both have since closed. Continue northward along the foreshore passing the old jetty which was the base for the fishing fleet. At the other end of the grove there is a pleasant rest area on the left of the main track with seats underneath a trellis.

6.1km Pass behind the Leichhardt Rowing Club and enter the grounds of Rozelle Hospital. Merge with and follow a road along the foreshore for 150m then, when it swings right over a spur, leave it and follow the grass above the shoreline northwards. There is no defined path, but it is easy walking around Callan Point. When the mangroves begin a rough path to the right climbs for 10m. This passes underneath a large fig tree where a nearby sign describes some of the aboriginal heritage of the area. Past the fig tree veer left and descend sandstone steps to paths along the foreshore. Continue for 100m to the exercise area where the walk started.

40 BONDI TO MAROUBRA

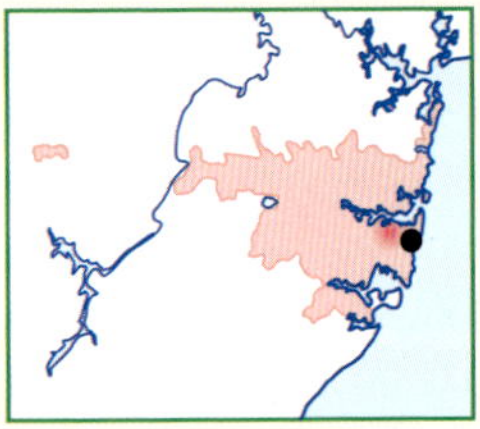

Length: 11.5km, one-way
Time: 4 hours
Grade: Easy-Medium
Total Climbing: 160m
Maximum Height: 30m
From Sydney: 8km
Closest Town: Bondi 0km
Maps: UBD p257, 277 or SYDWAY p298, 299, 318

The eastern coastline of Sydney is a mixture of sandy beaches, sheltered coves and dramatic headlands. The city has been built almost to the cliff edge and a very narrow strip of public land runs between the buildings and the crumbling sea cliffs. Walking along the coast is very popular, but this walk should not be attempted in big seas or with very high tides.

While this walk rarely passes through native bushland, it is nevertheless very scenic with plenty of views of the rugged coast backed by the tall buildings of the coastal suburbs. In warm weather there are many safe swimming places ranging from the ocean side baths to the sheltered waters of Clovelly Bay. For those who seek surf, the stormy beaches at Bondi, Coogee and Maroubra provide some famous surfing breaks. Some of Sydney's history is also seen along the way with historic pavilions at Bondi and Coogee and Waverley Cemetery that is the burial site of many famous Australians including Dorothea Mackellar and Henry Lawson.

Heading toward Mackenzies Point

Nelson Bay

Access

From Sydney follow Liverpool then Oxford Street then veer right onto Anzac Parade. Follow Anzac Parade south for 8km then turn left into Fitzgerald Avenue in Maroubra. Follow the avenue eastward for 1km and park near Malabar Avenue where there is all day parking. Fees apply for parking close to Maroubra Beach and is also limited to 4 hours maximum. The walk is not a circuit and buses are used to get to the start at Bondi Beach – there is no free, all-day parking near Bondi. From the parking area, walk east on Fitzgerald Avenue for 0.2km then swing north-east to the bus stop on Marine Parade. Catch either Bus 317 or 353 to Bondi Junction then change to Bus 380, 381 or 382 to Bondi Beach and alight the bus near the corner of Wairoa Avenue and Campbell Parade at the north end of the beach. Refer www.sydneybuses.com for timetables.

Public transport – from Sydney catch Bus 380 to Bondi Beach or a train to Bondi Junction then Bus 380, 381 or 382 to Bondi Beach and alight the bus near the corner of Wairoa Avenue and Campbell Parade at the north end of the beach. To return from Maroubra to Sydney take Bus 395 or 396. For timetables, refer www.cityrail.info and www.sydneybuses.com.

Variations:

1. **Bondi to Coogee**, 6.6km, one-way, 2 hours, Easy. Follow the first 6.6km of the described walk to Coogee Beach. Return to Bondi Junction on bus 313, 314 or 353 or to Sydney direct on bus 372, 373 or 374.
2. **Coogee to Maroubra**, 5.9km, one-way, 2 hours, Easy. From Maroubra catch bus 353 to Coogee Beach then follow the described walk from the 6.6km point to the end.

START
BONDI BEACH
Campbell Parade
Bondi Pavilion
rock pool
Bondi Beach
Bondi Bay
Bondi Road
Bondi Baths
The Boot
TAMARAMA
1.4
Mackenzies Point
Mackenzies Bay
Tamarama Bay
Bronte Beach SLSC
BRONTE
2.7
Nelson Bay
Bronte Baths
More information refer UBD 1:19,000 p257, 277 or SYDWAY 1:20,000 p298, 299, 318
See page 14 for legend
© JC/MC
TASMAN SEA
Waverley Cemetery
Boundary Street
CLOVELLY
3.8
Bowling Green
4.7
5.6
Shark Point
Clovelly Bay
Gordons Bay
COOGEE
Coogee Baths
Coogee Bay Rd
6.6
Coogee Bay
Ross Jones Memorial Pool
McIver Baths
Wylies Baths
Wedding Cake Island
222
Map grid is GDA 94
GRID
MAGNETIC
N
40a - Bondi to Maroubra
0
0.5
km
1:25,000
Contour Interval : 25 metres

0.0km From the bus stop near the corner of Wairoa Avenue and Campbell Parade, head south to the Bondi Pavilion. This grand, colonnaded building was large enough for 12,000 bathers – today it houses art shows and other displays. From the pavilion follow the wide, paved pathway south-west above the beach. At the end of Bondi Bay climb a ramp to pass above the Bondi Baths – the path past the baths leads to a dead end at a lookout. The baths are the home of the Bondi Icebergs, a bathers club, who swim every morning regardless of the weather. Above the baths turn left and follow a street for 100m to its end and descend steps to the 'Coastal Walkway'. Follow the concrete path around the small bay called The Boot then rise above cliffs to a track junction and veer left to a lookout on top of Mackenzies Point.

1.4km Mackenzies Point provides views of the coast in both directions. The track continues west along the cliff top and rounds the small cove of Mackenzies Bay then rises over a small point and descends gently to the sandy beach at the head of the narrow Tamarama Bay. At the back of the beach cross the grass and 20m right of the toilets climb the steps to Tamarama Marine Drive. Follow the wide footpath beside the road round the next point then descend steps to Nelson Bay and Bronte Beach. Follow the wide promenade above the beach to the Surf Life Saving Club (SLSC).

2.7km Continue to the end of the promenade and turn right to climb the steps 30m before the baths at the end of the beach – the track past the baths soon ends. The steps lead onto a minor road, follow this south climbing through Bronte Cutting – be careful to avoid traffic. At the end of the cutting turn left onto a paved walking track that soon enters the Waverley Cemetery. Follow the narrow walking track south along the edge of the cemetery passing very close to numerous graves. Continue to meet Boundary Street – this is the start of the Eastern Beaches Coastal Walk.

Waverley Cemetery

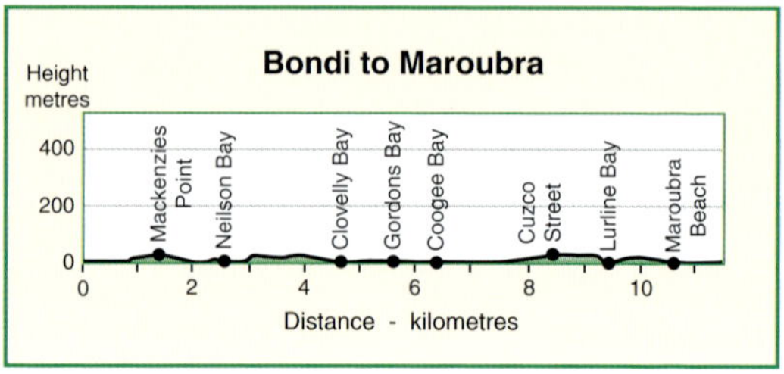

3.8km The concrete track passes between the bowling green and the houses of Clovelly. At the end of bowling green turn left and follow a grassy path around the top of Shark Point which provides a good view of the coastline. Continue around the cliff top to rejoin the concrete path near the corner of Ocean Street and Eastbourne Avenue and follow Eastbourne Avenue as it descends gradually north-west into Clovelly Bay. This is a very narrow bay with concrete platforms along both sides and a reef at the entrance providing a good swimming location.

4.7km The path rounds the end of Clovelly Bay then heads south-east along the other side. Either continue along at half height or rise onto the crest of the ridge above. Cross the large car park above the point to the south side and pick up the walking track again at the south end of Victory Street. Follow it for 30m then veer right when it divides (the left track leads to a diving trail – yes, it's underwater) and climb steps steeply to the end of another street. From there follow the timber boardwalk and steps west descending to Gordons Bay.

5.6km Gordons Bay has no beach and its major feature are numerous boats stored on timber slats. Pass above the boats and round the head of the bay then rise to meet Major Street. Follow this 50m then veer left leaving the concrete path to follow the grass beside the fence around the top of the point. Keep following the fence to return to the concrete coastal path and descend gently to Coogee Beach. Follow the wide promenade above the beach for 200m. The bus stop and shops are to the right near the traffic lights on Coogee Bay Road.

Gordons Bay

6.6km From Coogee Bay Road continue to follow the promenade to the end of the beach near the Ross Jones Memorial Pool. From here the walk consists of a series of short walking tracks between streets and is easier to follow than it sounds. From Coogee Beach the coastal track rises to a reserve and passes above McIver Baths then Wylies Baths. It continues just above the cliffs swinging around the coastal edge of Trenerry Reserve to a boardwalk. The boardwalk has been constructed to protect coastal vegetation in wet areas beside the track. The track rises to meet Alexandria Parade above Honeycombe Bay.

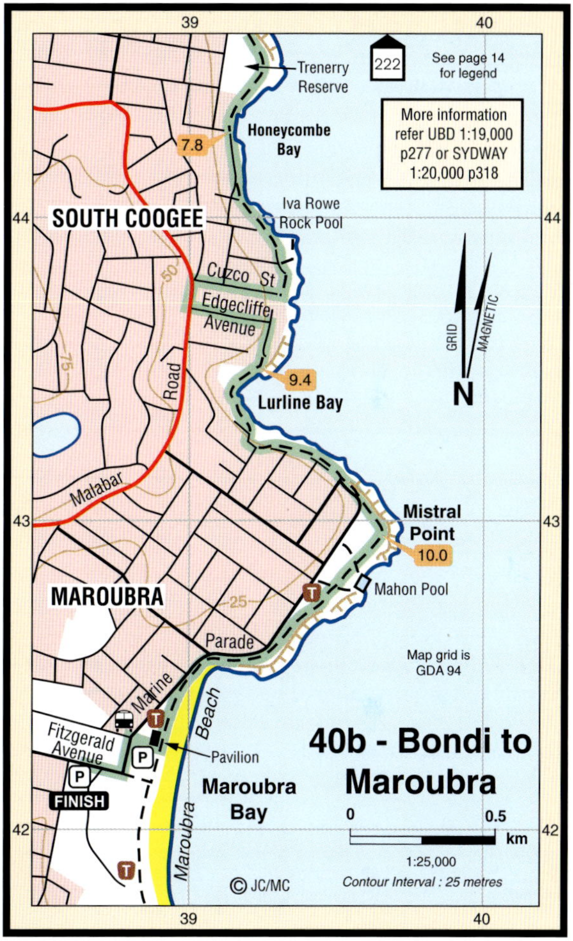

7.8km Follow the street for 200m then veer left below several houses to meet the end of Pearce Street. Descend steps on the left and pass above Iva Rowe Rock Pool – this is a natural, tear-shaped rock pool on the platform below. The track soon meets Bunya Parade which is followed southwards. Pass between the last two houses at the end of the street. Steps rise to Cuzco Street, turn right and follow the street west, turn left into Malabar Road then left again at the next corner into Edgecliffe Avenue. When it ends turn right into Seaside Parade and at its end veer right to the walkway steps between two houses. Descend these steps onto the rock platform below.

9.4km There is no track around the shore of Lurline Bay. Follow the rocky platform around the shoreline. Take care when crossing the narrow space between the cliff and a rocky gutter – it is safe except in big seas or very high tides. Continue along the rocky shore passing under the overhanging cliff then follow a concrete ramp rising to a street corner. A walking path continues along the clifftop passing below several houses then rising to meet the next street. Leave the concrete path and veer left to a survey marker on Mistral Point for more views of the rugged coastline.

10.0km Continue around the point to pass above Mahon Pool. Rejoin the concrete path and descend gradually towards Maroubra Bay. Follow the path behind the beach to the Pavilion then turn north-west and head to the bus stop on Marine Parade or continue to the car parking in nearby Fitzgerald Avenue.

JOIN A BUSHWALKING CLUB

Joining a club is often a good way to get started in bushwalking. Many clubs exist in the city of Sydney and its surrounding suburbs. They meet regularly, most meet monthly, and welcome visitors to meetings and on many walks scheduled on their programs. Walking with a club provides a safe and enjoyable way to learn and there is no shortage of members willing to provide tips and share experiences.

The Confederation of Walking Clubs NSW Inc is a state body that represents 66 walking clubs in New South Wales, 21 of which are in Sydney. The Confederation provides contact details of clubs, general advice for walking and also manages a volunteer Bushwalkers Wilderness Search & Rescue team. Contact details are:

Confederation of Bushwalking Clubs NSW Inc
PO Box 119, Newtown, NSW 2042
Email: admin@bushwalking.org.au

Website: www.bushwalking.org.au

Contact details for clubs in other states can be found via the website for Bushwalking Australia. This is a national body that represents the interests of recreational walkers. The website contains links to state walking organisations and other informative sites. The website address is:

www.bushwalkingaustralia.org

Cape Banks, Walk 1

THE AUTHORS

John Chapman, originally a civil engineer, worked for many years in bushwalking gear shops before turning to a university career in computer science focusing on graphics and multimedia. John has also worked as a professional walking guide in Tasmania, Nepal and India. He is now self-employed producing guide books. John is a keen photographer and a successful, international exhibitor winning many awards and medals. International photographic societies have awarded him the honours of FAPS, EFIAP, ARPS and PPSA. He has been a regular contributor to *Wild* magazine since its first edition and has self-published walking guides since 1978. John likes to explore new areas and regularly ventures into the bush.

Monica Chapman joined a bushwalking club in 1981 and quickly became an avid walker. She served on committees of two clubs, became President of Bushwalking Victoria (BWV) – formerly *Federation of Victorian Walking Clubs* and was its representative on the *Bushwalking and Mountaincraft Training Advisory Board* where she contributed to leadership training programs. More recently, she was convenor of *Bush Search and Rescue Victoria* and on the board of BWV. Monica's administrative career spanned the education, medical and biotechnology fields, but now she assists with guide book production full-time. She has also contributed to *Wild* magazine. Monica enjoys spending extended periods in the outdoors, both here and overseas.

OTHER BOOKS BY THE AUTHORS

Day Walks Melbourne, John Chapman, Monica Chapman & John Siseman, 1st edition, 2005

Day Walks Victoria, John Chapman, Monica Chapman & John Siseman, 2nd edition, 2011

Day Walks Tasmania, John Chapman & Monica Chapman, 1st edition, 2003

Bushwalking In Australia, John Chapman & Monica Chapman, 4th edition, 2003

Australian Alps Walking Track, John Chapman, Monica Chapman & John Siseman, 4th edition, 2009

Larapinta Trail, John Chapman & Monica Chapman, 1st edition, 2008

Cradle Mountain Lake St Clair and Walls of Jerusalem National Parks, John Chapman, Monica Chapman & John Siseman, 5th edition, 2006

Overland Track, John Chapman & Monica Chapman, 3rd edition, 2011

South West Tasmania, John Chapman, 5th edition, 2008

South Coast Track, John Chapman & Monica Chapman, 1st edition, 2009